The New Intelligence

THE NEW INTELLIGENCE

Artificial Intelligence
Ideas and Applications
in Financial Services

Jessica Keyes

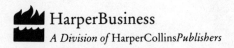

HarperBusiness
A Division of HarperCollins*Publishers*

International Standard Book Number: 0-88730-441-9

Library of Congress Catalog Card Number: 90–36096

Printed in the United States of America

Library of Congress Cataloging-in-Publication Data

Keyes, Jessica, 1950–
    The new intellegence : artificial intelligence ideas and
applications in financial services / Jessica Keyes.
        p.   cm.
    Includes bibliographical reference and index.
    ISBN 0-88730-441-9
    1. Financial services industry—United States—Data processing.
    2. Artificial intelligence—Data processing.   3. Expert systems
    (Computer science)   I. Title.
    HG181.K44   1990
    332.1'0285'63—dc20   90–36096
                                                                  CIP

90 91 92 93 PS/HC 9 8 7 6 5 4 3 2 1

To my husband and parents

Contents

List of Figures

List of Tables

Foreword

I've been on the shirt-sleeves end of technology for a long time. I've built hundreds of systems for dozens of companies. Being an insider colors your thinking about new technologies. Legions of salespeople ooze in and out of your office all day long. Everyone wants to sell you something. You're busy, you're tired, your users don't understand or appreciate you, you've been burned before by new technologies. So it's with a wary ear that you hear yet another sales pitch for yet another technological marvel that will "change the way you do business."

If you're a user, you are even more wary. You don't trust anybody. "How can it take so long to develop my systems?" you ask. "And why does it cost so much?"

This book is dedicated to those legions of the weary and wary. Look around you. What in heaven's name are you automating? Just plain data? Artificial Intelligence (AI) gives you the opportunity, for the first time, to automate knowledge and judgment. And in the competitive 1990s, you are what you know.

Artificial intelligence systems are no more mysterious than any other tool that you have in your toolbox. You just have to know how to pick up that hammer and bang in those nails. This book can be your guide.

In Chapters 1 through 4, we'll concentrate on the *hows* of using this technology. In Chapters 6 through 10, we'll travel around the country and take a peek at some pretty nifty expert and natural language systems developed by your brethren in the financial services community. And in Chapter 5, we'll learn how to go about auditing these systems once you've created them.

During my research for this book, I met many talented and creative people. I'd like to thank them for their patience in answering my numerous questions and enlightening me about their systems. Yes, there are some great things happening in financial services. So read on and get some good ideas.

Preface

ARTIFICIAL INTELLIGENCE (AI) IN THE FINANCIAL SERVICES COMMUNITY*

The winds of change blow slowly in the financial services community. But they blow at an even keel. At first AI was just a whistle on the wind. But the din grew louder and louder and finally could not be ignored. Quietly they waited and watched the brouhaha surrounding this miracle called AI. They silently cheered the successes and just as silently were saddened by the failures. And all this time they learned from all those who went before. And then finally they were ready. They entered the AI fray. And in a big, big way.

They really had no choice! Long the most paper-intensive of all industries, the financial services community was nearly crushed by the weight of all that paper in the mid-seventies. Their salvation—the computer. At the beginning of the 1990s, they find themselves crushed beneath the weight of—you guessed it—the output of all those automated systems. They automated paper to get information. They're now automating information to get knowledge.

Expert systems are funny. Users seem to have fewer problems in relating to a system that is knowledge-bound rather than a system that is data-bound. You'll often find that it is the user who champions the use

*This section has been adapted from "A Survey of Brokerage Systems" in the Spring 1990 issue of *Expert Systems*. Reprinted from *Expert Systems* (New York: Auerbach Publishers). © 1990 Warren, Gorham & Lamont Inc. Used with permission.

of expert systems in an organization. This is certainly what happened at Northrop Aircraft in 1983. Two engineers built their own expert system to advise in the manufacture of airplane parts and took the show on the road. They became the champions of expert system methodology at Northrop and developers of one of the earliest successful expert systems.

It's not surprising that users can be very opinionated about great uses for this technology. In the financial services community there is certainly fodder for the use of AI-injected systems. From the canyons of Wall Street to the gold coast of California, ideas have been sprouting like so many seeds. From trading to banking platform assistance to compliance to economic forecasting to underwriting to claims review, everyone has a great idea.

You'll note that trading is at the top of the list. It was certainly high on Tom Campfield's list. Tom, a VP in the investment banking sector, was one expert who wanted something better, and thus TARA was born. TARA (Technical Analysis and Reasoning Assistant) is used in Manufacturers Hanover Trust's Foreign Exchange Department. Successful? You bet, and largely because it was conceived by a user.

And it was a user who spearheaded Morgan Stanley's very successful Expert Tick system, which contributed many millions to Morgan's financial picture. Joel Kaplan and friends developed an expert system to monitor the ticker. With the volume of trades that a Morgan trader handles, it is impossible to check the ticker to determine whether the trade has been recorded. Expert Tick gobbles up the ticker information and matches it to the parameters of the order stream. The result: accurate and timely trades.

Accuracy, timeliness, consistency. All expert systems "sell" these buzzwords, which all have a profound effect on the bottom line. And are the driving force behind the growing flurry of expert system development activity.

A whole bunch of expert systems are being built today. According to a recent Coopers & Lybrand census, fully 43 percent of the largest financial institutions are delving into expert systems. Within the banking community, where expert systems are seen as a real competitive edge, the percentage grows to 60 percent.

The banking institutions have been particularly innovative in their application of AI methodology to their business. From financial planning to foreign exchange trading to pension processing, the banks are distributing AI far and wide in their organizations.

At Citibank, a rule-based system was developed that processes hundreds of thousands of pension checks each night. The *raison d'être* of this system was the necessity of calculating withholding taxes for the different states. Each state had its own rules, so a rule-based system was created that automatically advises the conventional system of the withholding calculation to make. The DOLS system is now quietly but successfully chugging away check after check after check.

At Chase Lincoln Bank in Rochester, New York, the Personal Financial Planning System was born to assist the bank's more affluent customers in planning their investment strategies. The customer answers an on-line notebook full of questions, and the system churns out one of 60 different investment options based on the criteria entered.

From systems to assist customers to systems to catch customers. Who said that expert systems weren't fair? In April of 1988, Security Pacific National Bank developed a bankcard fraud detection system. There are so many ways to "cheat" and so many early warning signals that this bank applied expert system methodology to cheat the cheaters out of their booty.

Another system that this innovative bank is fine-tuning is DEFEWS (Detection of Fraud and Early Warning System). DEFEWS will monitor all commercial accounts for irregularities in such areas as electronic deposits and withdrawals, wire transfers, and a myriad of other transactions. Batman, meet your match.

You know that Batman was really a wealthy dilettante who just loved to hang around. But this didn't stop him from scrutinizing his investment portfolio. He would have been proud of Chemical Bank's FXAA system, which audits potentially irregular foreign exchange trades. As a result of this system human auditors can examine up to 30 times more than what they had examined in the past. And all in the same amount of time.

Speaking of foreign exchange trading, Manufacturers Hanover Trust, known affectionately as Manny Hanny, is quite proud of its TARA system. TARA, mentioned earlier, is now deployed at the bank and becoming quite popular with some of the traders. TARA brought the world of foreign exchange trading to the trader all in one device. Using a workstation, the development team used a windowed approach to show live information. The expert system portion of the system monitors these feeds and makes recommendations that the trader can use or ignore. Nowadays, even if the traders ignore the advice, they are at least curious enough to take a quick peek at it.

Looking or scanning through reams of information is a potential bottleneck for any financial institution, but especially banks. Several of the large banks, Citibank and Chase among them, are working on natural language applications that will be used to interpret the text that constitutes electronic fund transfer messages and other bank messages.

In that same Coopers & Lybrand study, performed in 1988, it was determined that fully 65 percent of the largest one hundred insurers are into AI. For the most part, expert system technology is being applied to the rather complicated task of underwriting—the nerve center of the insurance business. But AI is making still more inroads. Blue Cross/Blue Shield of Pittsburgh, Pennsylvania, developed an expert system to check insurance claim validity. Taking claim monitoring a step further, Cigna has developed a Medical Management Information System that scans through claim reports and points out areas of concern. The system then proceeds to suggest possible solutions. So beware, your employer just might be scrutinizing your last medical claim. You know, the one for the hair transplant.

Deregulation. Globalization. Twenty-four-hour trading. Stop the world, we want to get off. By far the biggest bang for the buck will be in the securities industry. Firms up and down the street are busy at work developing trading systems, hedging systems. And one California company has even devised a way of predicting the next crash—after all, it actually predicted some of the signals for the last one.

The majority of firms are, at least, taking advantage of workstation technology and rapid prototyping to make the trader's life easier. Windows containing everything from prices on the different exchanges to plotting trends to the trader's position are being made available. Members of the brokerage community have watched with growing interest the expert system success stories in their sister industries. For the most part, they have looked to outside vendors to supply the application add-ins that can turn hum-drum conventional systems into something a bit more, shall we say, expert.

And their dreams are juicy. Why not have a system with a split-second reaction time for researching different opportunities and assessing the one with the highest return and the lowest risk? Why not have a system that evaluates external, current events from the news and predicts scenarios that could arise as a result? And why not be able to simulate the future market based on something more than past performance?

Why not?

The New Intelligence

1

Financial Services — An Explosion of Information

INFORMATION EVERYWHERE BUT NOT A DROP TO DRINK

Magic. Magicians are masters of optical illusion. They convince their breathless audiences that their tricks work by magic. But the tricks really result from precision sleight of hand, split-second timing, and careful planning. And Merlin's code prevents the brotherhood of magicians from ever whispering its secrets.

Knowledge. That's all that separates the knowing from the unknowing, the magician from the audience. Knowledge is an elusive creature, especially in large organizations. Inconsistent. Unripe. Buried in information.

BURIED IN INFORMATION

Pick up a *New York Times*. There is more information contained between the front and back pages than we can possibly digest. Add to this the other 99 papers we'll read this year. Or the 3,000 notices or forms we'll read or complete, or the 2,463 hours of television we'll watch, or the 730 hours of radio we'll listen to, and you have something called an information explosion.

1

According to Linda Costigan Lederman (1986), who devised these statistics for her piece, "Communication in the Workplace," this doesn't even take into account the number of hours spent exchanging information in conversations. And shouldn't we include information that is signaled by nonverbal means? Such as the wink of an eye, the firm handshake, or the nod of the head.

Soothsayers predict that the amount of information that we are expected to absorb will double every four to five years. Even now, more new information has been generated for mass distribution in the last three decades than in the previous 5,000 years.

Maybe it's more than an information explosion; perhaps it's more like a glut. And with this glut comes the breakdown of our ability to process or even retrieve the information we so labor to possess. Akio Morita, chairman of the Sony Corporation, believes that our capacity to retrieve this information is declining. In fact, he believes that out of all we absorb, we can retrieve from our memories only a paltry 5 percent.

Alvin Toffler (1970), in his much-acclaimed book *Future Shock*, paints an even bleaker picture. He writes of an actual breakdown of human performance under these extraordinary information loads and demonstrates its relationship to psychopathology. The resulting lament is all too familiar according to psychologist Bruce Baldwin (1985): "Even when I'm away from the office, my mind keeps on speeding. . . . I want to run away and live in the woods." Work is increasingly being done in one's head rather than at one's desk as we try to cope with managing this massive information overdose. The information we must assimilate has also become more and more abstract as technological innovators find new and clever ways to present it. And we don't just process one stream of data bits at a time. Dr. Baldwin refers to our need to deal with more than one information flow at a time as polyphasic activity. Picture Sam riding in his convertible on the way to his next meeting. He grips the steering wheel in his left hand, the cellular phone in his right, and on his lap rests his miniature tape recorder. And in the passenger seat sits his ultralite computer.

This increasingly large information flow is forcing people to adapt to mastering it and making judgments about it in shorter and shorter periods of time. Robert Jacobson, an information policy consultant to the California state assembly, likens this burgeoning quantity of information to an algae-infested pond that no longer has enough oxygen to support its fish. "We may actually be pushing the physical limits on the ability of people to process information," he says. "When that begins to happen, great amounts of information will be passing by, which people cannot evaluate."

Born of this glut is a new phrase that all agree has distinct meaning in our lives. Information anxiety, a nice turn of phrase coined by Richard Saul Wurman (1989) in his book of the same name, is that chasm between what we think we should understand and what we really do understand. As those papers and magazines and books pile up unread on our nightstands, we grow increasingly uneasy at our inability to keep up the pace. And exhausted, we fall asleep with yet another unfinished book at our side. Information anxiety, according to Wurman, "is the black hole between data and knowledge. It happens when information doesn't tell us what we want or need to know."

And perhaps there is no denser black hole than in the realm of information technology.

QUILL PENS AND VISORS

Sure, the more avant-garde among us have been toying with the strategic use of technology to turn the tide of information glut. But for the most part, we're still using the same tired old methodologies that we've been using since the computer took over the basements of our office buildings. According to Wurman (1989) these "old formulas and systems for data processing are impotent against the complexity of information we must assimilate today."

A regulatory agency automates a system that displays a profile of the entities that it regulates. This profile pours so much information on-line that it tops out at over 91 display screens. Rumor is that no one has ever seen the ninety-first screen.

The Securities and Exchange Commission must process thousands of free-form financial filings on a daily basis, far exceeding the capacity of the human reviewers.

The process of entering insurance underwriting data into the computer is so difficult, it takes one Midwestern company six months to train each new employee.

The process of credit authorization depends on dozens of variables and is fraught with human error. Things that are considered include payment history, seasonal variation, and even pattern of spending. Complexity grows exponentially as the number of cardholders rises and with it the request for more authorizations in a shorter span of time.

"The common denominator today is that the insurance agent is totally befuddled," says William LeStrange, the president of one of the largest of the independent insurance agencies. "He is no longer able to answer the questions that were simple to respond to only five years ago." LeStrange's complaint is due to the power of the computer, which spawned countless new policies. And with them, a whole new set of risk factors. The problem with the insurance industry is that companies can't get the information fast enough, can't process it quickly enough, and can't get it back in a format they can deal with.

So the problem is not in getting the information; computer systems solved that problem years ago. The problem is that once you get it in, you have a heck of a time getting it back out. Picture, if you will, a large black box pulsating with the sum total of information collected over eons. Humankind sits patiently around this glowing, buzzing object waiting for a shred of wisdom. Folks, welcome to the corporate data center. Soon the denizens of the corporate data center began to see the light. They realized that by changing how this information is "evaluated or aggregated, the dimensionality or structural content of the information may be altered to provide a different input to a different level of decision making." (King, Grover, and Hufnagel, 1989, p. 89). Hence, the birth of decision support systems.

FROM BATCH TO DECISION SUPPORT

In the twenty-first century we might achieve technological nirvana. For some, this might be the fusion of human and machine. A great debate has been raging on the technological, political, and even moral battlegrounds over the development of what we call, rather prosaically, an *artilect*.

An artilect would be a machine that would exhibit artificial intellect

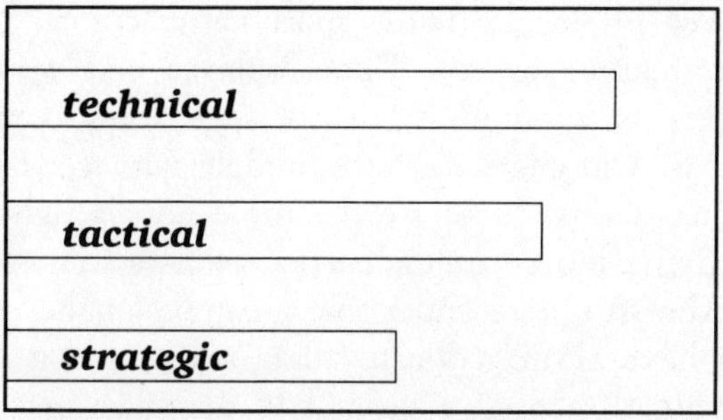

FIGURE 1-1. Types of Decision Makers.

to the degree of, one day, surpassing its creators. These ultraintelligent machines inspire fear, loathing, and a great deal of fascination in the scientific community as well as in the general public. Could we, humans that we are, bear living in a world "peopled by creations massively smarter than we are?" (de Garis, 1989, p. 17). But we jump ahead of ourselves. This is not the twenty-first century and there are no artilects to loathe *or* love. There is, however, the possibility of creating computer systems that are just about as bright as we are in narrower spheres of expertise.

The key is to create computer systems that present less, but more significant or germane data. Several methods can be used to present to the end-user the best mix of the detail with the composite data. All of these methods recognize a relationship between the type of decision maker and the detail presented, as shown in Figure 1-1.

Types of Decision Makers

There are three types of decision makers. At the bottom of the corporate hierarchy are the paper pushers. These are the people who *do* need to see all the data. They are the check processors, complaint takers, order takers, and customer service staff. These technical users need to input and review a wealth of data. Given the nature of the task, this is usually done in a rote fashion and not subject to complex decision making. At the other end of the spectrum are the organization's senior managers who use information gathered at the lower rungs for strategic purposes. A whole range of vendor-sold EIS (Executive Information

Systems) is now in vogue. These sport flashy colors, touch screens, and sparse information displays. Data displayed here would most likely be sales projections, profitability numbers, and key competitive data. In the middle is (you guessed it) the middle manager or tactical user. In organizational terms, these are the professionals right on the firing line who need the most careful balance of data. These are the poor unfortunates who sit buried under that great avalanche of information.

Companies have always collected data and stored it in diverse and hidden corporate databases. Automobile manufacturers keep massive amounts of data on file concerning their suppliers and dealership locations. For a long time no one saw any strategic value to this mass of detail. That is, until Chrysler fell into the black pit of insolvency. Lee Iacocca (1984) tweaked this very set of databases to save Chrysler from a fate much worse than rust. By moving to a different level of information analysis, Iacocca was able to convince members of Congress to support the loans that infused life into the veins of his company.

Filtering

There are a host of filtering methodologies for serving up this sort of strategic knowledge on a silver platter. For the most part, they are classified in three different ways.

The *monitoring method* serves up data to the user on an exception basis. This can be variance reporting, where the system produces only exceptions based on programmatic review of the data. For example, to review credit card payments and display only those accounts where the payment wasn't received or the payment is below the minimum payment.

The advent of the fourth-generation language (4GL), a tool enabling the end-user to access the corporate database with an easy-to-use query syntax, has thrust the *interrogative method* of system tailoring to the popular forefront. This method takes into account the many occasions when the user cannot identify the set of information necessary to handle day-to-day, ad-hoc analyses in complex decision-making environments. In these cases, all of the data elements need to be resident in an accessible database. And a tool needs to be in place to permit the user to easily and quickly develop queries and variations on these queries against this data.

When Banker's Trust decided to get out of the retail business in the early 1980s, the data processing effort to achieve this feat was enormous. One area that Banker's spun off rather quickly was the credit card subsidiary. The 4GL in use at that time was FOCUS (by Information Builders). The users and the accounting staff used this tool to great advantage to ensure a smooth transition of accounts to the many final resting places. Some accounts spun off to a bank in Chicago, some to Albany, while the high-rollers stayed behind in newly minted, privileged checking accounts.

A *model-oriented approach* comes in many flavors. Human resource or facilities departments are good candidates for descriptive models, which can be organization charts or floor plans. On the other hand, a normative representation of data is a good fit for budgeting when the goal is to provide the best answer to a given problem. Economic projections are a good target for modeling methodologies that have the ability to handle uncertainty. The operations management students among us gleefully apply game theory to those problems where there is a requirement to find the best solution in spite of a profound lack of information. An example of a problem that would use this type of strategy would be a competitive marketing system where data about the competition is scant or unknown.

Today's Technology Is Not Working

Unfortunately corporate data processing departments up until now have applied the "pitch, hit, and run" theory to most systems development. Little, if any, consideration is given to these diverse levels of informational decision making. Many *kluges* spew out unneeded and irrelevant data to users. These besieged users then unceremoniously toss the results onto the very crowded systems scrap heap.

Sometime early in the 1980s these users got wind of the phenomenon of personal computers. And with this hardware that they could control all by themselves came some novel software. This was the first instance of user-driven decision support software. And the data processing departments all across the country sat up and took notice.

In the world of the PC, the user is free to pick, to choose, to make mistakes, and then to gain insight from what was once chaos. LOTUS

1-2-3 was the inspiration that fired up the rockets. With LOTUS the user was, for the first time, able to perform the "what-if" analyses that so whetted the appetite. Now here was a decision support tool! But still only a support tool. One that is mired in the processing of data rather than the processing of knowledge. We still need to go one step further.

TRANSFORMING INFORMATION INTO KNOWLEDGE

Perhaps the industry with the largest share of traditional systems is the banking industry. No one personifies banking more, nor has done more for the banking industry than Citicorp's chairman emeritus Walter Wriston. In his 17 years as chief executive officer he revolutionized the international banking environment. And one of the tools in his toolbox of change was the computer. With over a trillion dollars a day changing hands in the New York market alone, the banking industry is gearing up for an alliance of technology and strategy. Wriston envisions a banking environment where the interface between human and machine permits easy access to complex information. Artificial intelligence, predicts Wriston, will become the norm and not the exception. He looks forward to a day when he can walk up to an expert system in a bank lobby that will be able to answer complex questions about his account. "Can I invest in a tax-free fund? Can I do brokerage transactions?"

Quaker Oats in Chicago was one of the first consumer goods marketers to realize the potential of strategic technology. More than fifteen years ago it set up its own computer program to analyze some 2 billion facts about different products and competitors. Use of this system permitted Quaker Oats to understand this data and to draw insights from it. This led them to the number one spot in such product categories as Rice-A-Roni and the ever popular Aunt Jemima Pancakes. More recently they began to realize that new technology was making the system obsolete. So without hesitation, out it went and in came Express MDB. With it they can perform the intricate "what if" analyses that will keep them number one.

This brand of filtering methodology is a technology very much in vogue as more and more entrepreneurial start-ups compete to slay the information dragon. MIT stepped in to become a knight in shining armor when it devised a novel way to separate the E-Mail wheat from the chaff. For many of us, electronic mail messages rate right up there with junk mail. The MIT system found a novel way to categorize messages as top priority if they come from certain people or if the message implies that it needs a response within a few days. Joining these "Knights of The Round Table" is a former LOTUS development executive. He started a company called Beyond Inc. based on just this technology. LOTUS itself has its own mail sifter. NOTES uses graphical displays to permit senders to imprint distinctive logos on their electronic missives. You can direct your mailbox to turn up its nose at certain logos and permit others access. I suppose some enterprising start-up company will find a comfortable niche in producing counterfeit logos for gate-crashing. Or will we call it logo-crashing?

Filters work for more than just turning up your nose at uninvited electronic guests. It is also a mainstay in the marketing arena. For years, marketers used technology to filter relevancies out of information glut. It started with the first totally computerized census back in 1970. The Census Bureau recorded demographic data on computer tapes. This provided a plethora of information on neighborhoods right down to your very own city block. By the time the 1980 census rolled around, these stats had ballooned into 300,000 pages of statistics. And a whopping ten times that amount sat patiently on computer tapes. Today the personal computer has put this same information on a desk top.

Some in the financial industry quickly followed suit. Investors Services, out of Bridgeport, Connecticut, has been collecting data for some thirty years. Today it manages Worldscope, an international database containing a wealth of information on some 5,000 companies. The key here is smart filtering.

A start-up company in Brookline, Massachusetts, seems to have found the key as well. Individual Inc. sifts through full-text articles and pinpoints items of interest to its subscribers. "We are operating an information refinery that takes a broad stream of raw data and turns it into actionable knowledge," says its founder Yosi Amram.

Dean LeBaron agrees to this approach. He was very much in the avant-garde in the middle 1970s. That's when he preached the use of computers to improve the quality of investing. Batterymarch Financial Management is one of Boston's leading money management firms with a portfolio of over $11 billion. LeBaron runs Batterymarch as one large expert system. It's "designed to operate the way an intelligent institutional investor would operate if put on a silicon substrate."

WHERE DO WE GO FROM HERE?

Wriston, LeBaron, and the rest of these folks recognized early on the advantages of using smarter technology. And each revels in the "number one" spot in his respective marketplace. What we aim to do is discuss ways of developing these smarter systems so you too can be "number one." In this book we're going to go where fearless others have gone before. Since examples of successful systems spur the rest of us on, at least part of this book is chock full of bright ideas whose time came and stayed. For those of you who are not quite sure how to get in on the act, the first several chapters of this book are for you.

A magician's secret revealed. Astound your colleagues at lunch by balancing an egg on one end. Sounds impossible? Discreetly pour a pile of salt under the tablecloth at the very spot where you will perform your magical feat. Press the egg, hard-boiled of course, onto the tablecloth atop the small mound of salt.

The magic here involves planning and sleight of hand; the magic in this book is artificial intelligence.

2 | AI and the Financial Services Arena

PUTTING AI IN PERSPECTIVE

I have three coins jingling in my hand. They add up to exactly 35 cents, and one of them is *not* a nickel. Guess what these coins are. This trick has been around a long, long time. You should know the answer: I have one quarter and *two* nickels. Artificial intelligence has been around a long time, too. So it's a wonder why it has taken this long to catch on.

But what is AI, really? There are as many definitions of what makes up AI as there are legs on a centipede. Back in 1956 when AI was still in its infancy, Marvin Minsky, who some consider to be the father of AI, was heard to say, "If it works, it ain't AI!" Elaine Rich (1983), who wrote one of the definitive treatises on the subject, defines AI as the study of how to make computers do things at which, at the moment, people are better.

At the moment. Now *these* are words to live by. I know we all agree that computers are better than humans in the art of numerical calculation. Quick, multiply 8,321 times 6,524 and what do you get (and no cheating!)? If you got 54,286,204 you're either using a calculator, you're an idiot savant, or an artilect. Once you get that number, store it away in your memory. Now store these six other numbers:

66,256,704	102,345,684	98,243,876
45,312,633	97,643,231	11,235,002

Close the book and try to remember these numbers without peeking. Were you successful? Psychological research shows us that humans can

11

successfully absorb seven pieces of information and recall them with no problem. Unfortunately, this doesn't seem to hold true with numbers. But feed these numbers into a computer and get instant access. In fact, store a million numbers in a computer and it will remember them perfectly. So okay, we humans are not as good as computers in some things like numerical calculations and information storage. To even things up, we are much better than that gray box at doing any activity involving intelligence, common sense, or ambiguity.

Artificial intelligence is a field of study in computer science that works at narrowing these differences between it (being the computer) and us. There are several branches of AI that pique our collective interest. The expert system branch is the one we seem to be interested in the most. In the financial services arena, *natural language* processing is running a close second. Add to this list robotics, speech recognition, automatic programming, and computer vision and we have bitten off more than we can chew. This list is sometimes longer, sometimes shorter as the AI gurus do battle over what AI actually is. So, let's take a short stroll through some of the fields of artificial intelligence and do some sight-seeing.

Natural Language Processing

Natural language processing enables people and computers to communicate on equal footing. There are two subfields: natural language *understanding* and natural language *generation*. For the most part, the work being done in the financial services industry is in the area of understanding.

Here the emphasis is on two areas: using natural English for database inquiry and deciphering textual messages. On the inquiry side, there are hordes of users out there who are less than comfortable using the computer. Couple this with the rigid syntax that most computer systems enforce and you have the makings of an information bottleneck. Information goes in but never comes out. Wouldn't it be great to just turn on that ol' computer and strike up a conversation like, "HOW ABOUT THOSE STATISTICS ON PROFITABILITY FOR THE THIRD QUARTER?" Well, later on in this chapter we'll see how an inquiry as easy as this is actually quite complicated. We'll also see a natural language's ad hoc inquiry capability in use at the New York Stock Exchange in Chapter 6.

More and more banks are working with natural language text deciphering and we'll see a prime example of it at Citibank in Chapter 7.

Robotics

A few years ago I visited TEXACO, which is located in New York's Westchester County. While sitting in a conference room, a beep-beep-beeping noise echoed in the hallway every 20 minutes or so. I finally jumped up to find out what that blasted sound was. It was a robot. A mail robot to be exact. Following a track around the office, it was programmed to stop at certain stations and wait for someone to pick up the mail.

Perhaps an even more exotic example of a robot is one under development by our very own Army. Called an Autonomous Land Vehicle (ALV), this $500 million-dollar baby moves at a snail's pace, some 12 miles per hour. Weighing in at the megaton range, this vehicle is completely automated, using computer vision to "see" the edges in the road and obstructions in its path. A bit after reading about it, I had a chance to see a demonstration of this robot on television. I tuned in to see a nervous reporter standing squarely in the middle of the road. He stood there assuring his viewers that this looming giant would stop short of crushing him. Every now and then, this reporter would glance over his shoulder. The camera would pan-in on close-up and you'd see a perspiring face twitching with fear. By the way, the ALV did stop short (very short) of our intrepid reporter.

Robotics is the most advanced branch of AI and the one that has probably been around the longest. It certainly has captured the imagination of our science fiction writers. Everything from Asimov's "I, Robot" to the evil HAL in 2001. In spite of our sci-fi writers' wonderful imaginations, most robots are programmed to do trivial manual tasks for purposes of increased productivity and reduction of cost. On the factory floor they alleviate the shortage of skilled labor.

As in every science, robotics scientists just love to provide naming conventions to their discoveries. The robot has arms, hands, and a power source. Let's get into the swing of things and learn a bit of robot lingo. An arm is a manipulator, a hand is an end effector. The next time you're at an important meeting why don't you just grab the CEO's manipulator and shake end effectors?

Robots are becoming ubiquitous. Even Burger King is looking for ways of robotizing its operation. Researchers at the University of Wisconsin–Stout in Menomonie put a robotic worker into action. The school has a "Burger King laboratory" which is a replica of a real one. School business program director, Tom Phillips, worked with a nearby high-tech firm to design and build what has become known as "Roboburger." What Translab built was only 22 inches high, 18 inches wide, and a bit over 3 feet long. It uses optical sensors, conveyors, and molded wire to grab, move, and assemble burgers and buns together. Roboburger can replace one person on the food line.

This process is harder than it seems. It takes perfect synchronizations to convey the bottom half of the hamburger bun and to wait for the perfect moment to drop a meat patty from the broiler, onto the bun. Using wire hands to situate the top bun just so on top of the burger—in just under two minutes a burger is born. Food (or burger) for thought: If someone had the bright idea to invent Roboburger, then why not a Roboteller or Robotrader.

Speech Recognition

The goal of speech recognition is simple. It is to allow a computer to communicate with a human being in the most prevalent mode of communication. That is human speech. The benefits are endless. Ease of access. Speed. Manual freedom. Remote access. Just imagine being on the road and calling up your office personal computer on the telephone. Imagine telling it to load up your spreadsheet, perform a trend analysis, and then read the bottom line to you!

The first foray into the world of speech recognition I ever made was in the middle 1980s with my office PC and something called a VOTAN board. Now *this* was an interesting product. You installed a board into your PC and connected up a microphone. Once this process was done you were ready to "train" the system to understand your commands. This was a process of joining a spoken command to a typed command. For example, one of the more common commands on the IBM personal computer is the directory command, which is typed as DIR. Once typed, you then press the enter key to have the computer display a list of all of your files that are on the disk drive in question. By training the computer to join the spoken word "directory" with the typed sequence DIR (enter), I could communicate with my computer by voice to do a command that normally requires several keystrokes. Now this was impressive. I set out to train my computer to understand by spoken command virtually everything. I began to get into trouble when friends, curious about the microphone attached to my PC, began to hover around my office making comments, snide and otherwise. Remember, the PC now listened for commands from human speech. With all the babble surrounding my office in those days, the computer, although well-intentioned, would occasionally misinterpret some of this background noise. It would invariably translate the gibberish it heard into an executable command. Unfortunately for my system. So it got to the point where I posted a large "SHHHH!" sign on my door. Folks who were visiting would try to communicate with me through mime lest they should set the computer off on a path of destruction.

Misinterpreting background noise was also the reason for suspension of the New York Stock Exchange's efforts in the area of voice trading-floor systems. The Exchange wanted to find a better way to jot down trades than by using a human reporter. The reporter function dates back almost to the beginnings of the Exchange. These are the folks who listen to the trade jargon and scribble the made trade onto a keypunch card for entry into a card reader. Not your most advanced form of technology. The Exchange's Research and Development Department, ever on the lookout for the new and the better, brought Texas Instruments into the picture. They wanted to see if there was a way to use speech recognition to replace the reporter function. If you make a pilgrimage to the visitor's center today, you'll still see the reporters, so obviously the speech recognition project was not exactly successful. In fact, what happened to me and my personal computer happened to them, too. The system could not distinguish between the spoken voice of the user and the very loud cries on the Exchange floor. Foiled again.

There are other problems, too. One of these is the computer's training requirement. You must train the computer to understand your voice. But your voice changes. This point was brought home at an ill-fated demonstration. The computer salesman had meticulously trained the computer to understand his voice early in the morning, for an afternoon presentation to some very high-level corporate executives. This salesman then proceeded to go out to lunch and have a couple of drinks to quiet his raw nerves. He then went back to the conference room to set-up the demo. When the big moment arrived, the salesman picked up the microphone with a flourish and spoke his command. Silence. With perspiration beading his brow, he cleared his throat and tried again. The computer just blinked at him. Now there were rumblings behind him. These corporate biggies were growing a bit impatient. He would try one more time. Clearing the frog from his throat he restated his command. Total failure. What had happened? Well, for starters, this system was very sensitive to changes in his voice. Our sorrowful salesman had trained the machine in the morning. By afternoon his voice had altered slightly. And after a couple of drinks and a bad case of the nerves, his voice had changed a great deal. The same thing happens if you train the system when you're well and try to use it when you have a cold. Now, it's true that the software used with this hardware device can make accommodations to these variations. In fact, that's exactly what I did. This enabled the computer to hear *everybody* and to try to process commands out of all the babble.

Perhaps the worst problem of all is the computer's need for hearing speech in a rather disconnected, robotized way. Most of us speak in a rapid-fire fashion and would find it irritating, if not downright painful, to have to speak to the computer S-L-O-W-L-Y A-N-D D-E-L-I-B-E-R-A-T-E-L-Y since these systems don't do real well at continuous word recognition.

Although we're not quite there yet, computer scientists are making terrific inroads. One of the most applauded uses of this technology is in the area of services for the handicapped. In fact, Stefan Michalowski, of the Stanford University mechanical engineering department, is doing just that in a Veterans Administration research project. He is working on a robot, equipped with speech recognition, to become the arms and legs for a quadriplegic. The user, equipped with a microphone, can verbally command the robot. Commands such as "Get me a drink of water" or "Answer the door."

There's application for speech recognition everywhere in corporate America. Data entry and security are some applications that come to mind instantly. Banking by phone will probably be one of the first uses of this technology in the financial services industry. And just think of what a combination of speech recognition and natural language processing would be able to do:

Banking customer: What was my checking account balance on
   December 15th?

Securities customer: Buy me 200 shares of IBM and sell 1000 of my Waste Management.

Insurance customer: What would the premium payments be for disability income if I wanted an income of $4,000 a month and I was willing to live with a 90-day elimination period? Also give me the numbers for a 30-day elimination period.

Computer Vision

How do we understand what we see? Believe it or not, visual images have been stored in computers since the early 1950s, so we've had plenty of time to perfect this particular branch of artificial intelligence.

It's done by the use of cameras. Images are received by the camera and then digitized (converted from analog to digital). These digitized signals are then stored as what we call pixels. Pixel is now becoming a well-known word, at least since the advent of desktop publishing. Most of us are familiar with the concept.

When you use your PC "paint" program, you might want to scan an image. Using your trusty scanner, scoop up an image that tickles your fancy. When you zoom in on it you see that the image actually consists of little dots that you can alter to suit your artistic palette.

These little dots are pixels and computer vision devices analyze them. What they're looking for are patterns to find visual clues. These clues include color, depth, texture, and motion.

Remember the Autonomous Land Vehicle that we met when we discussed robotics? The ALV used computer vision to keep track of the road. It did this by sensing patterns to look for the edges. Its goal in life is to look for the edges of the road and obstructions in its path. And it was the use of computer vision that saved that foolhardy reporter's life. The computer sensed an obstacle and refrained from crushing the intrepid newscaster.

Automatic Programming

In 1964 Arthur Samuels, developer of one of the first machine learning programs, predicted there would be no more computer programmers by 1984. Computers would have learned so much from executing so many programs that they would be programming themselves. In 1984, when he received a prestigious award, he retracted that prediction and promised to make no more predictions.

What really happened was that the demand for programmers actually went up because there were more and more things that people wanted computers to do. In fact, an IBM survey actually indicated that the number of applications is growing at the phenomenal rate of 45 percent a year.

Now add to this huge surge of applications the declining number of trained programming professionals. Finally, add the often cumbersome process of systems development and what we wind up with is a bottleneck.

Automatic programming may just be the answer. These tools can be thought of as systems analyst/programmer workbenches somewhat akin to the CASE (Computer-Assisted Software Engineering) tools that are being marketed today. The difference is artificial intelligence.

At the MIT Computer Science Laboratory, PROTOSYSTEM I became one of the first automatic programming tools to autonomously perform five stages of systems development. From soup to nuts, PROTOSYSTEM I automatically handles the steps of problem definition, specification analysis, implementation, coding, and compiling.

Not to be outdone by MIT, Stanford developed a system known by the moniker PSI. It was really several specialized programming systems integrated into one master automatic programming system. Included in each component was an expert system relating to each step in the development process.

Another automatic programming system from the land of sun and fun is University of Southern California's SAFE system. SAFE creates a program specification from natural language input. The use of natural language here is domain-dependent. This language understands the words of program specification but really wouldn't be able to converse about next Sunday's football game. Its transformation module translates this rather free-form English language specification into actual program code.

None of these systems ever made it to the commercial market. On the commercial end are the CASE products and although fewer than 24 percent of corporations are using these products today, CASE is most certainly a buzzword.

CASE can be thought of as a non-AI approach to automatic programming. The end objective is still the same: to automate the systems engineering process as much as possible. Index Technology's Excelerator product line is probably the best-known CASE tool in the marketplace today. It offers an integrated set of analysis and design tools to help a system guru define, verify, and document a system before coding actually starts. Giving the developer access to on-line dictionaries, graphical interfaces, and prototyping tools, gives the developer a head start. But it's not AI.

There's been more and more discussion about a merger between CASE and AI. On the one hand, CASE would obviously benefit from an AI infusion. And on the other hand, expert system development could sure use some better development tool sets. In fact, it is going in that direction. AION Corporation announced in late 1989 that it planned to produce a development management tool specifically for their ADS expert system product. This product can help in planning, development, testing, delivery, maintenance, documentation, and overall management of the entire systems development life cycle.

And more is on the way. Even Index Technology is working with Ontos, an object-oriented database sold by Ontologic, to *OOP-up* (I'll tell you what this means later on) its Excelerator CASE tool. And Bachman Information Services, Inc. has just announced an AI-infused CASE tool set.

Creative AI

It's well-known that, try as they might, AI researchers can't make computers creative. That's something reserved for humans. But try telling that to Harold Cohen. Professor Cohen has been an artist and computer scientist for over 20 years. Now he's managed to merge his two passions and create a distinct art form.

Using an AI program, Professor Cohen managed to infuse creativity into his computer. And what comes out is nothing short of art. Beautiful images of floral jungles and shy people paper the tall walls of Cohen's office.

WHY EXPERT SYSTEMS?

Over the last several years, over 80 percent of the Fortune 500 companies have explored expert system techniques. So there must be something to it. The usual selling point is that the expert system encodes the knowledge and reasoning skills of our resident staff experts.

It permits users to conduct dialogues with the automated system. It can provide an enormous boost to productivity and extend the power of the computer beyond your wildest imaginings. It's all this and more.

In the not too distant past, we had batch systems. Most are still running today and many more are on the drawing board. These systems are as far removed from end-users as expert systems are close to them. In the old days, bespectacled programmers sat in subterranean offices quietly punching little holes in keypunch cards. I should know, I was one of them. This motley crew laboriously keypunched each and every line of program code by hand. How I used to wish for some sturdy glue to paste back those little holes every time I made a keypunching mistake.

We would send that wad of cards on its merry way to an even lower level of the office building. Here the new and shiny computer (which had about the same capacity as today's personal computers) waited to be fed. One try a day was all you got as you tried to write and correct your program. It was much the same for the end-user. One try a day to "pull" some information out of the computer.

Not too much later those of us in the information processing field began to hear tall tales about some magic program that permitted files to be structured into something new and foreign. It turns out that this newfangled thing, called a database, actually permitted us to more easily store and retrieve our data. So now we could get information to our users more quickly.

And then on one winter morning when I walked into work, I spotted a green-glowing tube sitting atop my desk. It was a cathode-ray tube, also known as a CRT or terminal. It would serve to change data processing as we all knew it. You could now write programs without having to worry about gluing those little holes back into the keypunch cards. You could get your results turned around in minutes instead of hours. And the users thought that they had found The Holy Grail. Instant information. When we found ways to communicate this data to downtown San Francisco from downtown New York, the users achieved nirvana.

The migration from batch to database to communications-base seems a natural evolution. For those involved, each step was a revolution that required entrenched mindsets to change and new tools to be learned. The point is that change we did. So it should be no different with methodologies based on artificial intelligence. It's just the next step on our natural path of technological evolution.

But what are expert systems, really? Let's answer this by first explaining what they're not. They're not database management systems. Look at the left side of Figure 2-1. Here is a picture of a human resource database. This database contains facts and figures. It shows that John earns $26,000 a year. It also shows that Pete earns $67,000 a year. There's no knowledge here, just facts, all the facts and nothing but the facts.

Now look at the right side of Figure 2-1. This is a human resources knowledge base. There are no facts and figures here. It shows that if the salary of the employee is greater than $25,000 then the job title is manager. It also says that if someone is 35 years old or older then they are vested in the company's pension plan. This is knowledge in the form of rules. There are no mere lists of facts or figures, just knowledge about how this department works.

Some of you may use some very powerful tools on your PCs. LO-TUS is perhaps the most popular software package around. It's got so much power that you're certain it's got AI. Guess again. These software packages are just conventionally smart. They use traditional program-

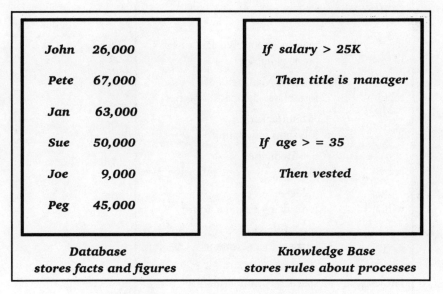

Database stores facts and figures	Knowledge Base stores rules about processes
John 26,000	If salary > 25K
Pete 67,000	Then title is manager
Jan 63,000	
Sue 50,000	If age > = 35
Joe 9,000	Then vested
Peg 45,000	

FIGURE 2-1. Database versus Knowledge Base.

ming techniques so that you can do your own brand of decision support. What they do have is the ability to let you enter information in any format. You can also write little programs or *macros* to arrive at new and different conclusions. Notice that you're still working with facts and figures. The program that processes these facts and figures is really no smarter than any of the other software programs you use.

So, what are expert systems? Let's try another tack. Let's explore some uses, financial and not, of this technology. Perhaps we can discern a pattern here. In the world of agriculture, an expert system predicts damage to corn due to cutworm. Another expert system manages apple orchards. In the world of chemistry, the expert system Dendral can determine the molecular structure of unknown compounds from mass spectral and nuclear magnetic response data. In the area of engineering, the Reactor expert system can help operators in the diagnosis and treatment of nuclear reactor accidents.

Expert systems are found in a myriad of areas. Look at Table 2-1 and peruse the many applications in the world of geology, information

	Geology
prospector	searches for oil
	Law
judith	reasons about civil law cases
LDS	product liability
	Information Management
rabbit	formulates database inquiries
	Manufacturing
isis	job shop scheduling
	Medicine
baby	monitors newborn intensive care
	Meteorology
williard	forecasting thunderstorms
	Military
adept	battlefield assessment
	Space
faith	spacecraft troubleshooting

TABLE 2-1.   Uses of Expert Systems.

management, law, manufacturing, medicine, meteorology, military, and space. And there are hundreds of others.

If we analyze the attributes of this short list of expert systems we can draw two conclusions. One is that some of these systems are used for packaging expertise for use by nonexperts. And the second conclusion we can draw is that the use of these systems serves the purpose of improving the performance of technicians.

Tosh-tosh, you say. You can use conventional programming techniques to do all of these things. You may be right! There is no precise demarcation between the expert system and traditional data processing. It is possible to use FORTRAN or COBOL, but perhaps there's a better way.

WHAT MAKES AN EXPERT SYSTEM TICK?

The secret behind an expert system is the "expertise." Instead of capturing the data surrounding a securities trade, you capture the knowledge of why someone makes that trade. Instead of just capturing data that is on an insurance application, capture the knowledge that the underwriter uses in determining whether to approve that policy or not.

Just as databases were a better way to store data than mere file systems, expert systems do a better job at storing and processing knowledge than do conventional systems.

Conventional data processing systems typically process large amounts of raw data. This data is put through a series of algorithmic paces and ultimately stored in some database somewhere. Let's look at a typical system, one that everyone is familiar with. Payroll systems are the backbone of any company. Just have a problem with it and you'll see a bunch of disgruntled employees. Inputs to this system are found on the employee master file, which stores information pertinent to each employee's wages. Now we need a deductions file, which accounts for each employee's extras, such as amounts deducted for the company savings plan, savings bonds, and even charity deductions. So what we have is a lot of data that needs some processing. The process of calculating correct deductions and tax rates requires many mechanical, mathematical computations. Most of us know little about taxes and might be tempted to suggest that this system does exhibit expertise. This expertise is little more than procedural information that is found in any manual. There's no explanation as to *why* or *how* these deductions work, they just work. The net result is the cutting of hundreds and hundreds of paychecks each and every week.

On the other hand, let's examine the creation of an expert system. At the Campbell Soup Company, a senior technician was about to retire. His job was to make sure that the cookers were in good working order. Campbell doesn't make soup by the pot-full, it makes soup by the vat-full. These cookers required constant monitoring. The technician in this true story had many years of experience on the job. Looking at gauges wasn't always enough. He could literally smell when there was trouble brewing. This ability is called gut feel, or heuristics, and all of us have it in some capacity. We get so good at something that we can do it upside down and blindfolded and it would still turn out right. This is what makes an expert, an expert. When Charlie was expert-systematized, he at first thought it a foolhardy idea. When all was said and done, he realized that the system built did indeed capture his experience. There is no data processing here. Of course, data is a component part of any system and it was here, too. Charlie analyzed data as he read the many gauges on the cooker. This system did not really process this data, the data was only a corollary. What it did process was Charlie. Or at least Charlie's knowledge.

YOU NEED A DIFFERENT TOOL TO PROCESS KNOWLEDGE

The tools of conventional programming make us comfortable. They're so familiar. Everything is so ordered. You put one line of code in front of another making sure all progresses in a logical sequence. It wouldn't do to have the chunk of code concerning payroll deductions fire off in the wrong spot.

So coding an expert system can be a rather unnerving experience. For expert systems are nonprocedural. Chunks of knowledge can go in any order. We'll soon learn, not too many pages from now, why it's not a good idea to cast all programming conventions aside. Even though an expert system will work no matter how you drop that knowledge in, it's a good idea to order that knowledge in logical chunks. Do this, and you'll keep your sanity during maintenance mode.

To code an expert system you need a software tool. There are many. There has always been a large selection of tools to choose from no matter what the programming problem. It is unrealistic to expect that one tool will solve every conceivable type of problem. Look at the computer language time line shown in Figure 2-2. My very first computer programming language was assembly language. This is about as close to the computer as you can get without having to resort to machine language. When COBOL was popularized, sometime in the 1960s, many programmers and their supervisors refused to give up the tool that they knew best. "Why use COBOL?" they asked. "Assembly language can do it all." They sure missed the point. COBOL was easier, more geared for business programming. Later on even higher-level languages were invented. Fourth-generation languages (4GLs) were born to permit less technical folk the happy experience of doing their own programming. When databases became popularized, specialized database languages began to make significant inroads. Oracle and Dbase are just two of this variety.

With all of this variety one would expect it to be difficult to make a choice. In data processing, the caveat for selection should be "fit the tool to the application." The keyword here is fit, mind you, it's not force. Most programming tools have attributes that make them labor-specific. That is, they are useful for particular tasks. Of course, most

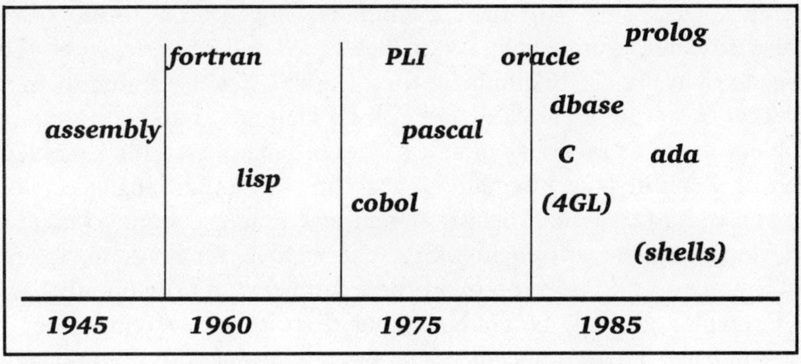

assembly	fortran	PLI	oracle	prolog
		pascal	dbase	
	lisp		C	ada
		cobol	(4GL)	
				(shells)
1945	1960	1975	1985	

FIGURE 2-2.　Computer Language Time Line.

tools are general enough that they are used for almost any task. You'll find features in each that tend to push them to be used in a particular way.

FORTRAN is an acronym for formula translation. FORTRAN is popular for those applications where an awful lot of calculation is going on. Your "quants" or your statisticians make this their programming language of choice. COBOL is an acronym for common business-oriented language. It has great facilities for bringing in large quantities of data, chewing it around a bit and then spitting it out to a database or a report.

There are four entries on our time line that are in vogue with those building expert systems. LISP is perhaps one of the oldest programming languages around. It also turns out to be the artificial programming language of choice for the American scientific community. Although uniquely powerful and well-suited for the job, LISP has its disadvantages. The first problem is the proliferation of LISP versions floating around. Although something called CommonLisp is becoming more standard, there are still enough variations of LISP around making it difficult to write *portable* (usable by any computer) code. LISP itself has some unique features that make it less than a perfect tool for the financial services community. Most AI research projects are done on workstation devices. While many financial services' AI systems also reside in workstations (we'll see some later in this book), standard financial systems traditionally run on a mainframe, minicomputer, or even a personal computer. LISP has a large memory requirement and is less than "neat" when it comes to something called "garbage collection." Garbage is created when variables are stored in the memory of the computer. Problems occur when so many variables are stored that there is no room to do any more processing. An efficient computer language has techniques to deal with determining when a variable is used and when it is not. The language may choose to eliminate these variables by discarding them altogether or storing them elsewhere. LISP's facility to handle this type of problem is not as robust as more traditional languages. Other problems with LISP are its poor integration capability with other languages. Let's say you've built a general ledger system and now you want to build in an AI component written in LISP. Although it can be done, it's not an easy thing to do. On top of all these problems add the one that says there aren't too many programmers out there that have experience in this language. These problems might soon disappear with the porting of LISP to mainframe and PC systems. So I'd stay tuned.

The European and Japanese academic, AI communities use a programming language called Prolog. It is a programming language based on predicate calculus. Instead of just listing individual processing steps in a Prolog program, you itemize a set of facts and rules. This is the type of logic programming that is best used to solve mathematical, symbolic problems, or those that exhibit many choices of the true/false variety. Where LISP is a procedural language, Prolog is a declarative language. More and more nonacademic AI programmers are turning toward Prolog, since its ability to handle symbolic problems makes it a natural for expert system applications.

It is the *shell* that most developers of expert systems will use. Shells are tools that you install on your computer that have been prewritten to handle all of the niceties of expert systems. All you have to do is dump in the knowledge, everything else is done for you. These tools are perhaps the easiest tools around, making expert system development available to the general data processing community. Some are so easy that even noncomputer people can build their own expert systems.

An owner of a dental laboratory had a problem. Only *he* had the instincts to figure out when a patient's false teeth would be ready. This presented a problem, since he was not always available. Then he had a stroke of brilliance. He had always dabbled in PCs. In fact, he set one up at the office and bought a few software packages to automate things such as inventory. Then he read about something called an expert system. So he ordered one of the cheaper PC versions and installed it on his computer. He then proceeded to collect his "rules of thumb" for figuring out how to determine the time needed to prepare dentures. He added these rules to the knowledge base that came with his expert system software. Now he's able to leave the office with a warm feeling. His staff can walk over to the system, punch in a few variables, and have the system tell them when the teeth will be ready. So smile everybody, this is a true story.

The C programming language is not specifically an artificial intelligence language. It seems that more and more projects traditionally done in Prolog or LISP are being done in C. There are two main reasons for this. The first is that C is a portable language. Since it is standardized, a system written using C for a DEC machine is easily transported to an IBM. For the shell manufacturers this is an overriding concern. The makers of expert system shells learned early on the error of their programming ways when they coded their systems in LISP. Buyers of the product kept on asking the same question, "Well, it's great that this shell runs on a workstation, but when will it run on a DEC? or an IBM?" Shell manufacturers began to realize that what people wanted were multiplatform tools. Most companies, and that includes financial services companies, run their business on different computers. It's not uncommon to have computer rooms with DECs, IBMs, TANDEMs and whatnot standing side-by-side. If developers are going to get into expert systems in a big way, then we need a tool that works for all of these platforms. Well, I'm happy to say that most expert system tool manufacturers *have heeded* this cry. Appendix B lists some of these expert system tool makers and their products. Since C is standardized and since it runs on all hardware platforms, it has become the language of choice for this mass migration. The other feature that makes it quite palatable to everyone is that there is broad familiarity with it. It's easy to hire staff to perform the necessary programming tasks.

The point here is that some tools do one thing well and some tools do other things well. For the expert system type of problem, these higher level symbolic languages and shells are the tools that are suited best for the task. Even though we narrowed it down somewhat to a few programming languages and shells, there are still a great many choices. And here I can't help you. Choosing a tool will be a function of the experience level of your staff, the languages they know, the operating concerns of your company, and perhaps most important—budget. We'll add a bit more insight to this process in Chapter 3 when we discuss how to build an expert system.

A SHORT COURSE IN KNOWLEDGE REPRESENTATION

The secret behind an expert system is its knowledge. So it makes sense that the secret behind an expert system tool is its method of representing or handling knowledge. We're going to take a quick tour now of some of the different ways that systems represent knowledge. The purpose here is to introduce you to the mechanics of expert system tools. For those who want a more intense discussion of any of the techniques discussed or want to read about other approaches, I direct you to the bibliography.

Rules

I'll start with the one that most people know best. Rules. This is such a natural that it's easy to understand. We lay down the law to our kids. We itemize rules of order something like:

IF I'm not home   THEN you can't have any friends over

IF it's past 4 P.M.   THEN no snacks

IF you get a C on your report card   THEN no TV for a week

Our lives are filled with decisions, so it's natural to turn these into decision rules. Try writing your own list for even something as trivial as getting up in the morning and you'll soon work your way up into the hundreds of rules. (By the way, your first decision rule would be something like: IF the alarm rings and its Monday morning THEN shut off alarm and go back to sleep.)

A rule has two parts. A premise: IF IT'S COLD AND IT'S CREAMY; and a conclusion: THEN IT IS ICE CREAM. Therefore a rule is a conditional sentence starting with an IF segment and ending with a THEN segment. A rule, or production rule as it is sometimes called, stems from a decision. Look at the decision tree in Figure 2-3. Here we're trying to decide whether a patient's bill for medical services should be reimbursed. Why don't you try your hand at turning this tree into production rules. I'll give you the first one. IF the patient is covered by insurance THEN proceed to determine payment schedule.

Of course, rules in real expert systems are a lot more complicated than our little examples. Look at this next rule:

If ?X is in class REACTORS and
* The PRESSURE of*
*   The PRIMARY.COOLING.SYSTEM of ?X*
* is DECREASING and*
* The STATUS of*
* The HIGH.PRESSURE.INJECTION.SYSTEM of ?X is ON*

Then   The INTEGRITY of
*   THE PRIMARY.COOLING.SYSTEM of ?X*
*   is CHALLENGED*

Do   ACTIVATE.ALARM
*   GET.VALUE X 'PRIMARY.COOLING.SYSTEM*

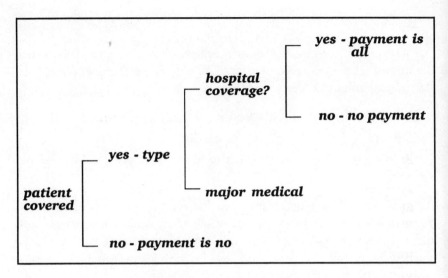

FIGURE 2-3.   A Decision Tree.

You'll notice a few things right away. First, this rule has three parts. The extra part is the DO. Now all expert system languages and shells are slightly different. They all permit the performance of a procedure. Here this is done in the section of the rule called DO. The instruction here is to activate an alarm. In another tool this function might be performed as part of a THEN or even as part of an IF. The second thing you notice is the funny ?X. This is called a variable. It gives the system a lot of flexibility so that not every detail has to be "hard coded." Here ?X is replaced by some class of reactor that is entered by the operator at the keyboard. Better yet, some function can be running somewhere that reads a database of reactor types and fills in this information as it executes this rule. The last thing you'll notice is the utter complexity of the rule. Most rules in most systems are equally complex. They might not be discussing nuclear reactors, but they are still quite complex in their own right. And not all rules have to be about the application, some rules can be coded about the operation of the expert system itself. These are called meta-rules and they state the ways in which the knowledge rules can be used.

Once you have these rules written up, there needs to be a mechanism to move around these rules, picking and choosing the ones that are to be "fired." Expert systems do not operate in the same way traditional systems operate. Traditional systems execute one statement at a time, unless of course there is a branch statement. Look at this little BASIC programming language program:

```
10    LET A = 10
20    LET B = 20
30    C = A + B
40    GO TO 60
50    PRINT C
60    GO TO 10
```

BASIC is a rigidly sequential programming language. Take a look at this code. Does the value of C ever get printed? Line 10 executes first. Line 20 always executes after line 10. Line 30 always executes after line 20. Even the branch statements in line 40 and 60 are rigidly applied. There is no room for variation here.

Inference Engine

The heart of an expert system is the inference engine, which is just a program that performs many functions. It controls modules that access the external databases. It controls the interface with the actual end-user. It also controls what we call a knowledge base. The code of the expert system is stored in the knowledge base. This code can take many forms, as we will discuss, but the most popular method of coding knowledge is in a rule format. In expert systems, the rules or code do not execute in any given order, therefore rules can be stored in any order. Rules execute according to a grand design called a control strategy, which prescribes the method of searching through the knowledge base. There are two major categories of searching.

Forward Chaining. The first is forward chaining. As shown in Figure 2-4, we move from a set of assertions or facts to one or more possible outcomes. The way rule application works is that the system searches for a value where the conditions in the IF part of the rule are

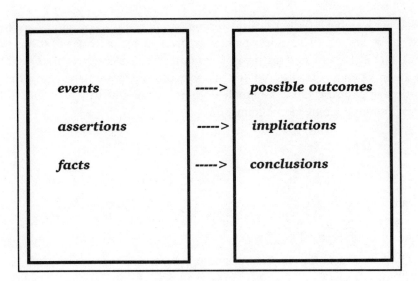

FIGURE 2-4.   Forward Chaining.

matched in memory (deemed to be true). If so, the THEN part is put into working memory. Applying a forward chaining control strategy to a list of rules forces the execution of the rules from beginning to end. This is a sort of top-down reasoning approach. It reviews all known facts that were either entered at the very beginning of the system or became known as other rules triggered or fired. After a rule is reviewed, if the premise is true, then it is fired. In forward chaining, every bit of available evidence is examined since the final goal is not predetermined.

A couple of examples might help in explaining a rather complicated notion. Suppose you have a personal computer. Now suppose the CRT goes on the fritz. It just doesn't work. The screen is black. Well there can be many solutions to this problem. Perhaps the plug is not plugged in. Perhaps the power is out. Perhaps the VGA board is bad. We go from an event, a bad screen, to one of many possible outcomes. Our forward chaining system would wind its way through rules that dealt with this topic trying to assist in figuring out what's wrong. Let's use another example. I call it "Convict on the Loose."

Suppose I tell you that a killer/bank robber and all around no-goodnik has broken out of jail. We know he hid the money, but we don't know where. We also know that three of his former cronies turned state's witnesses. While he was in prison, the killer/bank robber boasted that when he got out of jail he would retrieve the loot and seek revenge against his former cronies. We are a small police force. We need to know where to apply our meager resources. To solve this problem we apply a bit of forward chaining reasoning to come to a set of conclusions. What direction was the killer/robber heading? Was he armed? Did he have a shovel? Where do the witnesses live? Which witness does he have the biggest grudge against?

Backward Chaining. The opposite of forward chaining is backward chaining. Shown in Figure 2-5, this strategy operates from the perspective that you already possess an outcome and are searching for the conditions or circumstances that would lead to that result. Here the system tries to determine a value for the goal by identifying the rules that would conclude a value for the goal. Then the system backs up and tries to determine whether the IF clauses are true. Again a couple of examples to enlighten you. This time we know we have a bad VGA board and we leaf through our rules to find out if a black screen is indeed symptomatic of this problem. Or if murder tickles your fancy, we have a story called "Murder at Midnight" for your reading pleasure.

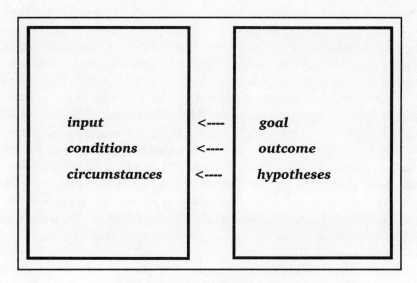

FIGURE 2-5. Backward Chaining.

Suppose we are called to the scene of a heinous murder. We have spent the last several months investigating the modus operandi of a notorious killer, Mr. X, who is still on the loose. The local constable asks, "Was this the work of Mr. X?"

We can apply a backward chaining control strategy to this problem. We already have a hypothesis about who did it. Remember that the constable asked the question about whether it was Mr. X. So, we backward chain through our rule base to determine if the inputs or conditions surrounding the murder really do lead us to the conclusion that it was Mr. X.

Search Features.   There are some very nice features that can be added to the inference engine's method of processing rules. One of the features that is an absolute must-have is "truth maintenance." This is the capability of stopping midway in a consultation, changing your mind, and having the system pick up and run with the ball without having to start over. In a conventional system, if you change your mind, you're out of luck. You must stop the program, reenter the new inputs and then restart the program. An inference engine with a truth maintenance facility keeps track of the maneuverings through the knowledge base. If you change your mind, the inference engine backs up and resets the rules and objects fired, giving you a clean slate. Now you can begin anew from practically any point you desire.

Along with having the ability to change your mind during a consultation there is always the chance that the session dredges up some rather uncertain decisions. Suppose that the police chief in the "Convict on the Loose" tall tale was not quite certain about how all of the evidence at the scene of the crime added up. He might reason as follows: "Well, if he had a shovel, then I'm about 75 percent sure that he went looking for the loot. On the other hand, I'm about 40 percent sure that a shovel means he's out to look for one of his old cronies and beat him over the head with it!" Isn't this the way we reason when we're not quite sure about something? Some expert system inference engines have this capability built right in to the rule declaration function. These are confidence factors and they are used to assign a percentage to a conclusion of a rule.

Rules are the backbone of almost every expert system tool out there. Most systems in use today use both backward and forward chaining, which we call a hybrid control strategy. If you think about it, most complex financial systems would need both approaches. For example, think of an expert system built to assist in the budgetary process. You'd like the system to be able to answer questions about how to perform the budgetary process (forward chaining). You'd like the system to also be able to produce a budget if you tell it to decrease expenditures by 5 percent (backward chaining). But, in spite of all you can do with rules, there's only a small subset of interesting problems that can be handled by a purely rule-based system. Add to this limitation another one. You simply cannot develop very large systems using a purely rule-based approach. You might run into something called combinatorial explosion. This is when the search space used by all of these rules becomes so large that it is impractical—actually impossible is more like it—to run the system. Let's look at an example that David Waltz of Brandeis University provides for us. The average number of moves possible in a chess game is 35. If you look ahead only three moves, you need to examine 1.8 billion moves. Trying to keep all of this knowledge in memory would make the ol' computer burst at its seams. The same holds true for expert systems. A large problem programmed in a purely rule-based format would necessarily need to support massive numbers of rules. Again that ol' computer would fairly burst its seams. Part of the problem is in the methodology that is used for searching through all of the "chunks" of knowledge in a forward chaining search strategy to find a match to a fact. There are several methods that shell developers use to cope with this problem. One way the developers cope with this problem is the implementation of what is called the RETE algorithm. This algorithm can be thought of as an optimizer for rule-based systems. In a nutshell, it keeps track of which rules are true for a given knowledge base state. In a very large system, even the RETE algorithm doesn't help. There must be a way to reduce the number of rules. There must be a more efficient way of defining knowledge.

Objects. To give expert systems the "oomph" to do complex problems, something more is needed. This something is called the *object*. Objects are the stuff of object-oriented programming, or OOP. This methodology concentrates on data structures, as opposed to functions, for problem solving. Believe it or not, this is not a new technique; it had its origin in the late 1960s. Objects give a nice neat way of defining knowledge. Look at the example of the object called CAR in Figure 2-6. The object CAR has several slots. Color is a slot, make is another slot,

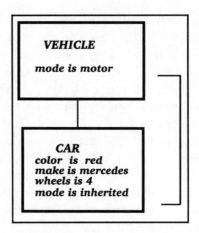

FIGURE 2-6. The Object CAR.

and number of wheels is a third slot. Each of these slots contains one or more values. The value of color is red, make is Mercedes, and the wheels slot has the value of four. Notice that the value of the slot called mode is *inherited* from its "parent" slot. Objects are hierarchical in nature, similar to hierarchical databases. There is a parent-child relationship between an object and the object beneath it in hierarchical order. Just as in a human parent-child relationship, where your child can inherit your hair or eye color, an object can inherit some attribute from its parent. In our example, this object car inherits the value of mode from its parent. Finally, let's look at the slot called Insurance in Figure 2-7. This slot has something called a demon attached to it that is not what you think it is. No, it is not from *Halloween Part V*. A demon is a rule or procedure that will fire whenever this value is accessed. If the slot Insurance is accessed, then a procedure named GoCalc, which will recalculate the insurance premium for this policyholder, will be automatically executed.

The attributes of object orientation make it perfect for developing expert systems. We've already discussed inheritance and the use of demons. Two other features are well worth noting. Each object can stand alone. We call this ability encapsulation. Looking at our example in Figure 2-7 you'll note that this looks like a mini-program. It has data and performs procedures. Since each object "hides" its data and procedures from other objects, one would expect there to be a communication problem in the use of objects. On the contrary, OOP is well-known for its ability to pass messages as either inputs or outputs. When an object is passed a

INSURANCE	
policy	life
age	under 25
premium	demon (GoCalc)
elimination	rules to determine value

FIGURE 2-7. Use of Demons.

message, it checks to see whether it can handle the request. If it can't, then it checks with its parent, who checks with its parent, until the message is satisfied.

So what you end up with is a loosely coupled network of virtual programs that mostly act independently. In a conventional programming language there is specific code that indicates exactly how to carry out commands. In object-oriented languages, the message is simply passed; it is left up to the object to figure out what to do next.

The reason why everyone is so excited over OOP is due to its extreme flexibility in creating new objects out of existing ones. This means that we can program new programs without having to do a whole bunch of recoding. We merely make a copy of the objects we're interested in, add new slots for new data and new procedures, and off we go.

ON SIPHONING KNOWLEDGE

What do Mozart and Christian Heinecken have in common? Both were prodigies. Mozart, as we all know, composed minuets at the tender age of four. Heinecken memorized the *Pentateuch* before the age of one, mastered sacred history before the age of two, and was a whiz at geography and history at age three. He spoke French and Latin, as well as being a master at religion, while little Mozart was hammering away at his piano. Sadly, he died (probably of exhaustion) when he was but five. Their brilliance was extraordinary. Since their expertise was so intuitive and was learned at such an early age, it would have been devilishly tricky to try to conceptualize knowledge acquisition had expert systems been around in the eighteenth century.

Fortunately the rest of us don't exactly qualify as prodigies. The task of knowledge acquisition is still a tough one to handle. So how do we do it?

The first hurdle to overcome is the realization of what constitutes expertise. It is not always necessarily connected to the "smartest person around." In a rather fun study entitled "A Day at the Races," authors Ceci and Liker (1986) found that even racetrack handicappers with relatively low IQs could beat the experts and "professionals." What this seems to be saying is that expertise may be less a function of intelligence and more the product of skillful coding of experience.

This coding of experience is not done consciously by the expert but is more the result of unconscious organization and structuring of new experiences.

Yes, experts are different from mere mortals. Most knowledge engineers do recognize this fact, but also erroneously believe that this major difference is in the quantity of knowledge the expert has managed to accumulate. Certainly quantity is one aspect, but there are qualitative differences as well.

The most obvious difference is that experts have experienced, according to Nobel Prize winner Niels Bohr, ". . . all the mistakes which can be made in a very narrow field." Experts have such depth of experience that when a new problem comes their way they can see the whole picture. Novices, on the other hand, possess little experience and thus "don't see the forest for the trees."

Perhaps the most interesting difference is that the expert's knowledge is organized more efficiently than the novice's. Even with the same stimuli, the expert is able to recall more readily the pieces of the stimuli than can the novice. This was proven in a memory experiment done in the early 1970s where novice and expert chess players were shown boards of games in progress. The experts were able to recall more piece positions than the novices since they were able to recall from their experience more patterns. A corollary experiment was done by showing both experts and novices gameboards with pieces strewn randomly about. Neither expert nor novice did better at this experiment, certainly proving the pattern recall hypothesis.

What this seems to indicate is that the expert, by virtue of a good deal of experience, learns certain patterns that seem to be almost "burned" into memory. A new problem exhibits traits that are similar in some ways and dissimilar in other ways to the set of experiences in memory. In fact, the patterning is so ingrained that sometimes it leads to decision-making by rote. This robotizing effect was demonstrated in a study by Frensch (1988) using bridge players as guinea pigs. In this study, the rules of the game were changed dramatically. Here each subsequent hand was to be led by the player who had played the *lowest* card on the last hand. This confused the dickenses out of the expert bridge players and adversely affected their playing skills. It didn't much bother the novices. Since their experience was not as yet ingrained, they had a much easier time adjusting to the new rules. What we have here is an indelible knowledge. The ramifications are significant for the knowledge engineering team.

For the most part, the first generation of expert systems relied on surface knowledge. This is knowledge obtained through a process of direct articulation, typically a series of loosely structured interviews. This laborious process is labeled a bottleneck by Ed Feigenbaum, who is one of the pioneers of the expert system trend. Here the knowledge engineer asks rather spontaneous questions as the expert describes a particular case or actually goes through the paces of solving the problem. The loose structure of this method of knowledge acquisition serves only to capture procedural knowledge at the most superficial level. It does not capture the expert's more abstract ability to apply this procedural knowledge at a more tactical level. Schon (1983) in his book, *The Reflective Practitioner*, has labeled this deeper knowledge as "knowing-in-action."

A second generation of methodology for knowledge acquisition comes from the research of psychology and computer science departments at various universities. Research has shown a better way of grabbing the knowledge residing deep inside the expert. These methodologies have been slowly creeping their way out of the laboratory and into some innovative, corporate, AI think tanks.

HOW TO WIN "KNOWLEDGE" AND INFLUENCE "EXPERT SYSTEMS"

There really is no best way to elicit knowledge from experts. The method used will be largely dependent on the circumstances surrounding the development of the system and the types of people involved in the project. Often, the combination of methodologies will do the trick when application of only one seems to miss the mark. There are many methods to choose from.

We already spoke of the most popular form of knowledge acquisition. This is the free-flowing dialogue between experts and knowledge engineers that can take place over several sessions or even one long brain-storming session. While this is not the best methodology for obtaining deeply seated knowledge, it is an excellent method for acquiring procedural knowledge. This most certainly makes up a large part of the expert's knowledge. Many engineers video- or audiotape the interview so that others can be involved in the interview process. While this is a great idea, be forewarned that transcribing these tapes into notes is time-consuming. One describer of this process noted that it took 100 hours of transcribing to capture 10 hours of interviews with an expert planner of airlift schedules.

Structured Interviews

A second form of interview is called a structured interview. This concept stems from the studies of social scientists and has been used largely in the area of the psychotherapeutic interview. The rule here is to plan the interview before you ever get in the room with the expert. First a meeting is called to discuss the problem to be expert-systematized. This general meeting will serve to provide enough information for the knowledge engineer to go back to the drawing board and carefully plan a second series of meetings, each of which will be structured around a specific topic. It is at these more structured meetings that a series of well-directed questions will be asked to elicit the knowledge that lies below surface level.

Task Analysis

In 1987 two researchers did a study of people working at a problem-solving task. In Bailey and Kay's study, they had people putting together a structure using an Erector Set. The methodology used by these experimental "construction engineers" was charted by the researchers. Hence, the logic was uncovered that was inherent in the problem solvers' reasoning.

This method can most certainly be applied to all classifications of problems. It can be done either silently where the knowledge engineer merely observes the process or by participation where the knowledge engineer asks questions and the expert comments on the task.

Learning Rules from Examples

This is how the *neural nets* and *inductive* expert system tools work. Instead of using various methodologies to directly elicit the reasoning behind the decision of the expert, a cadre of examples, when analyzed, should yield the same result.

Here a computer is fed automated cases or examples and their solutions. In the realm of expert systems, the output would be rules or decision trees. In the realm of the neural net, the knowledge is deeply embedded into the net.

Although this is probably the most preferable way of performing the arduous task of knowledge acquisition, this technology is still in its infancy.

Test Cases

A more human-like approach to the machine learning of rules by example is the "human learning rules from examples." In this methodology, a series of hypothetical problems are generated by the knowledge engineer that are based on the research of archival data or documentation. The goal here is to develop a.sampling of cases that will represent the depth and breadth of the entire domain and all levels of complexity.

This methodology is then used in conjunction with the structured interview. If the knowledge engineer is lucky, a test case will be developed that will be so tough that almost profound knowledge will be the result of its review. This happened to one researcher when a problem was presented to two expert interpreters of aerial photos. A radar image was so hard to decipher that their deliberations in trying to solve this unique problem were extraordinarily informative.

More Methods from the Annals Of Psychology

From the realm of problem-solving research, one of the most widely used tactics is to ask the problem solver to "think out loud." This requires the expert to verbalize procedures and reasoning processes that have been, up until that point, strictly at a subconscious level. This method has been used successfully by researchers with expert diagnosticians, expert physicists, and even expert computer programmers. In the same vein, researchers have used "decision analysis," in which the expert tracks the problems encountered and the type of decision made for each of these problems.

Perhaps the most interesting method in the group is *constrained* problem solving. Here the expert is given a problem to solve under rigid constraints. An aerial photograph that must be interpreted in two minutes rather than in a few hours. A loan application that has to be approved or not without supplying the expert with certain pertinent credit information.

Some 80 percent of the knowledge of an expert is easily obtainable through first-generation knowledge acquisition techniques. The other 20 percent though, that which is deeply rooted, requires a pick and an axe and a good set of second-generation techniques.

Financial Decision-Making

To successfully elicit the knowledge of the financial expert, it is important to understand how financial decision-making is achieved. Bouwman (1985) categorized financial decision-making into two discrete phases: familiarizing and reasoning.

In his study he used two groups of experts. The first group was composed of financial analysts who were given the task of evaluating a stock for possible investment. The second group was composed of loan officers whose task was to evaluate a multimillion-dollar participation loan. From studying how these two groups evaluated the information given them and their decision-making processes, Bouwman managed to dissect financial decision-making into four steps. In the first step the analysts did a general scanning of the environment looking for key identifiers such as sales or net income. The second step involved categorization through use of the evocation of templates remembered from their experience, such as

AI AND THE FINANCIAL SERVICES ARENA

"high-tech company." The third step was composed of a more detailed and specific reading of the information. The analysts tried to match the templates from memory to actual case specifics. Finally, the analysts evaluated all of the data and knowledge from the prior steps and reached a final conclusion. According to Bouwman, the first step corresponds to familiarizing, while the last three steps can be categorized as reasoning.

Knowing just how a financial analyst thinks through problems can assist the knowledge engineering team in the process of decoding the expert's knowledge. In fact, the firm Arthur Andersen used the Bouwman model when it developed the Financial Statement Analyzer system that we will discuss at length later on in this book.

MIMICKING THE BRAIN

The class only had nine pupils.

Three girls sat in the front row, three boys in the back one, while in the middle row the sexes sat alternately. Altogether, including the teacher, the sexes were equally divided.

When their home-work was returned marks were compared and the children were surprised to discover that the total marks gained by those in each row were the same, as were also those for each column from front to back and for each diagonal of the square in which they sat.

Excitedly they pointed out that fact to the teacher who replied that, when checking their work, which had been marked out of ten, he noticed that every digit had been used once and once only.

Three was the lowest mark awarded to a girl.

What was the highest mark given to a boy?"

From The Sunday Times Book of Brain Teasers, compiled and edited by Victor Bryant and Ronald Postill, 1986. Courtesy of © St. Martin's Press, Inc., New York.

Stumped? Confused? Embarrassed? For those of you who are one or all of these or those of you who just don't have the time or patience to figure this teaser out, the solution appears at the end of this chapter. Before you turn to sneak a peak you might wonder why your friend over there is chuckling. "I know the answer!" this former friend chuckles as you walk over to take a gander at the calculations on a cocktail napkin. "How'd you do it?" you ask trying to appear casual and even bored while inside you're dying of envy. "It's the gray matter," is the reply as your now mortal enemy points to your head.

Gray matter. The cerebral cortex, the grainy gray coating of the brain. Dipping and folding, what we know as convolutions: it is here that we do our thinking, our philosophizing, our perceiving, learning, and judging. What makes our brains tick? In our noggins are networks of trillions of interconnected neurons, joined by what are known as synapses. For example, neurons fire biological signals when stimulated by any of our five senses, such as something we see or touch or smell. Particular combinations of these signals trigger a specific firing sequence in the cells of the brain. Although scientists know little about the ways the brain actually works, they do know that the brain learns by strengthening or weakening the inter-cell connections. In this way, the brain begins to "learn" the pattern of the stimuli, making it much easier the next time around to interpret the same set of stimuli as, "I smell a pizza with anchovies."

So, it's no wonder that computer scientists in white lab coats work into the wee hours of the night developing hardware that can "think" just the way we do. On the hardware side, the concept of neural computers is being researched by the best and the brightest. Some researchers have even surpassed the neural computer and are working on what is known as a "living computer." At the University of Illinois in Urbana, a team of biochemists is using genetic engineering to produce protein molecules that together, act similarly to microchips. Professor Stephen Sligar believes that within the next ten years, the team will be able to create a quasi-brain by constructing a network of these molecules. Dubbed "biochips," this is the stuff of scientists' dreams.

Closer to reality and using software instead of hardware or bioware, the neural network has emerged as the concept that is slowly gaining credibility, even in the financial arena where the doubtful lurk in great numbers.

How Neural Nets Work

Neural nets simulate a network of hundreds of parallel processing, interconnected units, shooting messages to each other at a rapid-fire pace. The job of a neural net is to receive the input and respond. This may first seem like a task that can be handled as adequately by conventional means, but neural nets are computer programs with a difference. First, neural nets have the capability of recognizing downgraded inputs. What use, you ask, is this ability? What comes to mind right off the bat is handwriting recognition. We've been waiting for years for a user-friendly way to get information into the computer. We've tried menu-based systems, touch screens, and even icon-based systems. To the last one they're all unnatural and cumbersome to use. What could be more natural than the old pen and pad? Of course, handwriting entry into the computer has been around for years. For the most part these early systems were rigid and difficult to use, if not downright arbitrary. One system comes to mind where you used a tablet to enter information and commands into the computer. You had to have a very neat handwriting and I haven't had that since sometime around second grade.

A derivation of handwriting recognition is being attempted today at financial institutions, such as Banc-Tec. Deluged by thousands upon thousands of checks each day, the veracity of the check's signature is a big business. No one signs their signature exactly the same way each and every time. When you're relaxed and not in a hurry Ms. Smith, your penmanship teacher, would be proud of you. When you're rushed, in the middle of a typically frantic day your signature may resemble a long scrawl with the letters being somewhat distinguishable. Neural nets can be trained to recognize signatures even of those signers who got a D in Ms. Smith's class.

I know, you have visions of standing in line at the bank for hours and training that darn neural net to recognize your creative array of signature variations. You may have gotten this impression from your readings on voice recognition. Here each poor soul has to sit behind a microphone several different times during the day to train the system to respond to the tonal changes in a person's voice. Neural nets are smarter than that. They learn by themselves—this is what sets them apart from expert systems—from a user perspective. No more months and years of painstaking knowledge infusion.

Of course, this inclination toward being self-taught costs. It costs in the expense of the hardware involved or the amount of time the system takes to learn the ropes.

Why? Because it's more complex than it first appears. The alphabet is the first thing that we are taught as children. Andrew Meisel, a master linguistics specialist with a penchant for neural nets, explains how a simple net might work. Suppose that we represent each letter as a 5-by-7 matrix of binary values as shown in Figure 2-8.

Each matrix is a series of 35 ones and zeroes, therefore we have 35 input units. Each one represents one of the 35 positions in the matrix. The output of the analysis of each matrix would be an ASCII letter such as A or Z. Each ASCII letter is actually represented to the computer by an eight-digit code. For example, A would be 0100 0001. So what we have are input units and output units. We also need middle units, since these are the units that actually experience the activation that in turn triggers a response in the output units. All units, like the neurons in the brain, are joined by connections. Each unit has an activation value of either 0 or 1. Input activity triggers a pattern of activation across the middle units, which causes some sort of pattern of activation in the output units—sort of a ripple effect.

Say a perfect letter A is handwritten into the system. Activation of the units produces a numeric score that is calculated as a result of a weight being multiplied by the activation that passes through the units. Meisel gives an example of the output for this perfectly entered A:

0.001 0.977 0.002 0.002　　0.015 0.009 0.011 0.959

Using the rule that any output above 0.9 is considered a 1 and any output less than 0.1 is considered a 0 then we get the correct ASCII code for the letter A:

0 1 0 0　　0 0 0 1

Even if our handwritten letter A is less than perfect—that is, even if one or more of the 35 input units is faulty—it is still possible to produce the correct ASCII code.

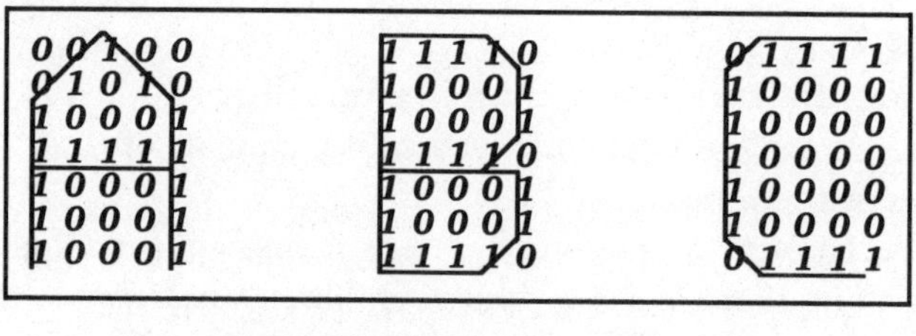

FIGURE 2-8.　Alphabet Matrix.

This is an example of what is known as a back-propagation net, which is probably the most popular and certainly the simplest. It is also one of the neural net strategies that can learn by itself. Simply stated, the input is entered and the output is calculated. This output is then compared to the desired output. Next, the real output of each unit is subtracted from the desired output and thus the net slightly adjusts itself toward correcting the error. This is a repetitive process that is performed until the net has learned a new set of connections that produce the correct output.

If the letter is so poorly written as to be unrecognizable, a more powerful net strategy could be employed to decipher even that.

Let's Consider the Possibilities

You don't have to write your own programs to handle the complex algorithms that are key to neural nets. All you need to do is go out and buy one of the many products that have been on the market for several years.

John Loofbourrow, chief of John W. Loofbourrow Associates Inc., based in New York, did just that. Using a $995-package that runs on an IBM PC, Loofbourrow was able to develop a system that forecasts the Standard & Poor's 500 index. It took Loofbourrow just 12 hours of entering the eight variables chosen as components of an arbitrary model. Data for 10-week intervals for the years 1974 through 1987 were entered for the high, the low, closing price, and volume. This was done for IBM stock, the price of gold, dollar/yen, dollar/Eurodollar. He also entered the result into the net and for this he selected Standard & Poor's 500 index. When the net is turned on, it searches laboriously for patterns on the input side that result in a particular output, in this case, a particular rise or fall of the S&P 500 index. A neural net is "hungry" for data. The more input it has, the more accurate it becomes. This, of course, makes perfect sense because a neural net mimics the way the brain learns. When confronted with many examples leading to a particular output, our brains learn that this is the normative response to these inputs. Soon, the brain can anticipate the answer even though the inputs might be slightly irregular. And just like the brain, we humans have no idea how the net performs its task. On its own, the net develops an algorithm to accomplish its task. In fact this has been one of the major drawbacks of using neural nets thus far. Up until now, neural net systems have been largely unauditable. In the financial services industry, auditing is a (nasty) fact of life. It is essential that all systems, neural nets included, be able to explain how they arrive at a particular conclusion. This lack of auditability, in spite of the impressive ease of inputting knowledge, is what has slowed the growth of this technology in financial services.

That may soon change: a San Diego-based company is hard at work on software that will extract an audit trail of the net's decision-making process. HNC Inc., using a set of patents obtained from a Northeastern University professor, is hot on the trail of software that will force the net to develop a set of production "if... then" rules. The concept behind this developmental miracle is the use of the net to input the examples and the resultant development, by the net itself, of easily understandable rules that will function as a more traditional expert system.

Loofbourrow wasn't looking for auditability. He was after a boost into the high-flying world of the stock market. And that's exactly what he got from his foray into the world of neural nets. The S&P net greatly improved its forecasting abilities as more and more examples were studied. In fact, he was so impressed by the S&P net's results that he's beginning to use a net to predict bond price swings.

Loofbourrow's pet net was NeuralWare's NeuralWorks Professional, but there are several others in this hot marketplace. Everything from the $100-BrainMaker from California Scientific to a souped-up $75,000-neural net, courtesy of Adaptive Decision Systems in Andover, Massachusetts. This $75,000-super net is being used, in pilot mode, for bank credit approval.

One of the first neural net vendors, Nestor out of Providence, Rhode Island, is the vendor of choice for Dallas-based Banc-Tec Inc. Banc-Tec's customers are the banking, retailing, and utility industries who have the awesome task of processing thousands upon thousands of handwritten checks. Manufacturing optical and magnetic recognition equipment, Banc-Tec wanted a smarter solution to interpreting the dollar amounts often scribbled on the face of the check.

One finance company that wishes to remain anonymous is using nets to evaluate loan applications. Taking inputs from a credit report and a written application, the net produces an expected loss-ratio score. This ratio represents the loss ratio that is calculated from a statistically reliable portfolio of loans identical to the applicant's. To develop a reliable net, this finance company entered tens of thousands of past loans. The results were quite interesting. Using conventional credit scoring methodology there was a ratio of 16 good loans to every bad loan. The neural net bettered the odds with 19 good loans to each bad loan. Even American Express, whose main business is credit, is using neurocomputers to appraise this risk.

David R. Aronson, president and cofounder of the Raden Research Group, describes several areas in financial services where neural nets are already being used or can be used. Tactical asset allocation is a perfect foil for the pattern-matching prowess of the net. Research into asset class performance can be made much easier using this sort of tool. There is a direct relationship between a particular asset class and market conditions, and the net can be the detective that makes these correlations. Neural nets can sort through huge amounts of historical pricing data to spot trends and report on indicators that signal key trend reversal points. And the net can be trained to filter through these signals and eliminate the ones that are falsely generated. With all of these ideas on the drawing board, the future of neural networking looks bright. The entire computing world is poised on the threshold breathlessly awaiting the next advance. There will be many. And in short order. From using nets to understand complex processes, to reading signatures, to understanding human speech. Even the defense department is proposing to spend $400 million over the next eight years on research. The sky's the limit.

NATURAL LANGUAGES

A woman seeking a divorce went to visit her attorney. The first question he asked was "Do you have grounds?"

She answered, "Yes, about two acres."

Perhaps I'm not making myself clear," he said, "Do you have a grudge?"

"No, but we have a carport," she responded.

"Let me try again. Does your husband beat you up?" he said impatiently.

"No, generally I get up before he does," she said.

At this point the attorney decided to try a different tack. "Ma'am, are you sure you really want a divorce?"

"I don't want one at all, but my husband does. He claims we have difficulty communicating."

This little tidbit came from United States Representative Pat Swindall of Georgia. He was using it to illustrate that Congress was not really listening to the people on the issue of the federal deficit. I like to use this story to illustrate how complex, and ripe for misinterpretation, our language is.

The ability to talk to the computer in one's native language has been the dream of computer scientists for more than 30 years. It's also the stuff of science fiction. Many of us grew up watching "Star Trek." With our weekly dose of Spock conferring with his computer it just seemed natural that we too should be able to speak to our computers without having to learn programmerese.

There are two questions that folks unfamiliar with the idea of natural languages usually ask. The first is "Why is it so difficult to teach a computer to understand what I type? Any six-year-old can understand me." The second, and perhaps easier question to answer, is "Why even bother? Of what use is natural language in the real world?"

We learn to speak our native tongues as if by osmosis. We're surrounded by it. Our mothers, fathers, siblings, and all of our relatives interact with us by using the same sounds, the same rules of grammar every day of our lives. Televisions and radios blare at us. Because this is such a natural process and because we were so young when it all happened we don't realize the enormous cognitive leap that we made when we first began to understand. Those of us who have studied a foreign language know what I'm talking about.

When you begin to learn a foreign language you really struggle. It's hard to shape the lips to force out the sounds of these hard-to-make words. Just like in learning to play the piano you practice interminable scales each and every day, in learning a foreign language you spend hours in school practicing. You drone, "je parle, tu parles, il parle, elle parle, nous parlons, vous parlez" for every tense, including tenses you never heard of before. All of a sudden, rules of grammar that we took for granted in our own language become so important to understand what is being said. So with this in mind let's take a look at what it's like to develop natural language systems.

Syntactic Ambiguity

Perhaps the biggest problem computer scientists working in this area have had to tackle is syntactic ambiguity. Especially in the English language. Many words can have more than one syntactic category. That is, some words can be used both as nouns and verbs. For example, let's look at the sentence, "Why don't you go outside and play?" Here the word *play* is used as a verb. In the following sentence the word *play* is used as a noun: "I enjoyed the Broadway play."

Some sentences are loaded with ambiguity such as this one provided by Schank (1972):

John saw the Grand Canyon flying to New York.

This is one of my favorites. It appears that either the Grand Canyon has wings or that John was aboard a plane, looked down, and spotted the majestic natural wonder. Take your pick. Of course, most of us would choose the latter interpretation since people have no difficulty in unravelling ambiguity. This example, by the way, was taken from Roger Schank, who has written widely on the subject of natural languages.

Professor Schank, when a member of the Yale University faculty, spent an enormous amount of time delving into the field of artificial intelligence, especially in the area of language. Professor Schank has always been interested in the problem of words that do not have precise meanings. He gives us an example in his essay "Intelligent Advisory Systems," which is included in the book *The AI Business* edited by Patrick Winston and Karen Prendergast in 1986:

John has a hand.
John had a hand in the cookie jar.
John had a hand in the robbery.
John is an old hand.
John gave Mary a hand.
John asked Mary for her hand.

The word *hand* has enough meanings to confuse thoroughly anyone attempting to learn the language—and that includes our computer.

Schank went on to build some of the first natural language understanding systems. His first, called MARGIE, was built in 1969. It served the purpose of making the Yale research team understand that the main problem was in getting the representation of the sentence right.

Getting the representation right is done in different ways by different AI researchers. Most agree, however, that any natural language system worth its salt has got to be robust enough to handle the syntactic and semantic meaning of a sentence.

Pronominalization

Along with syntactic ambiguity, there is a host of other grammatical rules that must be factored in a natural language system. One of the harder to handle is pronominalization. Several years ago I visited a software firm that marketed a natural language understanding system. One of the staff scientists took it upon herself to give us a demonstration of the product. She turned on the computer and logged onto the system. Rolling up her sleeves she typed in her first inquiry: *What does he make?* The computer responded with a rather cryptic message that we interpreted as: *I don't know what you're talking about. Reenter.* Our staff scientist reentered the inquiry and got the same terse response from the computer. Again she tried and again she failed. Finally, she saw her mistake.

To be fair, this staff scientist was pretty nervous and quite distracted by her visitors. She didn't notice that her first question contained a pronoun rather than a noun. Instead of asking the question, *What does Harry Jones make?* she asked *What does he make?* The computer had no way of knowing who *he* was. Her first question should have been something like *Which department is Harry Jones in?* The system would have responded with an appropriate answer and then she could have asked *What does he make?* At this point the computer would have tied the pronoun *he* to the noun *Harry Jones.*

This was an easy case of pronominalization. A harder one for the computer to understand would be *Give me a report on directors who have subordinates and their salaries.* Whose salaries do we want? The directors or their subordinates? An important capability of natural language systems is the ability to track conversational flow. We would readily understand the conversation that follows:

How long has Susan Jones been with this company?
   five years
Which department is she in?
   engineering
What does she earn?
   $24,000 a year
How much a month?
   $2,000 a month

It's obvious that we're having a lengthy conversation about Susan Jones. The computer must be able to keep track of the refer-backs to this person. Now let's add an extra layer of complication:

How long has Susan Jones been with this company?
    five years
Which department is she in?
    engineering
How long has Sheila Smith been with this company?
    six years
Which department is she in?
    administrative
How long has she been in engineering?

A person would answer for Susan Jones, but a computer would have a bit of a conversational flow problem.

Conjunctions

Perhaps the hardest word of all in the English language, at least for a computer, is the word *and*. Let's look at a couple of examples and you'll soon see what I mean. In the sentence *Give me a report on yesterday's profits and losses,* the word yesterday qualifies losses as well as profits. We don't want yesterday's profits and today's losses, we want both figures from yesterday. Consider this next sentence: *Show me John's last semester report card and address.* Should the computer search back in time to look for multiple addresses? I think not.

More Syntactic Lapses

And added to all this confusion is the very human penchant for speaking ungrammatically. You know what you mean, your friends know what you mean, but does this computer understand *profits for last month screwdrivers?*

Another syntactic area of concern is negation, in the event the computer is dealing with several levels of information. The inquiry *Show me a list of students with no extracurricular activities* is rather easy to process since the word *no* is straightforward. The sentence *Which students haven't taken all of their exams this semester?* requires the system to understand the design of the database. In this case, the *student* database lists exam grades by month. And what does semester mean? Some schools are on a three-semester basis and some on a two-semester basis. If we were to translate this inquiry down to its lowest and most understandable level, it would look like: IF SEMESTER = 1 THEN LIST STUDENT_NAME IF GRADE1 IS BLANK OR GRADE2 IS BLANK OR GRADE3 IS BLANK OR GRADE4 IS BLANK OTHERWISE IF SEMESTER = 2 THEN LIST STUDENT_NAME IF GRADE5 IS BLANK OR GRADE6 IS BLANK OR GRADE7 IS BLANK OR GRADE8 IS BLANK OTHERWISE IF SEMESTER = 3 LIST STUDENT_NAME IF GRADE9 IS BLANK OR GRADE10 IS BLANK OR GRADE11 IS BLANK OR GRADE12 IS BLANK.

And don't think we've covered everything. There's a host of: syntactic problems other!

Semantic Problems Are Worse than Syntactic Problems

An even harder nut to crack is giving a natural language system the ability to understand the use of semantics.

People refer to the same thing in a multitude of ways. Keyword searching systems force users to memorize exact formats, or else the systems refuse to give up the information. A robust, natural language system should allow for this type of ambiguity when processing these requests:

HOW MANY FIRMS SUBMITTED THEIR TAXES FOR 03/13/89?

HOW MANY FIRMS SUBMITTED THEIR TAXES FOR 890313?

SHOW ME THE TAX RETURN OF FIRM 890313.

In the first two examples, the system needs to interpret the various formats of date. Easy as it looks, date and time are troublesome to all natural language systems, no matter how robust. In the last example, we see that number again. Is 890313 a date, a tax identification number, or what? It's obvious to us that we're referring to an identification number, but the natural language system must do some pretty fancy semantic interpretation to figure this one out.

An Example of a Natural Language System

Perhaps the best way to explain the intricacies involved in developing a natural language system is to describe one that is being successfully marketed. Natural Language Incorporated, which is located in sunny downtown Norwalk, Connecticut, has developed an English language interface to relational databases. Running primarily in the Unix universe, its future implementations will take it to the world of IBM.

Natural Language™ can understand virtually unrestricted written English. It does this by employing a rather robust and well-integrated set of components, which when taken together, permit the system to understand many of the constructs in the English language that we just described.

The front end of Natural Language does spelling correction, dictionary lookup, morphemic analysis, and construction of the word lattice that is eventually used by the system's parser.

Much natural language research has concentrated on this one component. Figure 2-9 shows a representative parse tree that one would

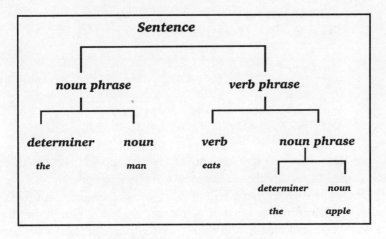

FIGURE 2-9. Standard Parse Tree.

find in almost any book on the subject. Natural Language decomposes the sentence into something akin to a sentence diagram. For example, the sentence "I need to fly to Boston tomorrow" is represented by the following diagram:

```
need nn
  SUBJECT:  i
  OBJECT:  fly nn
          SUBJECT:  i
          PREP:  to Boston
          WHEN:  tomorrow
```

Equally important to the understanding of a sentence is the system's capability of representing the knowledge contained within the parsed sentence. The NLI (Natural Language Incorporated) representation scheme is a combination of a semantic network and first-order predicate logic. Basic to this scheme are the grammatical components of predicates, objects, and descriptions. It turns these mere words into concepts by use of reasoning and expression of rules, among other devices. After applying this semantic interface, the parsed sentence above looks like:

```
*need nn
  SUBJECT:  g3  ISA:  *person
  OBJECT:  *fly nn
          SUBJECT:  g3
          DESTINATION:  g9 boston  ISA:  *city
                    *nameis nn
                    NAME1:  g9
                    NAME2:  g10  ISA:  *pname VALUE:  boston

          WHEN:  g12 tomorrow  ISA:  *date
          DAYOFWEEK:  3 MONTH:  5 DAY:  6 YEAR:  84
```

Other interesting components of this system include the Interpreter, which is used to reason about statements in the representation language. Then there's the Dictionary, which contains the English words. Concepts that are internal notions of predicates are next. Finally, we have: named objects, statements, and rules that capture common sense knowledge as well as specialized domain knowledge.

Like most other competing natural language products, Natural Language handles conjunctions, negation, nominal data, pronominalization, and a host of other natural language oddities, easily. Another thing it does well is the quick conversion to standard database interfaces. Hence an example that turns the English inquiry "Who makes more than their manager?" into standard, and in my opinion difficult to use, SQL (structured query language):

```
select distinct employees.ename1, employees.ename2,
    employees.salary, t1.salary, t2.ename1,
    t2.ename2, employees.dname
from employees, divisions, employees t1, employees t2
where divisions.dname=employees.dname
and divisions.manager=t1.eno
and (employees.salary>t1.salary
  or t1.salary is null)
and divisions.manager=t2.eno;
```

Perhaps the most salient feature of Natural Language is its deductive abilities, which provide a rule-based mechanism for adding application-specific knowledge to the system. What follows is a short scenario that NLI uses, to show this interesting feature:

Fred and George are men.

OK. Fred and George are men.

Mary is a woman.

OK. Mary is a woman.

If x hates y then x does not like y.

OK. If x hates y then x does not like y.

Does Fred like George?

Does Fred like George?

I don't know whether Fred likes George.

Fred hates George.

OK. Fred hates George.

Does Fred like George?

Does Fred like George?

No, Fred does not like George.

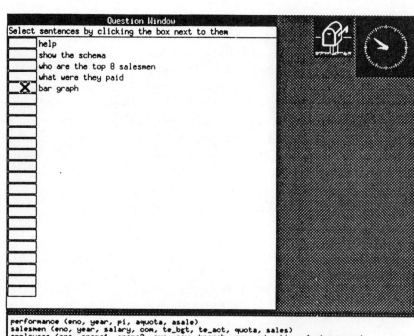

```
                    Question Window
Select sentences by clicking the box next to them
┌──┐ help
├──┤ show the schema
├──┤ who are the top 8 salesmen
├──┤ what were they paid
├─X┤ bar graph
├──┤
├──┤
├──┤
├──┤
├──┤
├──┤
├──┤
├──┤
├──┤
├──┤
├──┤
├──┤
└──┘
```

```
performance (eno, year, pi, aquota, asale)
salesmen (eno, year, salary, com, te_bgt, te_act, quota, sales)
employees (eno, ename1, ename2, axe, sex, branch, exp, education, last_company)
    ----  ----

Integers: exp axe sales quota te_act te_bgt com salary asale aquota year eno.

: who are the top 8 salesmen
Show the 8 salespeople whose sales are the highest.

The 8 salespeople whose sales are the highest.

first      last      sales
name       name
--------------------------
john       tower     3,200
frances    feldman   2,100
ellen      zorkin    1,800
hal        arles     1,800
horace     greely    1,700
maria      menendez  1,550
fred       jones     1,500
jack       smith     1,500

: what were they paid
Show those salespeople and the pay they were paid.

Those salespeople and the pay they were paid.

                                     year
                         1987                        1988

first    last    pay    commissions  salary  pay    commissions  salary
name     name
------------------------------------------------------------------------
ellen    zorkin  $50,000  $10,000  $40,000  $65,000  $25,000  $40,000
frances  feldman  45,000   20,000   25,000   57,000   22,000   35,000
fred     jones    45,000   20,000   25,000   53,000   18,000   35,000
hal      arles    47,000   15,000   32,000   53,000   15,000   38,000
horace   greely   70,000   25,000   45,000   70,000   25,000   45,000
jack     smith    40,000    8,000   32,000   44,000   12,000   32,000
john     tower    80,000   30,000   50,000   87,000   32,000   55,000
maria    menendez 42,000   10,000   32,000   45,000   10,000   35,000

: bar graph
Print a bar graph.


: []
```

FIGURE 2-10.   Natural Language's English Capabilities.

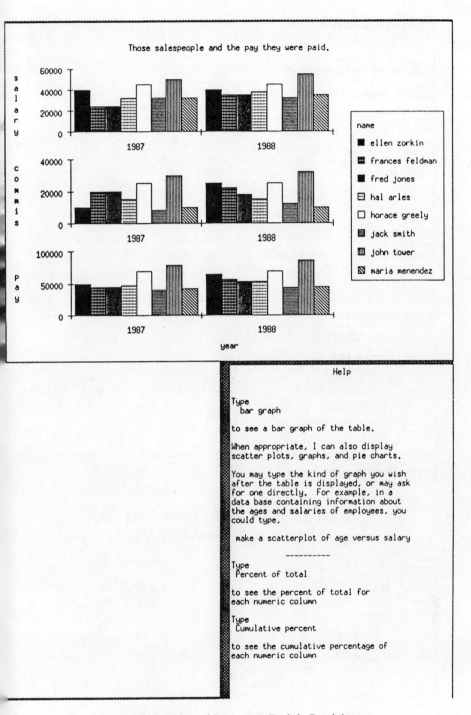

FIGURE 2-10. Natural Language's English Capabilities.

How do you know that?

How do I know Fred does not like George?

1. Fred hates George.
2. If x hates y then x does not like y. 1, 2 $\Longrightarrow$
3: Fred does not like George.

No person that likes George likes Fred.

OK. No people that like George like Fred.

Does Mary like George and Fred?

Does Mary like George and Fred?

No, Mary does not like Fred or does not like George.

Why?

How do I know Mary does not like Fred or does not like George?

1. Assume: Mary likes George.
2. Mary is a person. 1, 2 $\Longrightarrow$
3: Mary likes George and is a person.
4. If x likes George and is a person then x does not like Fred. 3, 4 $\Longrightarrow$
5: Mary does not like Fred.

But, best of all is Natural Language's interactive, and very graphic screen displays as shown in Figure 2-10.

A HOST OF OTHER NATURAL LANGUAGE FEATURES

$\mathbf{I}$t's nice to work with a computer system that corrects your mistakes. Many natural language systems do just that:

User: What is the total cas figure for firm 123.

Computer: I don't understand the word cas. Do you mean cash?

Even better is a natural language understanding system that dynamically grows much the way we do:

User: Give me a list of firms with total assets over 50 million dollars.

Computer: I don't understand the phrase total assets.
Do you want to:

1. quit
2. enter a definition
3. re-enter

Of course this is quite trivial, all of our word processors have this in their spell functions, but still it's nice to have.

The Uses of Natural Languages

Professor Schank built one of the first natural language understanding systems that demonstrated the utility of this branch of artificial intelligence. Called FRUMP (Fast Reading and Understanding Memory Program), this late-1970s program read the UPI wire and summarized its contents. FRUMP was given a broad understanding of world events—everything from earthquakes to oil spills to diplomatic crises. When the following story came in over the UPI wire:

> The State Department announced today the suspension of diplomatic relations with Equatorial Guinea. The announcement came five days after the department received a message from the foreign minister of the West African country saying that his government had declared two United States diplomats persona non grata.
>
> The two are Ambassador Herbert J. Spiro and Consul William C. Mithoefer, Jr., both stationed in neighboring Cameroon but also accredited to Equatorial Guinea.
>
> Robert L. Funseth, State Department spokesman, said Mr. Spiro and Mr. Mithoefer spent five days in Equatorial Guinea earlier this month and were given a "warm reception."
>
> But at the conclusion of their visit, Mr. Funseth said, Equatorial Guinea's acting Chief of Protocol handed them a five-page letter that cast "unwarranted and insulting slurs" on both diplomats.
>
> *The UPI story and FRUMP translation courtesy of The MIT Press.*

FRUMP was programmed to analyze each story on a content rather than word basis. It zeroed in on a broken diplomatic relationship and then worked on figuring out who broke relations with whom.

The translation took just 2515 milliseconds and came out as:

The United States State Department and Guinea have broken
diplomatic relations.

Schank envisioned great things from natural language front-end processors, including a very English-literate computer financial advisor. And although he made his predictions back in the late seventies, by the early eighties he was pretty much on the mark.

Today, natural language is being used for things such as database interfaces, text scanning for specific data, editing of text, and even front ends to expert systems.

The Users of Natural Language

The New York Stock Exchange uses a product called RAMIS-ENGLISH to access regulatory databases and Citibank uses a home-grown natural language system to figure out telex money transfer messages. We'll read about both of these applications in the second half of this book.

ATRANS was developed by one of the first natural language companies around, Cognitive Systems. Their product works similarly to the one developed at Citibank, but this one is for sale. The art of deciphering money transfer messages is important. We're talking millions and millions of dollars contained all on one little telex slip. A system of this sort needs to be able to distinguish between the different parties to a transfer. When you delve into the Citibank description, you'll see how fraught with difficulty this really is.

For a second, let's step away from the financial services orientation and take a look at a system developed for the Navy. FRESH is a decision support system with the goal of assisting in the scheduling of some 300 ships in the Pacific Fleet. Running on a Symbolics workstation with hooks to the Navy's mainline VAXs, FRESH cost some $10 million to develop. FRESH is actually an expert system written in Knowledge Craft with spurts of LISP and Prolog code. The natural language part comes in at the user interface. Texas Instrument's NLMenu product was chosen for this purpose. The FRESH front end provides the user with 19 screens that can be used to generate English inquiries.

On the other side of the profit margin is the Ford Motor Co. Their Direct Labor Management System is used to assist in the manufacturing planning process. Extremely detailed assembly instructions geared for the floor technician are generated from very high-level English descriptions supplied by Ford engineers.

Like its precursor FRUMP, General Electric's natural language SCISOR system is designed to read, understand, and answer questions about textual data. SCISOR provides a window into the use of artificial intelligence to winnow down the huge amounts of textual data that each of us has to cope with every day.

Just think of the possibilities. Today you arrive at your office with a desk weighted down by magazine subscriptions, newsletters, and various other exotic items. You make a grand attempt at reading what comes across your desk, but invariably end up thumbing through this pile of text and reading only what catches your eye. Imagine instead, coming into a neat and small pile of 8 ½ by 11 sheets of paper. This quarter-inch stack summarizes three pounds or five inches of daily reading. I don't know about you, but I'm sure voting for natural languages.

AND NOW FOR THE ANSWER
TO THE PUZZLE

Let's use all of our neurons to understand this rather convoluted answer:

Because the sexes are equally divided and the teacher is a man, the middle row is girl, boy, girl.

Every digit is used once and so the scores were 2, 3, 4, 5, 6, 7, 8, 9, and 10. These have the sum of 54 and will form a "magic square" with row-sum totals of 18.

The central digit must be 6. (Since the sum of the central column and two diagonals is 72, and this must be 54 plus three times the center.) Now 2 cannot be in a corner because there are insufficient large numbers to make up its three rows etc. to 18. Also, obviously, 4 cannot be in a line with 2. So the four corners are 3, 5, 7, and 9.

Mirror images (left to right) are not relevant to this puzzle, so we give below the four relevant possibilities, with the top row being the front of the class:

A			B			C			D		
9	2	7	5	4	9	3	10	5	7	8	3
4	6	8	10	6	2	8	6	4	2	6	10
5	10	3	3	8	7	7	2	9	9	4	5

As no girl gets less than three marks, A, B, and D are ruled out. In C the highest mark awarded to a boy is a 9.

Quick, where's the neural net?

3

From Information Systems to Knowledge Systems

A magician needs to know how to sell magic. Take several colored crayons and give them to an audience member. Have this participant choose one crayon and place it in your hands, which are held behind your back. With the crayon still behind your back in one hand, bring the other hand to your forehead to help in this divination. You will most certainly guess the correct color. How? While your hands are behind your back, rub the crayon across your thumbnail. When you bring your hand up to your forehead, sneak a peek. Your nail will be the color of the crayon chosen.

THE SELLING OF EXPERT SYSTEMS*

The selling of expert systems is not done by magic, sleight of hand, or trickery—it's almost an art. There are no tried and true formulas, no textbook methodologies, no seminars on what is probably the most important talent a computer professional can have. And that's the selling of new and potentially important technologies to users and to senior management.

The expert system is a mysterious art. At least to most computer professionals it is. This aura makes expert systems seem expensive

* This section has been reprinted from an article that I wrote for *Information Center Magazine*, June 1989, entitled "How to Sell Management on Expert Systems." I would like to thank Weingarten Publications for their courtesy in letting me use it here.

to senior management and confoundingly complex to everyone else. The secret of the sell is to push expert systems as just another integral part of the systems toolbox. So go databases, personal computing, so go expert systems.

Get The Product Known

The first step in any sales campaign is to get the product known. Expert system needs to become more than a buzz word by educating up and down the organization. There are many good one-day "getting started" courses being offered by prestigious universities. These afford a good overview of the subject and a general demystifying of the technology. IBM itself offers one- and two-day complementary courses to customers, although these are really marketing ploys for their expert system products. Whoever the trainer, attendees walk away with a good grasp of how expert systems fit into the systems puzzle.

In some organizations, an internal group can be called in to market the technology. At Du Pont the internal artificial intelligence R&D group offers everything from what they call management awareness speeches to four-hour management courses to two-day intensive courses. All are offered with an underlying expert systems marketing message.

At one organization, an astute seller of expert systems sent copies of a popular, PC expert system sampler diskette to users and management. Sampler diskettes are often programmed to be self-running or are tutorials with little understanding of the product's syntax required. In this case, the sample expert system performed an analysis of one's investment options. Everyone who received the sampler had a grand time playing with this new toy. It assisted them in intelligently picking investment and savings strategies based on their personal financial situation. To the last person, they called back our astute salesperson and begged for more.

For those with an aversion to hands-on—and many senior managers seem to be of this ilk—a fast-paced short videotape on the glories of expert systems can prove most conducive. Applied Learning Systems, formerly Deltak, has such a series in the James Martin Tapes. James Martin is one of the gurus of the computer industry. His videotape series is nontechnical, his on-camera presence magnetic, and the information quite illustrative.

Texas Instruments provides another avenue. TI is the yearly sponsor of a satellite symposium on artificial intelligence. The day-long symposium is captured on videotape as well. For a small fee one can order: the tapes, a set of 35mm slides, which can be used in presentations on expert systems; the Ed Feigenbaum best seller, *The Rise of the Expert Company*; and a set of sampler diskettes constituting Texas Instruments' Personal Computer Easy expert system shell. This is a powerhouse of sales tools. The tapes can be selectively shown to various levels of staff— from technical to users to management. Many of the tapes are case histories, which go a long way in selling the use of this technology. These case histories show users explaining the process and how it improved the company's bottom line. The videotape interview with the senior expert on Campbell Soup Company's "cookers" is the best of the lot and alone is worth the price of the package.

A more low-key introduction of expert systems to the computer jock's toolkit is dissemination of magazines and other literature. This approach is akin to flying over enemy lines and distributing propaganda leaflets. If it works for a government, it should work for you. Magazines such as *AI Expert* and *PC AI* are available at most computer-oriented magazine newsstands. These two magazines are aimed at the general computer-happy bunch and contain many articles about installed systems. Paul Harmon publishes a special interest newsletter aptly called "Expert System Strategies," which should stimulate the interest of most technical staff. In addition, this newsletter has back issues that list many of the companies that have developed and deployed expert systems. This list can be invaluable in contacting those who have already done it by those who wish to do it. Contained in the appendices of this very book is a rather long list of magazines, newsletters, and books with which you can paper your way to expert system heaven.

Prove Its Worth

Once the buzz words of expert systems are buzzed around the organization and interest in the topic is at a high, it's time to prove its worth. The sale of expert system methodology in a company often depends on successful implementation of the first demonstration project. Once a company experiences failure during exploration of new technologies, that avenue of adventure is often not pursued again for many, many months. If the technology is new within the industry, as is the expert system, a first-time failure can waylay use of this tool permanently. So, it's easy to understand why the selection of the first project is all-important. Now is when many of us will fall into the old Catch-22 trap. You can't build an expert system unless you have the right tool and you can't get permission to buy the tool until there is a successful system already installed.

There are many solutions to this sticky wicket. A sneak-it-in-under-disguise often works well in decentralized shops. Personal computer expert system shells can be quite powerful. Since PC software is comparatively inexpensive, there is usually no loud outcry over its purchase. This first expert system tool—or shell, as it has come to be known—need not be the final product. It need only give the flavor of the power of expert system methodology and most do that rather nicely.

The trial-period freebie may be used by those companies that carry a lot of "political clout". Many vendors of mid- to large-scale expert systems will gladly install their shell for a short period, and offer much assistance. From the vendor's marketing perspective they may think they have a hot prospect. If your company would look impressive on their list of customers, you have a real shot at this angle. If that fails, most vendors will offer their mid- to large-size products on a per-month, short-term lease. Since the large mainframe shells cost anywhere from $60K to $200K, a short-term trial lease can be less threatening.

Then there is the find-another-company-using-it-in-your-industry ploy. Most managements feel more secure if a peer company already has two feet in the pool. This copy-cat syndrome is pervasive and can be used to your advantage as a competitive force in getting the permission to enter the expert system fray. One trainer who taught a "How To" seminar at the CIA actually recommended that management be told that the KGB was using expert systems so why shouldn't they. This provoked a lot of laughter, but also a good deal of thought.

When all else fails, a cost/benefit approach can sometimes loosen the purse strings. The pitch here is to get the "cheaper not to reinvent the wheel" message across to management. If you remember the days of selling fourth-generation languages such as RAMIS or FOCUS, you remember selling management on the tool based on the queues of users waiting outside the cubicle door of some hapless programmer, waiting for him or her to write a program to sort and print a file in name order . . . in address order . . . in salary order. Use of 4GLs saved bundles of money for managements besieged with these trivial, but time-consuming, requests.

One cagey IS staffer costed out the COBOL development of many of the salable features of expert system shells. These included contextual help features, EXPLAIN and WHY functions, forward and backward chaining, objects, and truth maintenance. When all was said and done the COBOL bill was staggering and management sighed with relief when they signed the contract for the mainframe expert system shell.

For comparison purposes, the sample worksheet in Figure 3-1 can be used to calculate the breakeven point of expert system development. American Express, whose Authorizer's Assistant is one of the more successfully deployed expert systems, calculated their breakeven point at one year. AMEX management was much comforted knowing that the

---

1. **Current Costs:**
   Function   Hrs/Mo $/Hr   Cost/Month

1a. **Current maintenance costs:**

   Total (1 + 1a):

---

2. **Predicted cost:**
   Function   Hrs/Mo $/Hr   Cost/Month

3. **Projected savings: (total - predicted cost)**

   Monthly: **Yearly:**

4. **Development cost:**

   a. **knowledge acquisition**
   b. **rule encoding**
   c. **conventional programming**

   Function   Hrs/Mo $/Hr   Cost/Month

5. **Capital expenditures:**

6. **Monthly maintenance:**

7. **Breakeven months (Development + Capital) / (Monthly savings - monthly maintenance)**

FIGURE 3-1.   Cost/benefit Analysis Worksheet.

cost of their system, which assisted in green-card credit authorizations and is accurate 96.5 percent of the time compared to the human rate of 85 percent, would be paid back quickly.

Now that you have the organization speaking "expert systems", it should not be too difficult to target a user champion. Selection of this champion is very important to the success of injecting a new technology into a company. The real power behind the success of implementing expert system methodology in any company is with the users. Expert systems are unlike any other tool in that they perform, not clerical functions, but complex decision support functions. They assist in making the decisions that the user staff now make themselves. It's a whole different ball game when middle management staff are automated and a different sales tack must be taken. Getting them excited about the technology is only the first step. You must now get them to put their money where their mouths are by becoming involved in a small demo to test the waters.

At many companies, testing the waters is accomplished by targeting a small-sized, but politically hot, demonstration problem. To get the users' "buy in," it must be a problem that they themselves select. In one organization the users were disturbed over the lack of consistency in decision-making by the multitude of staff who were financial analysts. Peggy, a senior analyst, applied all of the good heuristics of her 10 years on the job. Peter, on the other hand, was fresh out of college and sometimes made less than perfect decisions—with disturbing consequences. An expert system that assisted in this process was the key and the firm's entry into the wonderful world of artificial intelligence. The development effort should be kept at a minimum, but care must be taken to employ those features of the toolset that dramatize its importance.

Once complete, this system becomes a very impressive sales tool. At Northrop Aircraft in California, this is exactly what happened as early as 1983. Two engineers who were fired up about the use of expert systems developed a demo system for the manufacture of airplane parts. For six months this show was on the road around Northrop selling the methodology at every stop. Note that the salesmen here were not on the computer staff but were user champions.

What this all boils down to is that the selling of expert systems (see list) requires a multifaceted approach coupled with the enthusiasm of a cheerleader, the tenacity of a bulldog, and the shrewdness of a politician.

1. Make expert systems a buzzword.
2. Network around the company—selling every step of the way.
3. Ferret out "friendly" users.
4. Target a user as champion.
5. Know the business.
6. Pick a "hot" first project.

WHY EXPERT SYSTEMS FAIL*

Oh! The magic of baseball.
It's the last half of the ninth inning. Two men are on base. Two outs on the last two batters. The crowd is hushed. A tall, skinny guy steps out of the dugout. He spits in his hands and grips the bat. He steps up to the plate. Fifty thousand pairs of eyes are upon him. Ball one. Strike one. Strike two. The fastball leaves the pitcher's mound, hardly visible in the summer haze. The skinny batter raises his bat and swings. It's an . . .

_____ Out   (check one)
_____ Homerun

Now that I've caught your attention, let's analyze the reasons for success or failure of no particular baseball game. Talent figures into it. So does teamwork. Weather (yes, believe it or not). Morale. Health/Injuries. Management. Not really as simple as it seems. Success seldom is. And failure lurks just around the corner. So too the development of systems. Particularly expert systems. Michael Stock, President of Artificial Intelligence Technologies (AIT), estimates that only 10 percent of expert systems of medium to large size are actually successful. And many, many out there in AI-land agree.

What are the reasons for a system to turn out less than . . . er . . . _perfect?_ Just like in baseball, they are many and diverse and oftentimes dependent upon individual personalities and cultures of organizations.

* This section has been reprinted from an article that I wrote for _AI Expert_, November 1989, entitled "Why Expert Systems Fail." Reprinted from AI EXPERT, November 1989; Copyright 1989 Miller Freeman Publications.

In sifting through the muck of failed cases, we can come up with gems of wisdom that will serve as red flags that we can watch for when we build a system.

No Expert, No System

The first red flag is perhaps the most obvious. Lack of an available and willing (keyword here) expert. Shearson American Express found this out the hard way in 1984 with their aborted attempt to implement an interest rate swapping expert system. The prototype had been successful, at least in theory. It assisted the traders in winnowing out the enormous gobs of data in order to pick out possible swap partners around the world (sort of like a dating service?). During start-up, the system appeared to have earned Shearson $1 million, but this cash cow soon dried up as the real experts—the traders—bowed out. You see, the system relied on the cooperation of the traders to enter information into the system. And anybody who knows anything about the psychology of Wall Street knows that traders don't share (they'd sooner sell their mothers-in-law). No expertise, no system.

Tom Campfield knows that. Tom was a senior official in the foreign exchange department before Manufacturers Hanover Trust's management decided that they needed to be a bit more aggressively innovative in the trading area. Tom, always ready for something new, became part of a team that built TARA, a foreign exchange trading system run on a Symbolics workstation with IntelliCorp's KEE (Knowledge Engineering Environment). And as MHT succinctly states it - No Tom, No TARA.

Management Support

But maybe we're jumping ahead of ourselves. We're presuming that we've already gotten management support for our AI endeavors and we're cavalierly discussing the "lack of an available and willing expert problem." So let's back up. Perhaps the greatest killer of expert systems (if not the system itself, at least enthusiasm for the concept) is management. There are two sides to this coin. Heads—management itself is ingrained in the "tried and true" mode. (Here's that COBOL inertia again). Millions are invested in these third-generation methodologies.

Staffs are filled with third-generation programmers, too. And for every Phyllis who wants to learn a new methodology there are ten Petes who want to stay true blue to the technology that they learned 20 years ago. Flip the coin to the tail side and we find an AI staff that just doesn't know how to sell this concept to management. According to Gavin Finn, a project manager of expert systems for Stone and Webster Engineering in Boston, Massachusetts, "You have to show some business or management benefit. It can't *just* be a neat idea... there has to be some pay-back." And Gavin should know. He's responsible for some very successful systems such as the Weld Defect Diagnosis System built using EXSYS.

For some, management support and a willing and able expert would be enough. There's another factor in this lengthy equation, and the user is not about to be left out. This should be a given: without the user, support systems won't work. One classic example of this is in the U.S. Postal Service. When the computer department automated the clerks who serve us at the windows, they met with enormous amounts of resistance, even sabotage, which delayed the implementation of this system for years. Although this was not an AI system, the reason for this wall of non-cooperation was due to lack of involvement by the users—up front— where it matters. So go conventional systems, so go expert systems. In fact, the result of exclusion of the end-users in expert system development could be even more calamitous. At the New York Stock Exchange, one expert systems development team knew the value of a good user. These users played a pivotal role, going so far as to being the actual spokespeople. They made their rounds to management and sold them hook, line, and sinker on expert systems in their division.

Our friend Gavin Finn agrees. In his experiences with building over 18 expert systems he has found the secret to success. End-users must perceive a need first. Then they must see the benefit. After all, we can't force them to use the system. And above all, Gavin insists that a user representative must be a (big) part of the development process.

The Knowledge Engineer

That's why the person who acts as the glue that binds all of these pieces together is so all-important. The knowledge engineer issue is one that is taken a bit too lightly at many organizations. "Hey, we're going to build an expert system. What's Karen doing on Monday? Nothing? We'll give her this book on *How to Build an Expert System* to read over the weekend." Comedy aside, it really does take a bit more than reading a "How to" book to build expert systems well. At one large Wall Street financial institution a COBOL programmer made an overnight metamorphosis into a knowledge engineer. Oh, he did take the requisite courses in how to use the tool that was selected. He even took courses in knowledge engineering. What everyone forgot was culture. Our programmer-turned-knowledge engineer had his brain cells patterned into COBOL. No, I'm not being facetious. Dan was a programming hacker. He loved his bits and bytes and data base calls. He was so wound up in worrying about the vagaries of data capture and manipulation that he really couldn't see the forest for the trees. When the users talked about stock prices, Dan was visualizing the programs he'd have to write to capture the data, reformat it, and pass it down to the PC where the expert system would reside. He was so absorbed in these details, he really didn't pay adequate attention to the nuances of what the experts where telling him. So the result of Dan's knowledge engineering effort was that he captured 80 percent of the expert's knowledge, but lost the 20 percent that was composed of the heuristics of what this expert's job was all about. In other words, Dan didn't capture the stuff of expert systems. And the system would have failed had the manager of the development team not noted the problem and reorganized the team. Noting that the company had no real experience in developing systems of this nature, this manager hired an outside consultant with years of practical hands-on tales of horror and success. Dan was cloned to this outside consultant—umbilical cord to umbilical cord. This mode of technology transfer worked like a charm. Dan began to concentrate more on obtaining knowledge and less on processing data.

Operations

Let's not leave out processing of data altogether. Michael Stock (AIT) thinks that one of the biggest reasons for failure of expert systems is the inability to fulfill operational requirements. "Expert Systems need to connect to real data. They need to keep up the pace with the real problem." Mike lists five criteria that we should use to ensure that our expert systems are operationally successful:

- rule firing speed
- system on-line requirements
- performance of system
- database activity
- networking

"AI stuff should never be minimized; operational stuff *can't* be minimized," so quoteth Mike. Lockheed Corporation found this out very quickly when they deployed their Medical Charge Evaluation and Control System. MEDCHEC's function in life was to check insurance claim validity. In theory, it seemed like a great idea. In reality, they found that it was cheaper and faster to send the claims out to be processed by human adjusters than to wait on the slow operation of the system.

We should never minimize the importance of the heuristics we all picked up from years and years of traditional software development. Back in the early 1980s, AI cast a long shadow. It was exotic: men and women in white lab coats with the words AI LAB on their office door intimidated the rest of us. Mike Stock (AIT) goes so far as to say that we allowed R&D people too much say in what was going on. Many of us got the impression that our "tried and true" methodologies of systems development just weren't appropriate in the building of expert systems. As Mike Stock says, the idea of a different methodology "is a myth. In reality, it takes a lot of traditional software engineering. It's here where the rubber meets the road." Well said. There's no mumbo-jumbo involved in knowledge engineering, as the process is called. It really is traditional software engineering, and then some. Bypassing the "development life cycle" can land one in a heck of a jam.

Capturing Knowledge

About the only difference between expert systems development methodologies and traditional data processing methodologies is the all important capture of knowledge, which is the essence or *raison d'être* of the system. Conventional systems contain minimal knowledge and loads of data, while expert systems process gobs of knowledge and perhaps even gobs of data. Knowledge capture is, in and of itself, a really fuzzy process. There are many ways of doing it and no single best way. Perhaps the most interesting case of knowledge capture took place at

Coopers & Lybrand during the knowledge engineering phase of system development of the ExperTax product. ExperTax is a knowledge-based system that provides expert tax advice (as if the name didn't give it away!) and we'll hear more about the development of this system later on in the book. A table was placed in a room with a curtain dividing the table in half. On one side of the table sat a junior member of the staff. He had spread out in front of him all of the tools and tomes of his tax trade. On the other side of the curtain sat several of the senior tax managers: experts in the field. They had nothing in front of them. The junior member was called upon to solve a complex tax question. He was able to ask questions of the senior audit managers who referred him to reference manuals and procedures. They solved the problem verbally; the process was videotaped. Later they replayed the videotape and captured the essence of this knowledge in the form of rules. You might have a willing and able expert, an experienced knowledge engineer, and unquestioned support from management. But if you can't distill real-world knowledge into something tangible, then you don't have an expert system.

Sometimes even the best knowledge engineering techniques and the most talented knowledge engineers can't get the job done. This is what happened to two Texas Instruments knowledge engineers who were signed on to "clone" Thomas Kelly. Tom, a civil engineer with Southern California Edison is a bona-fide expert. He can almost feel the presence of danger at the Vermilion hydroelectric dam. So in 1986 Southern Cal Edison plunked down over $300,000 to replicate Tom's knowledge gleaned from years of experience with the dam. Both sides grew frustrated right away. Time was ticking away and the knowledge engineers felt that Tom was not revealing enough. This was a complex task, relying on many rules of thumb. How did Tom know that a small stream of water on one side of the dam meant a blocked drain at its base? And Tom was unhappy, too. He felt that the two TI knowledge engineers weren't picking up on what he was saying fast enough. Too ambitious in scope, coupled with lack of the necessary communication between knowledge engineer and expert crippled the progress of this most interesting system.

Today, what is known as Project Kelly has wound down. A good prototype was built, but not a deployable system. Southern Cal estimates that another $100,000 would have to be pumped into the Vermilion system to permit it to become a generic dam-troubleshooting expert system. Now it just keeps Tom Kelly company during his lonely vigils watchdogging the dam.

Our Vermilion dam knowledge engineers hailed from Texas Instruments. TI's presence looms large in the AI field. Tommy Fox, Manager of Knowledge Engineering Services, has worked on quite a variety of expert system development projects since he began in 1985. Tommy distinguishes two broad categories of systems. Expert systems capture the rules of thumb of an expert while knowledge-based systems model problems. The key to successful development of these intelligent systems is to recognize which class of problems one has, because this will affect the tools and approach used. Expert systems are typically diagnostic or training problems. An example is the SwissAir system that checks for double-booking of reservations. From Tommy's experience, the biggest cause of failure of expert systems is the lack of an articulate expert or finding that the expert's knowledge lacks depth: that it's really just common sense. And no expert system deals satisfactorily with common sense. But a *little* common sense is a plus. Alas, there have been some notable cases of omitting even the most trivial common sense from a system. During beta (secondary) testing of a Ford Motor Company expert system designed to do credit analysis of car loans, the system goofed. It failed to notice that one 20-year-old applicant listed as 10 for the answer to the question of number of years driving experience.

Another pitfall is to corral too many experts (most of us would be happy to have just one). This is sort of a "too many cooks in the kitchen" problem. Tommy Fox of TI has a favorite war story. The expert system was DARPA's, the research arm of the defense department. The goal of the system was to create an aircraft pilot expert system. A whole slew of pilots showed up as experts. Some experienced and some not so experienced. It was impossible to achieve a consensus of opinion, amid all the crowing. And it was even more impossible to achieve a consistently high level of expertise.

And even if the system is successfully implemented, there are still hidden pitfalls. Probably the best example of this is one that is commonly thought of as a grand success. XCON is Digital Equipment Corporation's *pièce de résistance* expert system. It operates as a system configurator, piecing together working minicomputers that can have from 200 to 8000 parts. XCON replaced the function of the human technical writer. With the complexity of DEC systems growing, the technical writer was being left hopelessly behind, with the effect of delivering incomplete or nonworking systems. XCON changed all that by making sure each DEC minicomuter is completely and correctly configured. It now contains 10,000 rules and DEC spends upward of $2 million a year to keep it up to date. But even this injection of money can't keep the system current with the proliferation of engineering changes that XCON must keep track of. So is it a failure or a success? Is it an expert? Is it even accurate?

So, should we throw in the towel? Well, it's certainly not the ninth inning and we've got a few good pitches left in us. With good management techniques, good teamwork, a salable and workable problem, and the proper toolset we might yet hit a homerun.

THE SUCCESSFUL EXPERT SYSTEM DEVELOPMENT PROCESS FOR FINANCIAL APPLICATIONS

Now that I've scared you with all the ways a system can fail, I'll cheer you up with a set of procedures that will help you succeed. Financial applications are unique. At least for expert systems they are. The first expert systems that were ever developed were of the diagnostic or design ilk. These were the medical systems like MYCIN and the manufacturing systems like XCON. While these and other systems like them were most certainly complicated, the creation of a financial expert system is more so, due to the necessity of expanded domains.

Financial applications are necessarily broader in scope than manufacturing. They are typified by massive inputs, complicated and multiple processes, and variant outputs. In addition, financial applications undergo extraordinary amounts of oversight due to the public nature of the products involved (i.e., securities, insured bank deposits).

So even though expert systems make it easier for developers to drop some rules into a rule base, the design of these systems should undergo careful planning and testing, just as should be done in conventional systems development.

We're going to go through a series of some 10 steps that will serve you well, whether you are the developer of an expert system or the expert involved in the development process. Of course, once you get

your feet wet with the technology, shortcuts are invariably taken. However, be cautioned that unlike conventional systems, for some reason the
expectation with expert systems is that the system will work correctly on
the first try. I don't know why this is. Perhaps it's the aura of the name
"expert system." Perhaps it's all the hype surrounding the methodology.
Perhaps it's our hard sell to get the technology in the door. Whatever
it is, management expects a lot more than the usual 50 percent to be
perfected when the system is implemented.

I really don't want to air dirty linen, but most systems that are developed are put into production in a less than perfect fashion. Hovering
at about the 50 percent perfection rate. Why is this? First, the systems
development process is less than perfect. To caricature it, you'd find a
systems type walking into the office of a user and saying something like,
"Here's a piece of paper. Draw me a picture of how you want that report." The systems person doesn't have the foggiest notion of the user's
concerns or even what the user does for a living. Throw out the word
caricature: this *is* fairly typical. Don't you deny it.

Systems folks are too far removed from the user. This is the real reason
behind so many problems with our systems and why we find more money
spent on maintenance of systems than on development of the original
systems. If this is a *problem* in conventional systems development, it's
more a *crisis* in expert systems development. The word "expert" is key
here. As a developer, you are charged with pulling all of this expertise
out of the expert, choosing the right set of tools, and programming
the ultimate system. As an expert, your job is to make certain that
the developer understands your expertise and that what you see being
developed is what you asked for. All of the above requires a methodology.
While there are many to choose from, the one presented here typifies
them all.

Creating the Expert System Team

Well, you've already sold your management hook, line, and sinker
on the use of expert systems in your company. Bravo. You also arranged
to find an able and willing expert. Just make certain that this person is
really an expert, not just the first available "body" around. In Chapter
5, which discusses the auditing of expert systems, you'll find a whole
discussion on the topic of what expertise is. You might want to jump

ahead and read it, if you've got a problem with determining who in your organization really possesses true expertise.

The next step, then, is to select a systems team. Yes, just like in traditional systems development, it's a good idea to use a team approach. Expert system development projects need to be managed just as do other projects. On top of that, there are really two components of the task. The one that people are most comfortable with is the traditional systems work that must be done. All expert systems will have components in them that require access to real corporate data. Let's say you are building an expert system to do that budget, again. You'd need to be able to get to the corporate expense file as well as the accounts payable and receivables files to be able to make predictions. You may also need to do some networking. Let's say you've chosen to build your expert system on a workstation and you need to access some data in the mainframe. Someone needs to perform the programming tasks required to get this functionality. These tasks are data-driven and require a certain skill set. Another member of the team is the person or persons called knowledge engineer(s). They need a very different skill set that we'll discuss in a minute. The point here is that these two skill sets are quite different. While it is possible to find a unique talent that can do it all, my recommendation is that two people perform these two very different functions.

A good knowledge engineer will have certain, hard-to-find qualities. They must have the ability to converse with the expert in the language of the expert. This goes without saying, except that it happens so infrequently I felt that I had better say it. This person should also have the ability and the inclination to perform thorough research in the area chosen to be expert-systematized. In other words, no lazybones need apply. And finally, this gem of the systems world should have the literary capabilities necessary to document the results. What we have here is a rather unusual combination. And even though I'm running the risk of insulting a large segment of the systems development professionals, I must say that few systems people seem to possess these skills. At least, at first glance. But help is on the way.

For the most part, expert systems in production today have *not* been developed by traditional systems development staff. A large number of systems have been developed by the experts themselves (who obviously do possess all the skills listed above). An equally large number of systems have been developed by consulting firms, Big Eight, or otherwise.

It is possible to turn a data processor into a knowledge engineer. You just have to know how to do it. At least start with the proper ingredients. The candidate should have good written and verbal skills. Also this person should have tenacity because they're sure going to need it. Programmers who consider themselves hackers are too close to the code. They would not be the best choices for this sort of activity. A true-to-life story will serve to illuminate this point.

Peter (the name has been changed to protect the innocent or guilty— you choose) is one of the best programmer/analysts around. He can program rings around everyone. And he does everything so fast, but carefully. He's selected to become a "knowledge engineer." On his first assignment he begins to work with two experts in trying to wrangle knowledge from their brains into the form of rules. He sets up brainstorming sessions where he attempts to elicit this knowledge. At each session he listens intently to their pearls of wisdom. Unfortunately he doesn't really understand what they are talking about. Oh, he hears them and he does understand all the terminology. He's just so busy worrying about, "Gee, they're talking about pricing those securities. Now how do I write the code to get to the pricing databases and then import that data into my expert system tool" that he doesn't quite see the larger picture. In other words, he was missing the point.

The problem with Peter was that he was just too close to coding. So what happened? Because this project had a project manager, the manager decided to take some action. To solve the problem of Peter's worrying so much about data access, a new person was added to the team that would do all of this dirty work, freeing up Peter to do just the knowledge engineering. It worked like a charm. Freed from the burden of having to do it all, Peter began to concentrate solely on elicitation of knowledge. And someone else concentrated on the database calls and the actual coding of the expert system using the tool's syntax.

To counter this problem of being too close to the coding part to concentrate on the knowledge part, it turns out that the best candidates are those folks who have not programmed for a while. These are the project leader or system analyst types. They're far enough away from the process to be able to hone in on the big picture.

Perhaps the best advice I can give you is to make sure that these people are adequately trained. Sometimes in the heat of the moment, someone is tossed a manual and told, "Here Charlie, read this over the weekend. You have a new project on Monday." There are many ways to train staff in expert system concepts. Many universities offer courses. Vendors of expert system products typically offer training in their products. Even Texas Instruments down in Austin offers some top-notch knowledge engineering courses followed by courses in their specific tools.

Picking the First Problem

The very first time you build an expert system you want to be successful. Of course, you want all of your forays into expert systemdom to be successful, but the first will set the pace for this technology in your company. If the first attempt with expert systems is judged to be a failure by corporate management, it might be a cold day in the proverbial underworld before you get a second chance.

There are three simple rules of thumb to keep in mind when you select your problem. First, pick one that you know well. It's not a really good idea to pick a problem that is so vague and so "ununderstandable" to the team that successful development becomes a miracle of faith. Next, pick one that is small. Don't expert-systematize the *whole* office. Pick one department and pick one problem within that department. Last, pick a problem that matters. If you work for the Pentagon, then your first venture into expert systems shouldn't be with one to advise staff on how to generate internal requisitions. It should be a problem that has sell power; one that will make management sit up and take notice.

Not all applications lend themselves to expert system technology, just as not all applications lend themselves to being on a PC or being on-line or being database applications. Just where do you find these great ideas for expert system applications? Well, management is usually a good source of ideas. You might find some good candidates in the realm of reducing organizational complexity, which should tickle management's fancy. Other sources of good ideas are: customers of the company, a task force specifically set up to come up with ideas, the research and development department, marketing, operations staff, the knowledge engineering staff and last but certainly not least, the expert. If you're lucky, you might wind up with several good problems. At this point you want to pick the best of the lot and again there are some rules of thumb that you can apply to this procedure.

The most suitable problems for expert systems development require application of knowledge rather than data. In other words, choose a problem that requires decision-making over number crunching. An example would be a system that advises a planner on how to put together a budget. This is a better choice than a system that just calculates the budget. You also want to make sure that you pick a problem for which there is knowledge readily available. Don't pick as a problem, "Why were humans created?" It's an interesting problem, but no one really knows the answer so there isn't sufficient knowledge available to solve it. The availability of knowledge presumes there is an expert available. I've stated it before and I'll state it again many times before you finish reading this book—don't just pick the first John or Mary that has some free time. Make sure that expertise in solving this problem actually exists in your company. And if it does exist then that's the person you want to corral into this project.

Of course, if the problem you select is one which it takes the expert a few days to solve, you may have selected a problem that is too broad. If you have, all is not lost, just whittle it down to a manageable level. On the other side of the coin is a problem that takes the expert a mere pittance of time to solve. If this is the case, then you've chosen a problem that is just too trivial. So try to widen the problem. The best problems exhibit what is known as *depth in a narrow domain*, which is represented by the diagram in Figure 3-2.

Problem Identification

Now that you've successfully picked a problem and arranged for the appropriate folks to be the expert or experts and knowledge engineers, we can proceed with getting our hands dirty in problem solving. In other words, the fun has just begun.

We know what the problem is, but now we must define it. Believe it or not this is the most difficult part of the expert system development

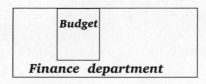

FIGURE 3-2. Sizing the Domain.

process. It can mean the difference between success and failure. If we define it too broadly or too vaguely, we'll wind up developing a bunch of incoherent rules making the system virtually untestable. On the other hand, if we narrow down the problem to the *n*th degree, the system ultimately developed will be too narrow and thus not cost effective.

Usually the problem is formally defined at the first working meeting of the knowledge engineering team and the experts. Let's use our budgetary expert system as an example again. Let's suppose that we've selected this as the problem to be expert-systematized. We've just walked into the first meeting of the team. What we want to end up with is a written description of what this system is specifically going to do. So we toss some ideas around over the course of the next few hours and finally come up with:

> The goal of this project is to develop an automated budgetary system that will exhibit the following features:
>
> **A.** Act as an advisor to the respective divisional budget administrators in leading them through the process of preparing the various forms required for the formal budget review.
> **B.** Act as an advisor to the central administrative staff in tying all the divisional budgets together.
>   **1.** Provide exception reporting and assistance in correcting these exceptions.
>   **2.** Act in an advisory capacity in determining how to apply budgetary constraints such that the least impact will be felt for the largest possible budget cut.
>   **3.** Perform budgetary calculation reporting and provide an audit trail of changes made.

After it's typed, we send it around to all the players involved to elicit their feedback. We don't want to keep anyone in the dark. Not management and certainly not the people who will ultimately use the system.

Expert systems are funny animals. If people feel threatened by being automated, they feel downright paranoid about having to work with an expert system. Just throwing a completed system at them and expecting it to be a success is downright suicidal. So get them involved. It might cause you some extra headaches, but they will be illuminating ones.

Maintaining Management Support

You've already been enlightened by our discussion on the selling of expert systems. Even though you've managed to get the expert system point across, you've now got to drive the point home. You've got to make them put their money where their mouths are.

An expert system is most certainly a "horse of a different color." With such a large investment in traditional software, many computer shops have become so fully entrenched with the old way of doing things that moving them onto a higher plane becomes difficult, if not impossible.

Most computer shops are a bit nervous about anything new. New software means new skills to learn, new programs to support, and new headaches to nurse. And most shops can do without the headaches.

Then there's the "bring the computer to its knees" syndrome. Most operations types fear what they do not understand. All new software has the potential of degrading system performance to unacceptable levels. For some reason, expert systems have garnered a bad reputation as a resource hog. Since expert systems do run on the mainframe this is an understandable fear. Unfounded, but understandable. Expert system tools *do* have a lot of features. And any misused tool with a lot of features has the potential of degrading performance. This is where project management and systems testing come in. A well-planned and executed system should have minimal impact in the production environment. In fact, you can probably do more damage with a wild COBOL program than you can do with an expert system tool.

To counterattack these fears I recommend doing what our foreign policy advisors often do: Meet the enemy! Form a committee of development, systems, and end-user personnel. The charter of this group would be to address, in an unbiased manner, the needs of the organization versus possible implementations for this type of technology. You'll find after a couple of meetings that Pogo was right, "We have met the enemy and he is us."

Conceptualizing the Problem

We've spent a good deal of time in lining up our pins. Now it's time to aim for a strike. In this phase of development, we need to concentrate on the specifics of the problem. A grass-roots understanding of the problem and all of its vagaries is absolutely necessary.

In order to do this, the knowledge engineer and expert should concentrate on the *who, what, where, when,* and *how* of investigative analysis. This is the beginning of the much heralded knowledge engineering process. The end goal is to develop a comprehensive view; what I like to call *conceptual documentation.* This is composed of several items.

The first thing we want to know is who will be the end-user. We want to know this because the consultation, which is the dialogue between the user and the system, should be tailored specifically for the level of worker using the system. A budgetary system geared for low-level clerks which would look different from one designed for accountants which would look different from one designed for senior executives. In our budgetary expert system, the users are accountant types so we'll design the system accordingly.

Now that we have the user figured out, let's take the time to understand the world we live in. By this I mean: Where is the budget process located in relation to the rest of the department in which it operates? Let's look at the generalized domain flow diagram of Figure 3-3. This is a thumbnail sketch of what the finance department looks like. For the knowledge engineers on the team, the diagram serves the purpose of introducing them to the area where the expert system will be used. For the expert, this sketch serves as a reminder of the relationships between the process to be systematized and the rest of the operation. In this way the team ensures that major inputs and outputs are not overlooked.

Now that we have the big picture, we need to finely tune it a bit to see the specifics of our chosen task. Figure 3-4 shows the problem area detailed flowchart. The keyword here is detailed. This diagram should

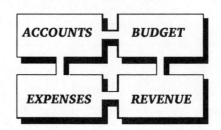

FIGURE 3-3. Generalized Domain Flow Diagram.

show the specifics of the functionality of the job. At a minimum it should show relationships to external sources such as outside databases, data manipulations to be performed, points of user interactions, and any areas of uncertainty. This exercise serves other purposes as well. For the knowledge engineer this activity will serve to make the job functions clear and specific. For the expert it will serve as a sort of checklist to make sure that all bases are covered during the development process.

Many developers of expert systems do not perform these tasks. They run a risk. Unless they themselves are expert in the area in question, they run the risk of leaving out some all-important tidbit that can dramatically alter the way the system works. So take out those rulers and crayolas and start drawing.

The last activity in the conceptualization phase is to develop a series of test cases. This is similar to testing the many branches of a conventional program. You need to develop several cases (no fewer than 10) that typify the process. This is the real meat behind knowledge engineering and there are many ways to do it.

The wrong way is retrospective analysis. Asking an expert how a solution was arrived at after it happens is like asking a bird how it manages

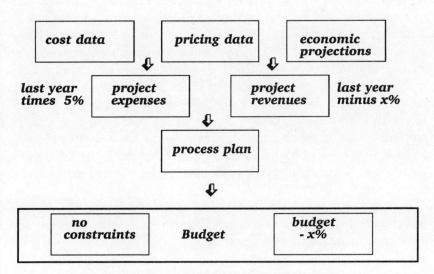

FIGURE 3-4. Problem Area Detailed Flowchart.

to fly. Nobody knows. Most people sequester themselves with the expert in a conference room and don't come out until all the knowledge is siphoned out of the expert. In this room a series of problems is discussed with the expert solving the problem verbally. Some tape-record this process and some even videotape the process.

There are many ways of eliciting or acquiring knowledge. We discussed a few at the beginning of this book and the Coopers & Lybrand example typifies the approach being taken by many firms. The point is that this is hard work and often very tedious. It's also cyclical. After you've uncovered a gem of knowledge, you should go back and review it with the expert. Around and around you go, where you'll stop only the expert knows!

Once you do complete the knowledge acquisition process be certain that you've kept a careful set of notes. These notes should include what was learned from the test cases, problems encountered, and conclusion or lack of conclusion reached.

Formalizing the Problem

At this point the team should *all* be experts. The problem should be so well defined that writing the specification should be a snap. This specification should be composed of an executive summary (naturally!) describing the problem and all of its assumptions, a description of who the user(s) will be, and the generalized domain flowchart. It should also include the problem area detailed flowchart. And last but not least, it should include a thorough description of the test cases that formed the base of the knowledge to be injected into the computerized system. When this is all done, send it out to all the folks who received the problem definition way back in step one. Do the usual. Hold a meeting and ask for feedback. It's better to get it up-front than at the end when it's too late. When you've overcome this hurdle you're ready to tackle the big one.

Roll up those sleeves. It's time to dig in and get that system written. Before we can actually code it we have to select the hardware and software with which to work our magic.

Picking an Appropriate Hardware Tool.   Expert system tools run on virtually everything. From personal computer to workstation to minicomputer to mainframe. The decision of which platform to run on is more dependent upon such conventional considerations as corporate policy, where the data resides, experience level of staff, or networking capabilities than on anything expert-system related. In a hundred different shops in a hundred different locations with a budgetary expert system waiting to be built, there will be a hundred different solutions. We'll choose one.

Right off the bat we should know that all corporate finance data is on the company's IBM mainframe 3084 MVS computer. (A bunch of Big Blue jargon for those not in the know; suffice it to say that all data resides on the big box in the computer room.) "But," you say, "this company has a plethora of personal computers floating all around the company. Why not save a bundle of money by off-loading this system to these PCs?"

Well, this certainly *seems* like a good idea. Upon much reflection and soul-searching, the designers decide to leave the entire system on the mainframe. Even though there are many PCs floating all around the company, they are not connected by any network. In addition, part of the requirement of this system calls for actual budget calculation, which the designers have already determined will be done on a conventional processing system. Since budgets are often done in crisis mode, when the users need immediate access to the data, the idea of waiting overnight to off-load mainframe data to the PC is unrealistic. So the designers decide to create a mainframe expert system that will be *embedded* into a conventional processing system. What's good for this team may not be good for you. If this is the case, read on to Chapter 4 for more insight on how you can make the right decision for your company.

With the decision made to run the expert system on the company IBM mainframe, the choices for software are narrowed down considerably.

Picking an Appropriate Software Tool.

There's a bunch of tools out there for you to peruse through. Some are extraordinarily good, some not so good. Some are extraordinarily expensive, some are quite cheap. So how do you pick a tool?

The first thing you should know is that not all companies use solely one tool. Different tools are appropriate for different types of problems. Look at the tool selection diagram in Figure 3-5. It shows the general categories of problems as paradigms into which you can place your particular problem. These words are important to know since they appear

TOOL SELECTION CRITERIA

INTERPRETIVE	*INFERRING SITUATION DESCRIPTION FROM DATA*
PREDICTION	*INFERRING LIKELY CONSEQUENCES*
DIAGNOSIS	*INFERRING SYSTEM MALFUNCTIONS*
DESIGN	*CONFIGURING OBJECTS UNDER CONSTRAINTS*
PLANNING	*DESIGNING ACTIONS*
MONITORING	*COMPARING OBSERVATIONS TO OUTCOMES*
REPAIR	*EXECUTING PLANS TO ADMINISTER REMEDIES*
INSTRUCTION	*ALTERING STUDENT'S BEHAVIOR AND KNOWLEDGE*
DEBUGGING	*PRESCRIBING REMEDIES FOR MALFUNCTIONS*

FIGURE 3-5.   Paradigms of Problems for Expert Systems.

in the literature that describes the software tool you are evaluating. An example: let's say you wish to develop an expert system, like XCON, that assists in the configuration of personal computers. This problem type would be one of design. As you stumble through the literature, you come across one package that looks interesting. It clearly states in the literature that it is used successfully for problems of the diagnosis category. Do you choose it? A resounding no! Actually most expert system tools adequately handle more than one of these paradigms and this fact will be mentioned in the product literature. It's still a good idea to determine ahead of time what kind of problem you have so you won't be surprised later on.

So now we have a decision to make. Which tool? We've already decided not to write it from scratch with one of the expert system programming languages of choice (LISP, PROLOG, C). We just don't have the experienced staff and "why reinvent the wheel?" Since we're running on the IBM mainframe, the field of choice narrows down to a select few. When going out to these vendors to evaluate their products, it's useful to go armed with a wish list so that you can find out exactly what features their product exhibits versus other products on your list. Figure 3-6 is one such list. You can expand it or narrow it down to suit your palette. One thing you'll find in evaluating these products is the tendency of vendors to invent their own terminology. You almost have to have a list of synonyms.

You'll see that the checklist has a lot of technical terms on it. Forward chaining, backward chaining, objects, rules . . . . Before you even get to the point of going out to the vendors and letting them compete with each other, it's a wise idea to review the attributes of your problem area and pick the features of the tool that you'll need.

Not all problems will need everything on this checklist. Buying a product that "has it all" is a good idea, however, but only in a research and development environment. Many companies, when they jumped into the AI pool, opted to create R&D departments to search out good uses for these tools. They set up rooms with the placard "AI Laboratory" on the door, and outfitted the interior with expensive workstations and more expensive software tools. In spite of the expense, most found it to be a good investment. Here prototypes could be developed and the proper set of features of the tool needed for the particular problem discovered. After the prototype the appropriate tool could be selected.

VENDOR:
ADDRESS
PHONE

COST: ONE TIME: **MAINTENANCE:**

CONSULTATION PARADIGM: DIAGNOSIS   PLANNING   DESIGN

KNOWLEDGE REPRESENTATION: RULES   FRAME   O-A-V   OBJECTS

INFERENCE: CONTROL: BACKWARD CHAINING
**   FORWARD CHAINING**
**   DEPTH FIRST**
**   BREADTH FIRST**

IMPLEMENTATION LANGUAGE: C
**   PASCAL**
**   LISP**
**   PROLOG**
**   PL/I**
**   OTHER:**

INTERFACES: DATABASES:
**   EXTERNAL EXITS:**
**   PROGRAMMING LANGUAGES:**

USER INTERFACE:
**   SCREEN:**
**   HELP:**
**   EXPLANATION:**

KNOWLEDGE ENGINEERING INTERFACE: EDITOR:
**   DEBUGGING:**
**   GRAPHICAL: SUPPORT:**
DOCUMENTATION
TRAINING

FIGURE 3-6.   Expert System Features Checklist.

In fact this is exactly what American Express did when it created its Authorizer's Assistant.

Let's look at our "planning/prediction" problem a bit more closely. We know that we need to use production rules and that objects would certainly make our system more efficient. In terms of control strategy, we would want a mixed-mode type of search capability. We want to be able to forward chain to instruct those staffers who need to learn how to perform the budget process. And we need to be able to backward chain when we ask the system to determine if we can meet our budget goals by taking a 5 percent cut.

On top of all of this we need to worry about connecting this system rather seamlessly to a conventional data processing system. This is known as embedding the expert system. There are several ways of achieving this end. You can "hide" the expert system beneath the wraps of a conventional system so no one even knows it's there. Or you can transfer control to the system when it's appropriate. Or you can even do it the other way around. You can embed the conventional system under the wings of the expert system so that the expert system calls the conventional system when appropriate. Our group of talented designers decide to start with the conventional system and then transfer full control to the expert system when necessary. To achieve this integration we need to select a tool that exhibits these sorts of facilities. We need to ask the questions: What types of database does this system interface to? What kinds of programming language can I use?

These considerations should not override some of the more fundamental attributes of a good expert system. One of the things that people like most about this type of system is its ability to interact with the user when a question arises. This has come to be known as an EXPLAIN feature. Some systems even have two functions: HOW and WHY. Think again of our budgetary expert system. A divisional user is working with the system when the system asks for the number of square feet of floor space the division occupies. Now this puzzles the user. Just by pressing the WHY function key on the keyboard, the expert system begins to explain just why that question was asked. This mid-run explanation enlightens the user, acting as a training device for these novices. Now let's watch our system as it concludes that a particular division is utilizing $20,000 a year of the budget for floor occupancy. The puzzled user presses the HOW function key and the system spews out the rule it used to arrive at this conclusion:

R1:
IF occupancy_footage is greater than 100 feet
AND Building_Loc is Miami
THEN TOTAL_footage is occupancy_footage x Miami_cost

HOW: R1: says to multiply the Miami cost per
*   square foot times the total footage used.*
*   Areas under 100 square feet are exempt from*
*   this calculation. This will calculate the*
*   total occupancy cost per year for your*
*   division.*

A rather simple rule, but still it serves to demonstrate the rather important feature of EXPLAIN. A feature you won't want to miss.

As you scan through the list you'll see a lot of nice things to have. Many of these features are absolute necessities, some merely are bells and whistles. Only you can make that decision as you match the tool to the problem.

Now that we know the features that we absolutely must have and the features we'd like to have, we are armed and ready to pursue those software vendors. At this point you turn into a deal-maker to have those vendors do their tricks to turn you into a believer. These tricks could be anything from loaning you the software to try it out, to having the vendor take a problem that you have already systematized on another platform and evaluate it or even prototype it on their platform. Eventually, though, one vendor will shine through for you and this is the one that will be selected, purchased, and installed. So at this point you're ready to prototype the system.

Prototyping — Always a Good Idea

During the formalization phase you developed a bunch of field notes during all of those interviews and videotaping sessions. Somewhere between then and this point these notes should have been turned into something a bit more formal.

Most expertise can easily be turned into pseudocode rules. One of the things I've learned over the years is that even if the project turns out not to be successful, or is never pursued with an expert system, the creation of those rules is valuable for the users. For what they've created is a procedure manual with that extra bit of expertise.

It is sound advice to build a prototype. Otherwise you run the risk of making an enormous investment in time and money only to find that the problem is not suited to an expert system. Or you may find the knowledge base is faulty, the hardware is all wrong, or the software is all wrong. Pick any one or more of these. A prototype will find all of these problems out for you *before* you make a large commitment of resources. And the word prototype is so comforting. Management expects a little experimentation, a few difficulties here. Not so with "real development." The expectation there is to do it right the first time. Of course, I'm not advocating or suggesting sloppiness, I'm just being realistic. Expert system problems are fundamentally more abstract than conventional problems, so the crutch of working with a prototype serves many purposes.

This prototype should certainly contain no more than 50 percent of the ultimate system: cut this number down more if you can. So if you developed four hundred rules during the formalization phase, prototype only two hundred of these rules. In the days of yore, AI scientists usually thought of prototype systems as "throwaways." Not so in the real world. The expectation is usually that the prototype will serve as a base for deploying the entire system. So keep this in mind as you go shopping for hardware and software.

Once you've managed to get this far you're entitled to once again roll up those sleeves. This time it's for some coding in the expert system tool of choice. Most expert system tools are different from each other. The syntax in one is different from the syntax in another, although similarities do exist. The syntax in an expert system tool is not like any you've ever seen. The syntax must reflect the features of the tool. Let's use Texas Instruments' Personal Computer Easy as an example. PC Easy is a rather nice, inexpensive tool having features that belie its bargain price tag. It uses a language called ARL, which stands for Abbreviated Rule Language. It contains the mundane such as equal and not; but it also contains the sublime in the form of these fun phrases: IS MIGHTBE, IS DEFNOT, IS DEFINITE, IS KNOWN, IS NOTKNOWN. It certainly whets the appetite with the possibilities of this type of technology. And if this inexpensive toolset contains these gems, you can imagine the punch that the more robust toolsets pack.

To do the prototype right, you want to make certain that all facets of the problem are somehow represented. Not only the representation of knowledge is important here. You want to make certain that you can get to the databases you need, provide a user interface in a manner that is useful and pleasing to the user, and a whole host of other features that you'd work out with your team.

In our budgetary example, we decided to code half of our 150-rule system. Since we've chosen an object-oriented expert system tool, this list of 75 rules is honed down even more. Our system needs access to several mainframe systems. We don't want to spend the time to code all the interfaces. Since we know that if one works then all should work, we work with only one of the databases that we need. We simulate the other one.

After several weeks of work we bring up a working prototype. Folks, we've only just begun.

Reformalization or Reassessing the Problem

Once the prototype is complete, run it to determine if the rules and objects are properly encoded and if, in fact, all of the rules are present that need to be present and if all the objects are present that need to be present. This phase is a reiteration of the initial formalization phase. The team must also make the determination whether or not the hardware and software chosen is indeed appropriate for the problem.

Although the prototype was checked out thoroughly while it was being built, it is important to run those test cases with the prototype. Then you must compare its conclusions against those manually derived by the expert or experts.

Since it is not possible to detail each and every tidbit of knowledge before undertaking this stage, running the prototype will uncover noticeable holes. Since these systems store their knowledge bases discretely from the rest of the system, it is a simple matter to enter the missing rules and objects. You may also notice that some of the rules are working incorrectly and must be changed. Really, this process is no different from any traditional system's testing methodology.

A stickier problem occurs when you find the expert system tool you've selected doesn't quite muster up to your expectations. This could be for several reasons:

- The shell is not able to process the final number of rules in the rule base.

- The user interface is not adequate.
- There is difficulty in getting to the external data needed.
- Too many *user exits* are required to make the system run. When you exit the expert system shell, it is usually to write your own code because the shell itself can't perform the functions that you need. Too many of these is not a good sign.

A hundred other reasons for replacement of the shell can be added to the list; these reflect the most common.

Along with taking a closer look at the software, it's also wise to scrutinize your hardware platform. You may notice a few problems:

- PC used does not contain enough memory (one megabyte or more is recommended).
- PC used does not contain enough disk capacity (if you're using the PC for other systems, have a 20-megabyte hard disk at minimum).
- PC used is not fast enough (use a speed-up board).
- Mainframe performance is degraded (could be that you're not really at fault, recommend a systems tuning first).

It may also be necessary to upgrade to a completely different hardware device. If the PC is found to be inadequate, you might need to upgrade to a mainframe or specialized AI workstation; although this is unrealistic in the era of the 386 and now 486 machines. On the other hand if mainframe response is seriously degraded and you are using your software tool properly, then this may be a result of the "straw that broke the camel's back." Some mainframe production environments just can't suffer one more burden. If this sounds like your shop, then you'd be wise to move this application to a mini, workstation, or PC.

Although expert system development tools are available on everything from a DEC to an IBM mainframe computer, you will find that the preponderance of them are available on the personal computer—notably the IBM personal computer. In the era of LISP-chip PCs, we've truly moved into the era of portable AI!

Okay. Our budgetary system prototype passed with flying colors. We created our prototype on the corporate mainframe with nary a complaint from the systems staff. We added a few new rules and objects when we realized we had omitted a process clearly represented on our problem area, detailed flowchart. We're glad we had that diagram. It ultimately spurred us into remembering that we needed to factor in the process of economic projection. We also found some conflicting rules that we fixed. Our dry run to see if we could access our corporate databases was successful since the expert system tool we selected had an interface already defined for our IBM DL/I database. All in all, our prototype was a success. Now it's time to see how really good it is. We're going to give it out to the users.

Testing

An expert system needs to be tested as thoroughly as a conventional system. It is hoped that through the use of a prototype and careful testing of this initial phase, the final testing period will be less than calamitous. In alpha (or initial) testing, the system needs to pass muster with those people designated as experts in the user group. All during this process you've worked with an expert or several experts, but there are other esteemed staff. And they should be given the opportunity to scrutinize the final system.

Once you've lived through that, the next phase of testing seems easy. In beta (or secondary) testing, which is probably the most important type of testing you can do, you send out the system to the actual end-users of the system.

Now remember that in the very beginning of this chapter I recommended that you do not keep these folks in the dark. If you do, then this phase just might become a nightmare. If you've been keeping them informed all along, then they're probably so revved up and excited about the system by now that this task will just glide along.

These users need to be given adequate time to "test the waters" by themselves. At the same time they should be given formal procedures for monitoring the session and noting any difficulties. Some of the techniques that auditors use to assess the correctness of the system can be applied here. They can be found in Chapter 5 of this book.

Use at least two to four end-users for this process. Set up the system to run in tandem with the current system or manual procedures that this expert system will replace or assist. They should be made to feel free to comment on any difficulties, opinions, suggestions, whatever their little hearts please. After all, a side benefit of this phase is to make the users "buy-in" to the system. And what better than to have users who know that their opinions count.

This phase should be called a pilot and should last at least one month. You should also branch out from this base of four users and present the system to nearly everyone within ear reach. Have presentations, serve coffee and donuts—believe me it works.

Maintaining the Expert System

Well, it's a bright new day. We're famous in the company for installing a working, budgetary expert system. Everyone loves it. Ah, success!

Let's not rest on our laurels yet. Have you ever heard of a system that didn't need changing? Since the development of expert systems is so new to a company, the chore of maintenance puts them in a quandary. Who should perform this function? The users? The development group? An AI group? The Information center? Unfortunately, I can't answer this question. It really depends upon the setup of the company.

In some companies, the AI team does all development and maintenance. In other companies the AI team does just the development and an operations group does the maintenance. Still in others, where no AI team exists, the development team does it all, just as with any other project.

I like this solution the best of all. Expert systems development, if you haven't noticed, is somewhat akin to traditional development. It's just more detailed. The expert system tool should be thought of as just another tool in the developer's toolkit. It's wrong to segregate this function from the rest of systems development: It's not more scientific; it doesn't require a Ph.D from MIT to perform it. Just use it like you would any other tool and maintain it in the same way.

WHERE ARCHIE AND FILMORE LEARN ABOUT EXPERT SYSTEMS

For those of you still not quite sure how to use this brand of technology, let's follow in the footsteps of two hypothetical computer folks who are new to it, too.

It's 1964. It's the era of the miniskirt and the Beatles. Bespectacled, serious, young men stand ogling a pristine steel box rising up a full 10 feet off the floor.

"Came in from IBM last week. The guys from R&D call it an IBM 360 computer," explains Archibald, scratching the bald spot on top of his head.

"Well, heck, Archie. What are *we* supposed to do with it?" asks Filmore with a puzzled expression.

As the lights flicker on this strange gray box in the dim light of the basement where it has been installed, our two heroes circle the intruder with frowns on their faces and fear in their eyes: for Archie and Filmore are the very first data processors in their company and this is the very first computer they have ever seen.

"Eureka, Archie, I've got it! See this little trap door? It's a great place to store our slide rule manuals."

Twenty-five years ago. And most of us are in similar situations. New technology and we can't quite figure out what to do with it. With the data processing wagon train securely circled around the campfire, it's hard for our expert system indians to break through to roast their marshmallows. With the courage of a great modern-day warrior, Archie offers the flag of peace—a committee.

Gathering emissaries from the development group, the systems group, and most importantly, the user group, Archie and Filmore begin their latest mission. The purpose of this committee is to match the needs of the organization with implementation tools. A sort of coupling of what's out there with what's needed here. Committee members are instructed to clear their brains of day-to-day data processing needs. The concern is not with "change report FH111 to print number of employees" but with how can we be innovative and competitive as an organization using technology. Using the techniques of wish-lists and brainstorming yields far-out ideas. But every so often amid the laughter of the process, a gem is found.

The committee explores these gemstones carefully, discussing tangible benefits to the organization and technologies that would need to be utilized. Archie and Filmore's committee is really "cooking." Ideas galore are being generated. But every time Archie or Filmore mentions the term *expert system*, the group's collective eyeballs glaze over. They just don't understand what this newfangled expert system methodology is.

"No amount of explaining can really do justice to what expert systems are," Archie explains to the committee. "This approach is so conceptually different from traditional data processing that it takes a grand leap of cognition to grasp it. So, as a start, why don't we compare the two types of systems," continues Arch as he begins to draw up a chart to pinpoint the similarities and differences of the two technologies.

Filmore remembers that he really did not understand the technology until he started actually working with it. So he recommends following the advice of the old adage "a picture is worth a thousand words." Or being precise, the data processing version of it would be "hands-on is worth a thousand manuals." Filmore sends sampler diskettes to all committee members and waits for their reactions. Leafing through the trade magazines he had noticed that many of the manufacturers of expert system software would send sampler diskettes of their tool for very little money. So he bought; and he hopes the committee will too.

The users, the systems group, and the old-fashioned programmers are thrilled over the power and flexibility of the sampler expert system shells. They "play" with an investment advisor, a restaurant advisor, and use an expert system to choose a wine. Finally they understand the dynamics of this type of software and are able to appreciate the different approach to data processing that it represents. So the committee at Hook, Line, and Sinker Inc. is reeled in by our intrepid expert system champions, Archie and Filmore.

Our heroes have successfully overcome the first obstacle, and all too often the *last* obstacle to a new technology—resistance to change. Now they have to roll up their sleeves and organize a pilot to prove the worth to management. Now the fun begins.

Now that the committee, long since having become a team, is willing, our friends decide to assure that they are able. The first bullet of their plan addresses this issue. The staff has a good inkling as to what expert systems are, but no real hands-on experience. They look at the diverse hardware and software platforms available and know that it would not be very wise to select just one. To put all of their eggs in one basket, so to speak. They solicit management support and are able to fund a small "Artificial Intelligence" lab. Archie wants the hardware to be representative of the firm as a whole, so he opts for purchase of a powerful workstation, a revved PC, and a slice of time on the company's IBM mainframe.

Filmore goes shopping for the software. He decides on one symbolic programming language, one PC expert system shell, one workstation hybrid tool, and one mainframe expert system shell. Filmore shops from a catalogue of many, many tools. Too many to mention here, but they can be categorized as symbolic programming languages, expert system shells, and hybrid environments.

Symbolic programming languages are of the LISP or Prolog variety, although sometimes C is used. These languages possess the richness that permits the programmer to represent knowledge, as well as get close to the operating system. The only problem is that "the wheel" must be reinvented continuously. Expert system shells provide the "wheel" that the system can be based on. Already possessed of code to interface to the user, to interface to various files, to provide mid-run explanations, help, and so on, these shells save gobs of time and are easy to use. Their negative aspect is that sometimes they preclude customized systems, unless *kluge* programming is resorted to. Last, but not least, hybrid environments such as ART and KEE are mostly used for high-power systems. Often, R&D departments use these tools on workstations for prototyping because these tools contain every advantage in expert systemdom. Typically the deployed expert system is redone on a less costly platform after the prototype stage. However, many a high-powered system has remained indefinitely on the initial platform.

With a veritable smorgasbord of tools, the newly formed AI team can sample the richness of the toolset and elevate themselves on the learning curve before a project begins.

"Whew! We just spent bundles of money. Personal computers, workstations, software, training. You name it, we got it. I think it's time to put up or shut up. Let's pick a project," says Filmore, carefully organizing the shelves upon shelves of computer manuals.

Way back in the initial committee stage, the team brainstormed a set of projects that seemed exciting to the company. These problems are now carefully screened to find one that is not only sexy but has a positive return on investment. Archie knows that even though the development of a system to assist the finance department in budgeting is a great idea, it's not a great, first idea. It has no payback. Another member of the team, Marie, has an idea to develop an expert system for the credit department. Hook, Line, and Sinker extends credit to thousands of fishermen. The current system requires a customer service worker to look up all records of a particular customer before credit is extended. This can take up to 20 minutes and requires the customer service representative to scroll through screens and screens of data. The current success rate, that is, the rate at which the representatives extend good credit versus bad, is hovering at an 83 percent level. Marie thinks that this could be improved with an expert system. The team evaluates this problem and "Lo and behold, an expert system idea is born."

Now that the team has picked an appropriate problem, they work hard to get the definition of the problem down on paper. They understand that the success or failure of this project depends upon selecting the optimum segment of this domain for expert system development. Too broad a definition and the system will become unmanageable and untestable, too narrow a definition and the return on investment will be minimal. Credit authorization is a meaty process. It entails access to many data files and perhaps to outside data sources as well. Hook, Line, and Sinker has many different types of credit plans—preferred customers, new customers, small business, large business, individual. And there are different criteria that can be applied to each category. The group decides that the biggest bang for the buck will be the individual account because this is where Hook, Line, and Sinker experience the biggest risk.

Hook, Line, and Sinker is buzzing with excitement. Most of the staff has had a chance to read the Credit Assistant problem definition document. They are excited by the possible cost and time savings. The customer service department is especially eager to get started. So now it's time to pick a willing expert.

Archie and Filmore know that this step is crucial. They can't build an expert system without able and willing and ready expertise. They can't afford to wait for little pockets of five minutes here, five minutes there. They need a full-time expert. Unfortunately, the senior credit authorizer is just not interested. Even though users are represented on the committee, this one is just not buying. Filmore knows that many users are resistant to share their banks of knowledge with something as cold-blooded as a computer. ("Dang, it took me some twenty years to get to where I am today," thinks Charlie the expert). So Filmore uses Plan B and shows the reluctant expert a videotape, obtained from the Texas Instruments Satellite Symposium on Expert Systems, of case histories of successful projects. The one in particular that he shows is the interview with the expert soup tender at Campbell Soup who went from doubter to believer after an expert monitoring system was implemented. Once

Filmore showed *his* expert this videotape, the expert was convinced
that the system would be a worthwhile effort. The key here is that
another expert convinced him. If you can't get another live expert, try
a videotaped one.

With the expert convinced and ready to participate, the team can begin to conceptualize and then formally specify the problem. A thorough
understanding of the problem and its relationships to external processes
is all important. Archie performs a data flow analysis that yields a nice
flowchart of the current process. Filmore creates a data dictionary of all
data to be used. Marie sketches out the manner of user interface to the
system. They all decide upon the representative test cases that will be
their gauge throughout the whole system. They use the test cases to
walk through each stage of system development.

Although similar to traditional system analysis, which consists of
techniques the team knows, the process of developing an expert
system—or knowledge engineering as it has come to be known—is about
90 degrees different. "You know, it's gonna be easy to get at 80 percent
of what Charlie knows. A lot of this can be found in the credit department's procedure manual. It's the other 20 percent—Charlie's instincts,
his gut feeling—that is necessary to make this a true expert system.
And this other 20 percent is really, REALLY hard to get," says Archie
scratching his bald pate.

The team knows that retrospective analysis is not sufficient, so they
try a different technique. They videotape the expert as he goes through
the paces of several problems. Some of these problems are complete and
some are constrained. This forces the expert to "dig deep into his inner
resources" to come up with a solution. The team also spends much,
much time in the credit department documenting actual cases as they're
happening. With cases in hand and a profound understanding of the
process, the team, which now very much includes Charlie the expert,
is ready to roll.

But wait, surely they don't decide to build the entire system all at
once. This problem is very large and they aren't sure which expert system
tool, much less the hardware to run it on, to use.

Charlie suggests that they create an expert system for just one facet
of the problem. He recommends that they choose a segment of the
problem that is representative of the entire problem. One that accesses
the needed files. One that demonstrates the user interface and that
recommends credit decisions. His suggestion: Build a system that would

authorize credit for individual customers using their 30-day payback plan. The other team members gleefully agree.

When the dawn breaks over Hook, Line, and Sinker the next day, the team is found standing in the AI lab looking from the PC to the workstation to the mainframe terminal. Choices, choices, choices.

"Well, where should we build it?" puzzles Filmore.

"Since this is a prototype, we really don't have to build it on the platform it's ultimately going to run on. In fact, since it is only a prototype I expect that we are going to find out a lot about what is appropriate and what's not appropriate for this system. So it really doesn't make a difference where this system runs during the prototype stage," answers Archie.

"Well, I'd like to at least make an intelligent guess. This way, if we're right, we won't have to make so many changes to get the prototype into implementation mode," counters Marie.

"Okay, let's look at the requirements of this baby! Does it need mainframe data?" asks Archie.

"No, we can download to PCs and use our local area network to hook 'em all up. So I guess we can use the PCs," answers Filmore thoughtfully.

"Yeah, but which software tool do we use? I would like to use a shell. It's already prebuilt. I'm not sure of the functionality that we'll ultimately need. Are we gonna need both backward and forward chaining?" responds Marie scratching her head.

"Well, at this point, we're not real sure what we're gonna need in terms of software. Let's prototype it on the workstation using ART. It's got a bit of everything in it and the workstation has lots of juice, so it'll be a good gauge of the hardware requirement. When we're done, we'll take an inventory of the features we used and look for a shell that is less expensive and comes with exactly what we need," suggests Filmore.

And so they all agree. And the prototype is built in 30 days and 30 nights. They work with Charlie the expert to turn the case analyses into rules and enter them into the system, a few rules at a time. Then they sit back and note the results. This iterative development method permits them to test and test and test until it works in the manner that they expect. It also permits them to make changes dynamically. When they have developed all of their 250 credit rules and the user/database interfaces work smoothly, they deploy the prototype to a friendly user on the credit floor. This user agrees not only to perform his own normal routine, but to pivot over to the prototype system and "shadow post" the same transactions so the system can be tested in a "live" mode. When this has been done for a week successfully, management approves the full usage of the prototype by the friendly credit authorizer.

At the end of the prototype stage, the team regroups and evaluates the measurement statistics that they have been collecting. The system has been "right on" and has approved and declined credit accurately. In fact, all of the other credit authorizers are clamoring for the system because they can see that it cuts down on the voluminous amount of work that they have to perform and boosts their success rate. The team, buoyed by their success, requests that the prototype be expanded. They add more functionality and increase the number of workstations out on the floor. They solicit additional rules and ideas from the other credit authorizers and find that including them in the development of the system boosts the acceptance rate of the system.

Four months later, to the day, Archie and Filmore are sitting in Marie's office, with their feet propped up on top of her desk.

"It's time to re-look at our platform. There are 25 credit authorizers out there. If we supply each one with a copy of ART and a workstation, we're talking big bucks," gasps Marie.

"Well, we know that we don't need the power of a workstation. We can downgrade to a less expensive PC," mumbles Archie, who is lost in thought.

"And we've narrowed down the requirements for our expert system to one that has the capabilities of backward and forward chaining, interface to graphics, and an interface to a database such as dBASE. That should lower our costs considerably!" adds Archie.

"Okay, let's get our act together. We need to show our pilot to management and to discuss the costs for developing a complete working system. And we also need the time estimates," orders Marie.

And so our expert system team goes back to the drawing board to develop the specification for the complete system. One year from the beginning of the prototype, the Hook, Line, and Sinker Credit Advisor was deployed to all credit authorizers. Marie wrote the user manual, Filmore gave demos, and Archie trained the masses.

"Well Archie, we've come a long way since we started out together in 1964," reminisces Filmore.

"Yeah. I wonder," ponders Archie. "Did we get smarter or did the machine?"

4

Connecting Data Systems to Expert Systems

OVERVIEW

In 1985 Keith Gormezano created a business empire that wound up thirty-fifth on *Inc. Magazine*'s list of the fastest growing companies (Marsano, 1987). He was chief executive officer of at least five companies and earned millions. Actually, he earned only $200 from his far-flung enterprises. He hoodwinked everybody with little money and a lot of *knowledge* about how to fill out forms and financial documents with the right *data*. He was a magnate only because he said so. He simply supplied the right information and his fame grew. But he did nothing wrong. He took no money and broke no laws. About the only thing that got hurt was the ego of the financial press. He did it because he wanted instant celebrity. And he got it.

Even though it's the knowledge that makes an expert system expert, it's the data that makes the system work.

What good is an expert system that can't process the insurance underwritings, the securities trades, the loan applications that are the stuff of financial systems? And what good is an expert system tool that has no links to the automated databases that we use in our day-to-day businesses?

In the very beginning there were the computer scientists. During the early 1980s quite a few of these gurus got large amounts of venture capital and started companies with the goal of vending AI software to the commercial sectors. It wasn't until the computer scientists added team members with some business savvy that the idea of artificial intelligence began to look appealing to those west of the Silicon Valley.

The first expert system tools were a bit like the first personal computer tools—they gave a flavor for what was ultimately going to be developed. These first tools certainly had powerful enough inference engines, although most were purely rule-based. What they didn't have was "data-grabbing" flexibility.

This inability didn't seem to matter in the beginning. Most expert systems were stand-alone. They were developed on workstations and personal computers and data was minimal, oftentimes being entered by hand. As time progressed, the problem sets being addressed increased in complexity. Data complexity increased as well.

Gradually the products began to sport interfaces to well-known databases or file structures. On the personal computer side, it was uncommon to find an expert system tool that did not have the ability to interface to LOTUS, dBase, or at least ASCII files.

These paltry linkages did not assuage the hunger for data. Of course, it was always possible to write an expert system in a programming language like Prolog or LISP. If this was the case, you merely wrote extra code to access your database of choice. The problem was that the tool of choice was more often the expert system pre-written shell. And this is just the place where this dearth of linkage interfaces existed.

The majority of financial services systems reside on corporate mainframes. These mainline databases are often extremely large and quite complex. Added to this database complexity is the growing trend toward distributed processing. It is not uncommon to find networked personal computers accessing mainframe computers, minicomputers acting as servers, or workstation nodes performing special functions.

Expert system vendors had to change their errant data linkage ways. More and more databases and file types began to be supported. For those aberrant files, expert system vendors supported user-defined programs to exit out of the expert system for access and then opened the door to the data that was being transferred back in. Mainframe expert systems were announced as was cooperative processing between personal computers and the mainframe. And on the horizon we're sure to see knowledge and data sharing across the multiple and diverse nodes in the networks of the future.

THE EARLY EXPERT SYSTEMS—BIG
INFERENCE ENGINES, LITTLE DATA*

Expert systems were lowered, like a boom, on the unsuspecting financial services community in the early 1980s. Academicians, long on theory (with green sawbucks dancing in their eyes) but short on practicality, ventured into the commercial arena with products that whetted the appetite. But like Chinese food, financial services found itself still hungry after the feast.

Corporate CEOs around the country were ushered into mauve-colored conference rooms to see the grand-daddy of demonstration expert systems—the Wine Selector. For some very peculiar reason, most early expert system packages came equipped with one or two sample expert systems that were so trivial it is a wonder any expert systems packages sold at all. Somehow corporate types were supposed to understand that the expertise of wine selecting mirrored the corporate experience. At one large financial institution in New York that was (un)lucky enough to see this demonstration fail, the senior VPs went around for months laughing at the mere mention of expert systems. Industry experts such as Harvey Newquist, editor of *AI Trends Newsletter*, agreed, "Up to now, expert systems have been on the lunatic fringe of the computer industry."

For those companies that took the bait, the tool was bought and made the rounds of the R&D staff as a tool in search of an application. Systems were built here and there, small and necessarily stand-alone. For the most part, the early systems were PC-based shells—though heavy-duty R&D was being done on the workstation platform with symbolic languages such as Prolog and hybrid tool sets such as ART (Automated Reasoning Tool).

Some interesting systems were conceived and developed on these early platforms. American Express's Authorizer's Assistant, developed as a prototype on a stand-alone system using ART, is a classic example of the power and utility of this new tool. At the Air Force Institute of Technology a decision-support expert system was built as a scheduling and planning tool for Space Command launch operators. Insight 2+,

*This section was extracted from a February 1989 article that I wrote for *Database Programming and Design* that was originally titled "Mainframe Expert Systems: The Holy Grail." I wish to thank *Database Programming and Design* for their courtesy in letting me use it. Courtesy *Database Programming and Design* ©1989.

an early version of Level 5, was used. At the same time stand-alone prototypes galore were being written. Delco Products with their Fan Motor designer, Coopers & Lybrand with their Insurance Underwriting expert system. Systems for hardware configurations like DEC's XCON, NCR's OCEAN, and Hitachi's Machine Room Floor configuration module.

Good systems. Cost-effective. Increased productivity. But what else do these systems have in common? Most, if not all of these systems and dozens of others out there, were stand-alone. These systems were not in areas typically requiring integration into corporate databases.

There is no doubt that XCONs and OCEANs are valuable systems and valuable examples of the proper usage of expert systems. XCON proved that an expert system could make an unmanageable task manageable by creating a system that could configure a working computer out of over 7000 possible parts. Looking at the case histories of deployed expert systems, one asks the question: How many computer manufacturers are there? How many NASAs are there?

Followers of expert systems everywhere yearned for one more thing. Connection to their mainline data. But mainline usually means mainframe. Therein lies the problem and perhaps the solution.

Although the trend is toward distributed environments, corporate data almost always resides on a mainframe computer. While there are millions of personal computers in "Lotusland," over a hundred thousand Vax minicomputers in "DECland," there are somewhere around *ninety-five hundred* "Big Iron" MVS licenses in "IBMland," according to DEC marketing manager David Love (see Figure 4-1).

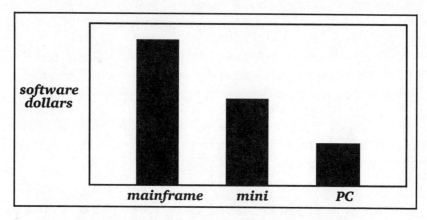

FIGURE 4-1. Corporate Investment in Mainframe Applications.

MAINFRAME EXPERT SYSTEMS— BIG BLUE

$\mathbf{A}$lthough few in number they represent billions of dollars in corporate software investment. Big Iron, Big Dollars, Big Corporate Databases. It is clear that while enormous progress has been made in distributing decision-making prowess to the end-user workstation, in terms of downloads to stand-alone systems, the tough nut to crack is in read/write access to corporate data. Yes, there are those companies who have developed gateways between the workstation and the mainframe, but so far these solutions are non-elegant and none-too-easy to use. The seams between the two environments are all too evident to the user. They're also prone to failure and slow transfer rates of data through the gateway. Dr. Allan Scherr, an IBM Fellow, sums it up by saying, "I don't know how to do shared data applications except in a centralized environment."

Except in isolated instances, most users of information systems use more than one automated system. A Finance department might use a terminal or PC device to access a budgetary system—an accounts payable/receivable system among others. This user might even use the same device for electronic mail. The key point here is that this user is familiar with the device and system interface currently being used. An expert system in this environment would do well to fit nicely into this same environment. In fact, John Landry of Computer Associates, formerly Cullinet, sees little difference between conventional environments and expert system environments. He describes all conventional applications as a series of interconnected expert systems where the expertise is buried in the code. The expression *embedable expert systems* arose from the ashes of systems that failed because of their "stand-offishness." In other words, they failed because of their nonintegration into the standard business environment.

Many corporate entities have not even considered the many benefits of expert systems because of this pronounced incompatibility with conventional environments. Astute vendors quickly took note of this resistance and with an "if you can't beat 'em, join 'em" attitude, announced the first expert system shells that run in mainframe environments.

The current leader in the IBM mainframe marketplace is AION's product, ADS (AION Development System). However, the products are changing so rapidly and are being marketed so aggressively that today's

last-place is tomorrow's leader. IBM joins the foray with several products: Expert Systems Environment, Knowledgetool and IBM KEE, which
can be rated as low, medium, and high, respectively, in terms of richness and capability. Never one to rest, IBM has an even more powerful
tool up that big blue sleeve. The Intergrated Reasoning System (TIRS)
is the latest and greatest of the expert tool sets. Information Builders
got into the act by acquiring Level 5 Research's, Insight—a $95-dollar
product—and rewriting it onto the mainframe. This product provides
powerful features like forward and backward chaining, an easy-to-use
English syntax in rule development, and ability to partition rule bases
and objects. Information Builders seems to understand the power behind
availability on many platforms. Level 5 runs on IBM PCs, Apple Mac-
Intoshs, IBM mainframes under both TSO and CMS, as well as on any
VAX/VMS configuration from the MicroVAX to the VAX 8900. From
a distributed-processing perspective this packs a powerful punch.

One of the more exciting offerings is AICorp's KBMS, the new kid
on the block. Starting with a natural language front end (AICorp's other
claim to fame is the natural language Intellect product) and ending with
a data dictionary permitting the Expert System to easily interface with
a host of database and file systems.

The original PC version of Level 5 was $95 when I first purchased it
"many eons ago." The mainframe version sells for $48,000 to $57,600.
The KBMS goes through the roof at $200,000. All of the others lie
somewhere in-between. If we set the mean price of PC shells at $495
and the mean price of a mainframe shell (single CPU, since the more
CPUs a shop has, the more the license costs) at $95,000, we get a PC-
to-mainframe ratio of 1 to 190. So, it costs about 190 times more to
purchase a mainframe shell than a PC shell, and oftentimes the features
of the two platforms are the same.

And let's not forget that bane of the user community—production or
CPU charges. There is definitely an overhead cost to using expert system
methodology on traditional computers that use charge-back mechanisms
that are I-O sensitive. The costs are great in terms of CPU efficiency
and charge-back production costs. We should also mention the large
dollar outlay for the mainframe shell. Given these sticklers, an intensive
cost/benefit analysis should be done to make sure that the tool resides on
the platform that provides the optimum fit. Table 4-1 lists key criteria
that should be evaluated during this "mainframe or not" decision-making
process.

1. Do you need to read corporate data real-time?

2. Can your system survive with reading overnight download of corporate data?

3. Do you need to write corporate data real-time?

4. Can your system survive by writing to the corporate database via overnight upload?

5. How much data would need to be downloaded as compared to PC or workstation capacity?

6. Is there an absolute requirement for embedding the expert system?

7. Does this application require high-resolution graphics?

8. What is the first year's cost per user of the system if developed on the mainframe?*

9. What is the cost per user of the system after initial software has been amortized?

10. Evaluate features of tool selected for long-term requirements—not just features required for prototype.

*Cost per user = (cost of software shell/no. of users) + estimated charge-back cost for production usage

TABLE 4-1   Criteria to Use in Mainframe Evaluation.

Traditional data processing systems, such as our example in the finance department, are relatively noncomplex. These applications are composed of simple Gets and Puts and employ few sophisticated search stratagems. The inference engine of a typical expert system is a powerhouse of sophistication. Complex control mechanisms for object manipulation and rule searching coupled with such CPU-intensive features as truth maintenance, confidence factors, and even Bayesian probability capabilities may be the straw that breaks the camel's back. All you systems engineers are probably quaking in your boots by this time. Yes, mainframe expert systems do have the potential for bringing the CPU to its knees; but, so does a conventional COBOL program.

Like a tailor with a pair of scissors cutting away excess material, the expert system designer should excise all features of the tool that are not required by the application. Using the standard, systems development methodology of prototyping and optimizing, it is as easy to create

an efficient mainframe expert system as it is to create an efficient conventional system. Interestingly, this may soon be a moot point within
an IBM mainframe environment. IBM's NETVIEW product, part of the
heralded Systems Application Architecture (SAA) long-term strategy,
has a hook into their Knowledgetool expert system shell. To masterfully
control increasingly complex IBM networks, systems engineers may use
this expert system tool themselves. So goes systems engineering, so goes
the world.

And many companies believe this to be true. More and more are
jumping onto the mainframe bandwagon. Herb Schorr, once IBM's expert systems guru, predicts that businesses will one day be pumping as
many million instructions per second at expert systems as they do now
at conventional systems.

A medical malpractice insurer in Los Angeles, California is using
Cullinet's Enterprise Expert on an IBM 4381 to process a deluge of
malpractice claims. With over one hundred rules, this system ultimately
determines why claims occur and will possibly revamp the way they do
business. Why did they go with mainframe expert systems? All of their
data was already resident in large Cullinet IDMS databases. They saw
no reason to mix and match systems and hardware, so mainframe it was.
A bank in Indiana felt the same way. The re-insurance division of this
bank, with twenty to thirty users, was already using the mainframe for
a multitude of systems. They wanted embedability and they got it using
AION's ADS. A large New York Bank found themselves in a pickle
not too long ago. The pension processing department, the largest in
the country, was required to modify their system due to a change in tax
law. And they needed to do this in a very short period of time. And
they were constrained by the corporate decision to stay within the IBM-
MVS/XA environment. Using IBM's Knowledgetool, they managed to
create a rule base of over one hundred rules and meet that target date
successfully.

So it seems that mainframe expert systems are a viable alternative and
somewhere along the line a decision has to be made about the approach
to take. There is a thought-provoking caveat here. Does a company
take one approach or multiple approaches to expert systems? In other
words, does the data-processing top gun make a generic decision to go
workstation (or mainframe or PC) expert system and hang all doubters
and dissenters? For an answer to this question let's take a stroll down
memory lane. When the corporate data center was first built it was a very

"vanilla" operation. One type of hardware, one programming language, one database. Look at that data center now, or to be more accurate, look at a company's multiple data centers now. It was found that a vanilla solution did not work. Alternative hardware and software alternatives were required in each data center for the very different types of applications that were being built. DEC infiltrated IBM shops. PL/I found it's way into traditionally COBOL shops. Database administrators found themselves supporting different brands of databases. PCs proliferated, workstations made their entry. In other words, a kluge of choices. Why should expert systems be any different?

So, does the poor designer flip a coin: heads it's mainframes and tails it's PCs? Here again, traditional systems methodology has a way to assist in the decision making. It's called a requirements analysis. In this phase you fit the tool to the application rather than forcing the tool on the application.

There are many solutions to the question "Where shall my expert system reside?" There is no right answer, but there is a best answer and it depends on so many technical, cultural, political, and practical considerations that one might be tempted to give up and go back to batch systems.

In a picture-perfect technical world, the optimum solution would be a flexible solution. A system that can be ported easily and fluidly among several platforms would provide economies and efficiencies not possible in a single-device approach. Shells such as Information Builder's Level 5 and Nexpert Object have made a commitment to provide portable shells in as many environments as they can muster. It won't be long before the other vendors march to the beat of this same drummer. Picture a system that starts out on the mainframe computer. Due to response-time considerations and cost, it is moved over to a minicomputer easily overnight. Picture a system that is resident on a host or a mini that runs concurrently with a sister system on a Mac or an IBM PC. Now our reception is a bit fuzzy, the horizontal must be off. To get it back to picture-perfect we need something to string all this together. And in a way not visible to the users. *This* is a network.

There are networks and there are networks. Most of us have our personal computers connected either to the host computer by a point-to-point network or are connected by a LAN. The marketplace is just now waking up to a type of "any-to-any" network that provides access to dissimilar devices in a transparent manner. In this way Archibald the clerk can turn on his PC and access data from far-away places with little or no technical knowledge. Vendors such as DEC and Sun espouse this cause and have made corporate headlines with their success. Couple this brand of network with expert system knowledge bases and a wealth of opportunities for cost savings and enhancement of features presents itself immediately. Corporate database on the mainframe, expert system running on a workstation or PC device, grabbing and updating data swiftly through the network: all are invisible to the user save for the smart interface now afforded.

So, are mainframe expert systems the answer? Well, maybe yes and maybe no. Let's take a good look at the different options in using mainframe data.

EXPORTING MAINFRAME DATA*

Back in the "Neanderthal" days of early computing, programmers waited in long lines to get to the computer where they "hardwired" the instructions of the program they were interested in running. These early relics ran in the pristine state of accepting no real input, producing no real output, and certainly never heard of the term databases. This was over thirty years ago, and to quote some arcane advertising, "We've come a long way, baby!"

We're a *long* way away from those early days. Where computers were once exiled to tiny, office building basements, there are now millions of square feet of prime space loaded down with buzzing, whirring, blinking iron boxes. Where once only the most critical applications were automated, we now automate everything from accounts payable to risk assessment to the company football pool. Nowadays third-generation computer programmers are sharing resources with fourth-generation users who use simple but powerful tools to make computer magic. And every-

---

*This section was extracted from a May 1989 article that I wrote for *AI Expert* that was orignally titled "Expert Systems and Corporate Databases." I wish to thank *AI Expert* for their courtesy in letting me use it. Reprinted from *AI EXPERT*, May 1989; Copyright 1989, Miller Freeman Publications.

one agrees that the three most important keys to computer success are access, access, and access.

There have been volumes written on successfully installed expert systems. These trade papers put the average, Joe data processing director to sleep. Why? He's got ten billion dollars worth of corporate data sitting on some mainframe. He's also got no good explanation of how to connect his highly-touted and occasionally expensive, expert system tool to this goldmine of data. In a word, access.

Buried deep within the bowels of expert systems manuals are the answers to Joe's questions. Before he begins digging a trench to find this little pot of gold, Joe better make sure that he's asking the right questions.

The very first question that he should ask is, "Where should this expert system reside?" As in any decision, there are a myriad of choices. Figure 4-2 show how complex this question is.

Some of us might be tempted to toss a coin or throw darts to select a suitable platform for an expert system. Others of us are all too happy to use whatever is available. Still others of us sit and scratch our heads and never make any decision at all. Since logic is supposedly the forte of systems people, let's apply a bit of logic to the process of selecting the proper environment for our expert system. Our quest for truth can be broken down into three broad study areas: expert system *features* required by the application, *data dependence*, and *network capabilities*.

Platform	*Selections**	*Examples*
PCs	*Many*	*Guru*
Workstation	*Moderate*	*ART*
Mainframes	*Few*	*KBMS*
Multiple	*Few*	*Level 5*

* Selections indicates the number of tools in that environment.

FIGURE 4-2. The Multiple Platforms for Expert Systems.

Features Required

It should come as no surprise that not every tool exhibits the same features. Picking a tool that omits the very features that your application needs is foolhardy indeed. The best bet is to do a thorough analysis of what you require BEFORE you begin tool selection. Table 4-2 is a sample checklist to use to assist in this very important first step. Of course, filling out this checklist presumes a very intimate understanding of the problem and of expert systems in general. Many of the terms on the checklist identify specific expert system stratagems that require understanding to apply properly.

You may find that given ten applications you get ten very different responses to this checklist. This does not necessarily mean that one needs to purchase ten different tools. It only means that one must find a richer tool that exhibits many if not all of these features. Caveat One—do not perform this process in a vacuum. It is conceivable that more than one group in your organization is looking into the use of expert systems as well. It is also conceivable that after your successful

```
[] Control Features
   [] Backward chaining
   [] Forward chaining
   [] Depth-first search
   [] Breadth-first search

[] Knowledge Representation
   [] Rules
   [] Frames
   [] Semantic nets

[] Consultation Paradigm
   [] Diagnosis
   [] Planning
   [] Design

[] User Interface
   [] Help feature
   [] Explanation feature
   [] Screen
```

TABLE 4-2 Checklist for Selecting
an Expert System Tool.

implementation of the system, you'll have many requests. Don't build yourself into a corner; keep an eye toward the future.

Data Dependence

With the feature set firmly established, you're ready to tackle data dependence. Since this section deals with the problem of linking expert systems to corporate databases, we're presuming that you require hooks into the mother lode.

With pencil poised, try tackling Table 4-3, which will help clarify your specific needs. It should be becoming clearer as to what you can get away with in answering the question of data access. The best solution is always the simplest solution. If real-time access to data is not required, then why go through the labor pains of making this delivery?

The Network

The last piece of the puzzle is the weakest link—*network* capabilities. The ultimate system to deliver to the user should be easy to use, with the seams transparent. What we don't want is a system so complex it needs a user manual the size of the *Encyclopedia Britannica*. Remember, system worth to a user is inversely proportional to the weight of the user manual. Table 4-4 is a checklist you can use to determine just what level of network your data center supports. If it is difficult to access data via your network, then explore different alternatives.

"Disclaimer"—A savvy designer will also take into consideration corporate culture. Conventions in the organization about company-wide technological strategy and cost constraints are important to note. It would do little for the designer's career if he or she made a pitch for mainframe expert systems when the company had just spent millions in distributing to departmental computers. Making a pitch for an expensive solution in times of corporate slump is equally uninspired.

How to Pick the Optimum Hardware Platform

With those words of wisdom in mind let's lay out those checklists side-by-side and make some real sense out of them.

Figure 4-3 is a matrix you can use to assist in determining the optimum platform for the system you are designing. Now, to set the groundwork

[] Files required to access:

   [] Mainframe database:
      [] IMS
      [] DB2
      [] IDMS
      [] ADABAS
      [] Total
      []

   [] Minicomputer databases:
      [] Hewlett-Packard
      [] DEC
      [] Wang
      [] Tandem
      []

   [] PC files:
      [] Lotus
      [] dBase
      [] ASCII

   [] File structures (nondatabase):
      [] indexed
      [] sequential

[] Real-time access:
   [] real-time inquiry
   [] real-time update
   [] redundant file okay

[] Time delay:
   [] immediate access to date
   [] overnight
   [] weekly
   [] monthly

[] Data elements required:
   [] all data elements required
   [] subset required (list): _____

[] Level of computer literacy of users

TABLE 4-3   Database Checklist.

[] What needs to be connected?
   [] Mainframe   [] Minicomputer
   [] PC   [] Workstation

[] Is there a working, tested network in place?

[] What software packages are being used to transport data from one node to another? Assign a level of complexity (1 = easy to use, 2 = moderate difficulty, 3 = difficult to use)

____   _____

____   _____

____   _____

____   _____

[] Are any scripting packages in use? (scripting packages can balance out the complexity of difficult-to-use packages by automatically generating many of the keystrokes necessary to do the transports)

[] User Base
   [] Level of computer literacy of users

TABLE 4-4 Network Capabilities.

	1	2	3	4	5	6	7	8	9	10	11	12
Complex tool	x	x	x	x								
Moderate tool					x	x	x	x				
Simple tool									x	x	x	x
Real - time access	x	x			x	x			x	x		
Data download			x	x			x	x			x	x
No network	x		x		x		x		x		x	
Network		x		x		x		x		x		x
Order of Solutions	1	1 3	3 1 2	3 1 2	1	1 2	1 2	2 1	1	2 1	2	2

1 Mainframe expert system
2 PC - based expert system
3 Workstation - based expert system

FIGURE 4-3. Expert System Platform Decision Matrix.

before we get started, we must define the rules of thumb. A complex tool is defined as one requiring many features as exemplified by the checklist in Table 4-2. It follows that moderate and simple tool sets require proportionately fewer features. Table 4-3's checklist gauged our database requirements. Obviously, if the database is a dBase file on an IBM PC, the expert system would naturally default to a PC-based system. The database exercise hinges on one very important question. Does the user absolutely require immediate read/write access to corporate data? Or can the system survive with downloaded data? Our last set of criteria is the network issue in Table 4-4, defined here as the ability to port data fluidly between diverse computers. This is not just a simple PC or workstation to mainframe download that we presume is "omnipresent."

Applying our guidelines we can quickly see how the following expert system decisions were made. The Airline Seat Advisor was developed by Sperry and Intellicorp. The purpose of this system is to assign discount fares to airline flights. Those of you who have made an airline reservation lately know how tricky and complicated this process can be. We also would assume that this application is not dependent upon gobs of corporate data. A complex tool and no real-time access would lead us to a workstation decision. In fact, the platform chosen was the software tool, KEE (Intellicorp), on a workstation device. Similarly, the National Agriculture Library of the USDA built an expert system to help library users find references. This Expert Agriculture Information System requires moderate tool complexity and little data outside of reference-desk information. The choice was the product, 1st Class, which runs on a personal computer. At the other end of the spectrum is the Doctors Company in Los Angeles, California, which uses Cullinet's Enterprise Expert to process malpractice insurance claims. Mainframe data and moderate tool complexity pushed them to a mainframe tool.

When the decision is made *where* the expert system should reside, the *which tool* decision should be addressed. Using our checklists we already know the required features of the tool set and the types of data that must be accessed. These should not be ignored, for picking an inappropriate tool is as foolhardy as picking the wrong platform.

Figure 4-4 shows the general categories of integration between expert system and data. Again, for our discussion, we are presuming that we want to integrate an expert system tool and a corporate mainframe database. We refer to this as a *native database*; not to be confused with the databases resident on personal computers and workstations.

Reads ASCII, Unix file	*PC*	*Workstation*	
Reads Lotus, etc.	*PC*	*Workstation*	
Reads via exit	*PC*	*Workstation*	*Mainframe*
Reads native database			*Mainframe*

FIGURE 4-4.   Common Integration Modes.

The Patent Leather Widget Company

It now boils down to a choice between a set of alternatives. For this exercise let's use a common (to all alternatives) case study. The Patent Leather Widget Company, or PLWC for short, maintains all of its corporate data on an IBM 3090 mainframe using IBM's DB2 relational database. They want to build an expert system to track inventory at their many warehouses. They want the system to be able to automatically reorder parts, when necessary.

Alternative 1:   *Download corporate data to an ASCII or Unix file. (Unix is the accepted format for most workstations.)*

A mainframe program must be written to read the DB2 database and create a file in a format acceptable to the expert system on the PC or workstation. Once this extract file is created, communications software is then used to download the file onto either a hard disk or a floppy disk. If this downloaded data is still not in the format required by the expert system, another program—this time resident on the PC or workstation— might have to be written to reformat the data. Once the reformatted data is ready, it can be accessed by the expert system.

For PLWC we need to download part number, warehouse location, inventory on hand, and point-of-reorder number.

This is a small subset of the 200-element DB2 database. Our expert system of choice for this example is Texas Instruments' Personal Consultant for use on an IBM PC. The READ-DOS-FILE command reads data from an ASCII file and assigns the values it reads to parameters. It may also assign the values read to an EXPECT PROPERTY list, which is a set of values for a given variable.

Our PLWC PC file is named WIDGET.DAT. Reading this file into our expert system is done similarly to reading a file in a conventional program except for a slight twist. Accessing external files is normally done within the context of a rule.

```
IF INVENTORY-LOW-PART4
THEN READ-DOS-FILE "WIDGET.DAT" INDEX 4
     PART LOCATION INVENTORY REORDER
```

Our expert system has determined that the inventory level is low for widget part 4. It issues a read command to the ASCII file.

Since our ASCII file is sorted in the order of part number; that is, the first record is part 1 and the fourth record is part 4, we can use the INDEX option, which permits us to read the appropriate record directly.

Most expert system tools have a somewhat similar feature, the syntax might change but the concept is the same.

Alternative 2:   *Reads dBase or LOTUS or other*

This alternative has many of the same features as Alternative 1, but the back end is a trifle easier.

PLWC still needs to have a program written against its DB2 corporate database. Communications software is still needed to download the file.

In this example PLWC Systems has decided that it will run this expert system in two places. It will run on the mainframe against the DB2 database and at the distributed, warehouse locations on personal computers. They want to be able to use the same tool on both the corporate mainframe and on their many warehouse IBM personal computers. They are already downloading data in the appropriate format to the PCs for use in dBase applications by the warehouse supervisors.

The decision is a combination of ADS/PC and ADS/MVS both from AION Corporation. A big bonus is that ADS/PC and ADS/MVS are almost identical.

Since the data has already been loaded into dBase, we can proceed to use this formatted data in our expert system.

Beginning with version 4, ADS/PC provides record I/O, which is more efficient than the earlier releases. All releases permit READ DBASE and WRITE DBASE statements, which process the entire file in memory. Obviously this won't do for large databases. Record I/O permits sequential and direct access to files created by LOTUS 1-2-3, dBase II, dBase III and R:Base. Prior to access by ADS/PC the dBase file must be translated to a file in the Standard Data format (SDF). The dBase COPY

TO command does this nicely. The ADS/PC FIXLINES utility is then run to verify that the file is indeed in the correct format. The code to access our dBase file to find part 4, where widget_dbf is the dBase file, is as follows:

```
loop
   getrec(widget_dbf)
   breakif eof(widget_dbf)
   if filestatus(widget_dbf) <> 0 then
      closefile(widget_dbf)
      return
   end
   if widget_dbf->.widget_part = 4 then
      closefile(widget_dbf)
      found_flag = TRUE
      return
   end
```

Alternative 3: *Reading via an exit.*

For file or database structures not supported by the expert system tool of choice, reading an external file or database through an exit in the expert systems tool may be the best solution.

Our PLWC systems designer has decided to access another company-wide file to determine warehouse personnel. IBM's ISAM (now unsupported by IBM but still in use) is the file and AI Corporation's KBMS is the expert system tool.

AI Corp's KBMS has the ability to directly interface to IBM's DB2 and SQL/DS databases. For databases not of those two flavors, KBMS has an extraordinary feature called a User Defined Object (UDO) interface. The UDO permits KBMS to interface with any and all database or file structures.

KBMS' UDO permits calls to application programs written in either COBOL, PL/I, or Assembler. Our PLWC designer decides to write a COBOL program to access the Human Resource ISAM file. In KBMS terminology the designer is creating what is known as an Access Module.

Data from the Human Resource file is considered an object. If the designer is to read data from a salary file as well, another COBOL Access Module must be written to define the salary object. The specific Access Module, or in this case the actual COBOL program, is linked to the definition of the object (the Human Resource file) via the ACCESS/

MODULE property of the Detailed OBJECT screen. The real power behind this facility is that this file is now defined as an object. KBMS' sole data structure is the object. Database objects, knowledge base objects, and UDO objects (with some restrictions) are handled on an equal footing during rule processing.

The Access Module COBOL program is really no different from any other program that OPENS a file, PROCESSES until end-of-file (or direct read) and then CLOSES a file. The KBMS requirement is contained within the linkage section, which is the data passed between KBMS and the Access Module.

UDOs are initiated via rule. One must write a rule that operates on the UDO object. This is equivalent to calling a program, which is a familiar concept in modularized programming.

The typical declaration for linking to a COBOL UDO is:

```
Procedure Division Using Appl-Control-Data
                         Anchor
                         Function
                         Obj-Control-Area Cursor-
                         Control-Area Buffer-Area
                         Cursor-ID
                         UDO-Status
```

where   Appl-Control-Data contains data that may be set by an application program, which calls KBMS. In cases where KBMS is not called by an application program, this parameter will not be used

Anchor is a pointer to a portion of local storage for use by the Access Module when the object is opened

Function contains a character string directing the UDO's process option—such as Open, Close, Delete, Fetch

Obj-Control-Area is a pointer to a structure that describes the object and its attributes

Cursor-Control-Area describes the next call to be performed and the search strategy for access to multiple occurrences of the file

Buffer-Area points to memory storage for one occurrence of the object

Cursor-ID is used for data retrieval or manipulation

UDO-Status is the status code for all UDO calls

This COBOL UDO is then used to open the ISAM file, process the desired records that contain employee information, and return the required data to the expert system. The UDO is very similar to your garden variety "called program," the only difference is the caller of the program, which happens to be an expert system.

Alternative 4:   *Reading a native database.*

The simplest approach is to read the database directly using a mainframe expert system tool facility, if provided. Most mainframe shells provide hooks into DB2 and SQL/DS, some access Cullinet's IDMS and IBM's IMS.

This time, the PLWC systems designer wants to access his DB2 database directly through AI Corporation's KBMS. He knows that he will retain the DB2 functionality of different views of the data for different users. He also knows that KBMS can automatically generate the initial object and attribute descriptions directly from a DB2 table or a stored view. This ADD (Automatic Data Definition) facility will save lots of time, which is at a premium for the designer.

Figure 4-5 shows how a KBMS define Detailed Object session screen appears. Once the object is defined, its attributes or columns are then defined such that each column (or field) has a unique name, data type, width, and other pertinent information.

Accessing DB2 data through a rule construct is transparent, it looks no different from any other rule construct. For example, if the Widget DB2 table has a key of PART NUMBER, then the following rule would access one Widget occurrence at a time:

```
IF PART NUMBER = DESIRED PART NUMBER
   THEN....
```

KBMS represents the state of the art in data/expert system integration, making it one of the most versatile tools being marketed today.

We've gone through four rather lengthy descriptions of accessing corporate data, and we've used three different tools to do it. There is much variation in the methodologies that the different vendors use as well as sometimes fuzzy documentation supplied with the product. The point is that just a few years after expert systems' Neanderthal beginnings when data was entered via keyboard, no self-respecting tool is being sold without several alternatives for accessing corporate data.

```
DETAILED OBJECT Screen     Create Mode     Application: s1
Created attributes for 'Widget.DB'
PLEASE DEFINE YOUR NEW OBJECT AND HIT ENTER
Object: COLUMNS                    Object Type: DB2
                                   Occurrences: 900


Parent:
Class Description:
When Created:
When Deleted:
When Needed:


Everything:
Key: NAME    Default: NAME    Always:
Who:         Where:           When:
How:         Why:             Count:
Sort:        Statistics:      Summarized:


             DB2 Specific Information


Table Name: Widget.DB
Database Name: DB2WI              Tablespace: SYSDBASE


13: Help/Expand    15:Return    16:Editor Menu    17:Lookup
```

FIGURE 4-5.   Simulation of a Detail Object Screen in KBMS.

DISTRIBUTED AI

Mainframe computers are powerful, but expensive. Personal computers, workstations, and minicomputers are less powerful, but they're comparatively cheap to buy and operate. Long before artificial intelligence stuck its foot in the door, corporate computer centers began to unload "Big Blue" onto little blue.

It all started with the minicomputer. And in minicomputers, DEC is king. Applications that were large and discrete from the mainframe began to be bundled off to DECland. Factoring systems, credit card systems, collection systems, all ran on the ubiquitous DEC or any one of a number of competitors in the mini marketplace.

Then a couple of guys in a Californian garage made big headlines and bigger waves with something called a personal computer. At first, these PCs were used for word processing or stand-alone, spreadsheet packages. As more and more software began to be developed, more and more data processors and their users opted to move permanently into the PC environment.

Software developers saw an opportunity to develop programs permitting the PC to emulate a terminal attached to a mainframe computer. This program was then modified to permit a user sitting at a PC to enter a series of complex commands that permitted the downloading of corporate data right to the PC. This new facility spurred data processing departments galore to write little ditties. These would access corporate databases to create a file in the correct format for downloading to a PC. You see, most people had the erroneous perception that just by having this download facility all you had to do was activate it and all the data on the mainframe would be yours for the asking. Nothing could be further from the truth.

Stand-alone emulation and download programs were, obviously, not the total solution. Something more had to be added.

Cooperative AI

And it was. It was called cooperative processing. It started innocently enough. Conventional software developers knew there had to be a better way to permit personal computer users to have access to mainframe data. This was particularly so for the vendors who sold software that ran on both the mainframe and the personal computer.

RAMIS, the fourth-generation language we met in Chapter 3, developed a very nice, neat facility that permitted personal computer users access to mainframe data. They merely entered into a RAMIS/PC session and requested mainframe access. Now this may seem humdrum but there were some very interesting features that were offered way back in the middle of the 1980s. The first feature was a scripting language. One of the main problems with mainframe-to-PC links was the amount and complexity of keystrokes that were necessary before anything meaningful could be gotten from the mainframe. Now, this may have been fine for the high-tech user, but the low-techie just gave up. Scripting features permit a series of keystrokes to be captured and stored so that the end-user merely needs to press one key to execute a series of commands. So all of the convoluted PC commands that were necessary became invisible to the user. The other interesting feature was the ability of the system to jump right into RAMIS on the mainframe. Here a RAMIS command could be executed and with a simple TRANSFER command, this data could be downloaded right into the PC session. This meant that the end-user didn't have to wait for some programmer to have a bit of free time before a program was written to extract data from the mainframe into a file compatible with the download program. So what you had there were two sessions that were fundamentally the same, one on the PC and one on the mainframe. Each cooperating with the other to provide the user with an ultimate solution. This was a very early use of the concept of cooperative processing.

In the fourth quarter of 1989, AICorp Inc. introduced a cooperative processing capability that permits the cooperating distribution of applications developed with their expert system product or their natural language product. KBMS and INTELLECT, respectively, have been injected with the intelligence to know how to route requests for data to the correct hardware platform. "A person who needs additional data from a KBMS/PC application can simply request the data and not be concerned about whether it is on the PC or a remote machine. KBMS will automatically route the request to the computer where the data is stored and bring the response back to the PC," is the gospel from AICorp President Robert N. Goldman.

They call this remote, knowledge base processing. It uniquely allows the actual application logic to be distributed over multiple machines. What this means is that the user can be using a personal computer when the expert session decides it needs to get some more data. It discovers that this data is not on the PC at all, it's on the mainframe. Without so much as a whisper, KBMS/PC will route a request to the mainframe. It then grabs some data and downloads it into the expert system session, without the user ever being bothered.

Concurrent AI

Concurrent AI tries to achieve more than just invisible mainframe-to-PC data grabbing. *Concurrency* provides for the sharing of knowledge across discrete processors such that AI computations are necessarily handled in parallel. According to Gasser (1989), "faster and more efficient computations are the usual reasons for investigating concurrency, but higher levels of abstraction provide more rationales."

In the world of academic AI, one way that concurrent processing is being achieved is through a "blackboard" architecture. A blackboard architecture is typified by a common area that is shared by many different data sources. The blackboard is divided into different semantically segmented areas called levels. On each level, a knowledge source may read or write. The levels are controlled by a supervisor that functions similarly to the control program in a conventional computer system.

Each knowledge source may be composed of a rule base, a subset of rules in that rule base, or a procedure. Each knowledge source has access to all of the data contained within the blackboard. As in conventional data processing systems, multiple access to data can cause concurrency problems. These blackboard systems use synchronization locks to prevent inconsistent and erroneous update.

Hence, this blackboard permits a common area for the concurrent interaction of multiple knowledge sources.

THE BEGINNINGS OF DISTRIBUTED AI

Blackboard architecture is the basis for many distributed AI research projects. Concepts related to coordination and control are equally true for distributed architectures as they are for concurrent architectures.

Why is distributed AI even necessary? Along with the trend toward off-loading corporate data to smaller and smaller machines came the business trend of distributing work units across multiple geographic locations. The era of the downtown, centralized office building was dead.

In its place was built a cadre of office parks clustered in suburban communities.

Now groups of people across multiple locations need to work together
to come up with a solution for a joint problem. From a data processing
perspective, this poses no problem as long as one centralized processor
is shared remotely by all locations; but the trend is toward multiple
processors, one for each location.

This is being done for several reasons, cost being chief among them.
Off-loading departmental data to a distributed processor provides the
response time upgrade, the isolation of data from other possibly corrupt
sources, and the use of specific tool sets that fit the nature of the process.
With the proliferation of tools (i.e., many different types of databases,
multiple 4GLs, spreadsheets, AI), the mainframe at the central location
was becoming increasingly burdened with this wide variety that had to
be installed to support the variety of users. By off-loading departmental
data to distributed processors, not only the data would be off-loaded,
but the tools would be as well. Here, distributed computers do the bulk
of the work, with the centralized computer acting as a server to gather
back summary information for corporatewide decision making.

An extra level of difficulty is encountered when the system to be distributed is an AI system. And although distributed artificial intelligence
is not quite here yet; it's on the way.

For more than a decade there has been much research underway to
make this concept a reality. Using the blackboard approach as a base,
one group of computer scientists designed a system where a network of
processors can exchange messages by writing on each other's blackboards
as shown in Figure 4-6. Rules resident on each independent processor
can function to notify that particular system that a message has been
passed to it. In this way, distributed AI can be achieved.

Perhaps the approach that will make the most significant inroads will
be the one based on the building block of expert systems—the object.

A full object-based system in a distributed environment is called a
distributed object-oriented system or DOOS. In a conventional object-
oriented system, there is a single controlling agent and objects are accessible through a shared space.

This is not true for distributed environments where there are several
processors and, accordingly, several object spaces. While it is a trivial
matter to use pointers to link parent and child object to keep track of
an inheritance attribute, it becomes much more involved across multiple

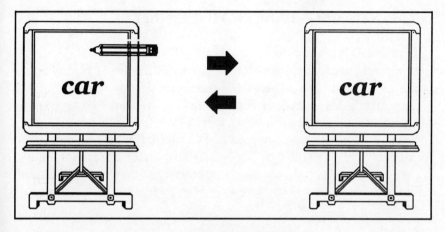

FIGURE 4-6.   Blackboard Architecture.

processors where memory pointers cannot be used. In this case messages must be passed between the processors. This forces the additional overhead of increased expense as well as the danger of timing problems such that the messages are out of sync.

Synchronization problems can occur very readily. Real-time expert systems infer that the knowledge base is rapidly changing. If the distributed environment is widely dispersed, it might well be that the messages cannot keep pace with the rapidly changing knowledge base.

There are a host of other problems. Gasser discusses load balancing where the goal of the system is to optimize clustering of objects for enhancement of processes such as message-passing or inheritance. Objects being passed across processors must be embedded into operating system structures carefully. This becomes difficult since objects may form a network with pointers reaching out far and wide into memory. Once this web is formed, it may even be necessary to completely reconstruct the object to transport it.

Distributed AI, to date, is purely theoretical. Much work has been done in the area of parallel architectures that will serve to expedite the implementation of distributed AI. Special-purpose hardware, such as The Connection Machine, and special-purpose programming languages such as Concurrent Prolog are being used to achieve this end.

In the financial services environment, where the majority of applications are resident on conventional processors the wait for distributed AI will be longer.

The Network—Tying It All Together

Distributed AI is one facet of a puzzle. The trend toward decentralization, and therefore distribution of databases, creates a patchwork of puzzle pieces that must somehow be connected together.

True, the LAN market is burgeoning, but the links being effected today are trivial compared to what is necessary for the future.

Level 1 networks are composed of PCs and CRT devices connected to a host. The propensity of networks today are of this variety. Level 2 networks link several processors, possibly DEC VAXs, and PCs and CRTs to a centralized host. Here PCs using emulation boards can easily

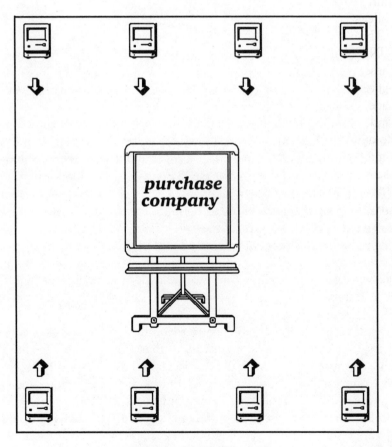

FIGURE 4-7.   Distributed AI.

communicate across the network, and processors speak readily to other processors. Level 3 networks carry variant processors as nodes. Here you could find a DEC VAX linked to an IBM 9370 linked to a SUN workstation, although the mainframe host is still central to the network. Effecting this sort of network is an exercise in tenacity. Grit those teeth as you're forced into re-wiring miles of cable and installing multiple communication packages on the mainframe and node processors.

Level 3 networks are in vogue today as vendors such as DEC and SUN market their networking expertise. But it is the Level 4 network that is going to take the collective brain power of all the DECs and SUNs to figure out how to support it. Going back to our discussion in Chapter 2 on neural networks we had a short discussion on the brain. The brain is composed of trillions of neurons that are networked together. Collectively, these neurons work in parallel to make a decision.

Think of a company that has eight variant processors (some DECs, SUNs, IBMs). Each of these processors can be thought of as a neuron. These eight processors together are the company's brain as we see in Figure 4-7. At each of the eight locations, part of a decision is being made to (perhaps) purchase another company. Each of the processors handles its part of the decision but must effectively communicate with the other seven. This is necessary to be able to send messages, get some common data, and review other decisions-in-progress. Although we've discussed concurrent and distributed AI we've omitted one crucial detail. That is that the network architecture to support this brand of AI does not yet exist.

5

The Auditing of Expert Systems

THE REGULATORY CLIMATE

October 19, 1987. On a cool, crisp Autumn morning thousands of Wall Streeters were wearily making their way to work after the weekend. Nary a smile among the sea of faces that turned up Broad Street. Ties not yet knotted, scruffy sneakers and socks on the opposite end of Chanel-suited executives. By 8 A.M. the cavern of buildings that is Broad Street was lit up by the glow of the countless dealing rooms up and down the street. Over at 11 Wall Street the members of the New York Stock Exchange were already on the floor, checking their posts for Friday's closing prices. All eyes turned toward the big clock on the wall, which was fast approaching 9 A.M.

The opening bell. The signal of a new trading day. It all started so slowly. Blue-frocked specialists seemed to dreamily make their deals with the crowd of brokers who surrounded them. The din of the hundreds of floor brokers making thousands of deals seemed like the quiet roar of the rolling ocean waves. The intensity increased, at first imperceptibly like the calm before the storm. But then the storm hit full force. The dream turned nightmare, the crowd turned screaming mob as the very foundation of the New York Stock Exchange quivered.

By the time it was all over, a high of 608,148,710 shares of stock had traded hands; a high of 20,993,000,000 dollars had been traded on one day. Some won, but most lost.

Many watched the events of that Black Monday and Tuesday from the potato belts of the Midwest, the avocado fields of Northern California, and the retirement communities of the South. Eyelids puffy from crying they sat, eyes glued to their television screens. For this was no docudrama they were watching. Many were watching the end of their dream.

There have been many explanations as to just what caused what has been labelled a market break by the securities industry but called a crash by most small investors involved. Greed. A market that was just too high, and bound to fall sooner or later. Whatever the reason, it helped in pushing the small investor out of the market.

But this was by no means the only factor that Joe and Alice and Mary used in making their decision to dump their securities and tuck their money away safely in a bank. They also remembered Ivan Boesky.

The government sat up and took notice. From the white marble floors of Congress to the back offices of the Securities and Exchange Commission to the cubicled- enclosures of the GAO, Washington spread out its tentacles and encircled Wall Street. There was such a flurry of activity that the Washington elite and the Wall Street power brokers alone kept the Pan Am shuttle in business. If nothing else was accomplished, at least a heck of a lot of people managed to amass gobs and gobs of frequent flier miles.

Early in 1988 the various government agencies lowered the regulatory boom. A number of recommendations were made to strengthen the financial marketplace, which if put in place could alter the very essence of the financial markets.

In spite of all this brouhaha about change, the investing public continues to look cross-eyed at the hubbub surrounding the financial services industry. They distrust Wall Street, so they take their hard-earned money and try to stash it in a bank. They quickly withdraw it at the very first hint of a problem. And in an environment still reeling from the savings and loan disasters, more and more money is being stashed safely under the mattress.

There is perhaps no better tool that can be used to restore confidence in the industry than the demonstration of stringent controls over the inner workings of a bank, a brokerage firm, or even a securities exchange. And perhaps the strongest control is the use of auditing.

THE FACTORS OF EXPERT SYSTEM AUDITING

It's no secret that computers make mistakes; or rather the programs had been written with misconceptions in design or errors in the code. In very large systems, especially those in financial services where the code is complex and the programs are very long, the possibility for error is very high. Enter the EDP (Electronic Data Processing) auditing department. EDP auditors are charged with ensuring that the process of creating and running computer systems is consistent with recognized development practices.

Complexity

Expert systems are both harder *and* easier to audit than your garden-variety computer system. The wind can blow in either direction depending on what building tools were used. When you build a log cabin, you clear the land and lay the foundation; although our forefathers often used the sweet-smelling earth as their very first carpets. Log after log is joined together inching upwards toward the sky. When it's done you can walk about, inside and out, rubbing your finger along the neatly stacked logs. You can see at a glance just how the log cabin was made.

Then there is the skyscraper. Acres of dirt are hauled away to lay the foundation, often as deep as a dungeon. Steel girders are hoisted heavenward by groaning cranes. Hundreds of hard-hatted workers scurry around on high crossbeams. The skyscraper rises as does the log cabin — the difference is complexity. Many expert systems are built to be as easily understood as our log cabin. And many systems are built to skyscraper levels of complexity. And many more are built somewhere between the two extremes. There are three factors that determine expert system complexity.

The first factor is tool complexity. There are hundreds of expert system tools in use today: from programming languages to expert system shells. Many of these tools are simple and self-documenting. By far the most simple tool would be any of the expert system shells that process only rules and do not deal with uncertainty. Building a system entails only entering the IF... THEN structures that make up the knowledge on which the system is founded. IF it rains ... THEN take an umbrella. IF the amount of the withdrawal exceeds the customer's balance ... THEN deny. The system deals only in definites. Moving up the complexity scale would be an expert system shell that deals in uncertainty. IF it rains AND the location is the Caribbean... THEN take an umbrella (certainty factor of 50 percent). And once we get into object-oriented programming we have met with a level of complexity that warrants extreme care.

The second wicket that makes it a sticky wicket is the level of expertise being snared in the expert system fishing net. A system that makes wine selections is simpler than a system that determines when your false teeth will be ready, is simpler than a system that makes recommendations in personal investment, is simpler than a system that authorizes loans, is simpler than a system that makes buy-sell decisions for foreign exchange dealers.

And not to forget the third factor—the most vital and the most problematic. Poets have dedicated odes, philosophers have wondered, and debaters have argued over this one wisp of significance in our tiny universe—yes, us. Will we adhere to the decision of the expert system, or won't we?

Audit Questions

We live in an era when all things computer are deemed to be correct. Why do the uninitiated place their faith so readily in those ubiquitous green-and-white listings that so clutter our offices? They say, "The computer can't make a mistake." Oh no? All computer systems should be audited. Since expert systems are a level of complexity greater than the conventional system, the audit should be of a level of complexity greater than a conventional system audit.

Where did you get the knowledge for this system? Now
if we're dealing with a medical expert system and the answer to our question is Dr. Kildare,* the auditor should roll up those sleeves, because they're in for the duration. Expert system knowledge should come from (surprise!) an expert. No compromise here, no "Let's use Mary because she's here." The audit process should check to ensure that the best possible candidate for stardom was chosen.

It's substance that is at the heart of an expert system. So how do we get it? Unfortunately, for many expert systems the expert selected is the person who has the most free time. For other expert systems, the top guru in the department is selected, who is then taken off the line for several weeks or months in an attempt to wrest the knowledge from its very

---

*For those of you too young to remember or too old to care, "Dr. Kildare" was a televised medical show in the 1960s.

roots. Some very smart systems use the combined expertise of several experts, which gives the ability to incorporate differing or competing viewpoints. Perhaps the most brilliant of expert systems incorporates the views and opinions of experts external to the company itself. The degree of expertise selected should be proportional to the level of strategic competitiveness the system is expected to display.

Functions within an organization are often graded proportionally to their worth to the organization. In a bank, those responsible for approving mortgage loans are often at a higher grade level within the organization than those that authorize credit on major credit card purchases. The organization inherently recognizes the complexity of the mortgage authorization process as compared to credit card authorizations. American Express, in its development of the Credit Authorizer for their green card, appropriately used a senior authorizer as the basis for the rules governing their very successful expert system. The rules governing this sort of credit approval may be many but are noncomplex and based on a moderate number of variables. Mortgage approval is a horse of a different color. Many variables come into play here, some vague or fuzzy. This process must take into account such things as amount of mortgage, down payment, security, primary income, secondary income, rate basis, rate spread, term of loan, and the list goes on. There is obviously much more risk associated with this process. The seedlings of this brand of expert system must come from a much more senior staffer and from more than one staffer to boot.

Most corporations have been quite perceptive about the failings of their own internal organizations in certain areas of expertise. Many raid competing organizations for their most experienced personnel. Many hire "big names" such as past members of presidential cabinets for their unique perspectives on world events. So too, expert systems. Interest Rate Insight is one of those rare expert systems that encompasses brilliance. Developed as part of an interest-rate advisory service run out of Menlo Park, California, it employs the combined expertise of over forty-eight erudite and renowned individuals in such areas of Fed policy, inflation, central bankers, government deficits, the dollar, risk, and uncertainty. Horace "Woody" Brock, president of Strategic Economic Decisions Inc., holder of five advanced degrees from Harvard and Princeton, is the pivot around which this system swings. There is no single person who possesses the expertise to determine such esoteric and probabilistic characteristics as interest-rate swings. It takes the combined expertise of many. This is what Woody had the insight to see was necessary. To be competitive, or more precisely, to provide the premier economic forecasting service, Woody knew that even his five advanced degrees were not enough.

Interest-rate forecasting is on the high end of the expertise-required scale as shown in Figure 5-1.

Perusing this figure makes it readily understandable that there is great risk in building a so-called expert system that utilizes the wrong level of expertise. Once the label of expert system is hung on a product, expectations are raised to a high level. This can possibly damage a company's reputation and even its competitive position in the marketplace if the knowledge contained within the system is at an inappropriate level.

At one prestigious Wall Street firm it was decided to build a trading system that would provide expertise in the time-honored tactic of hedging. Since hedging is more of an art than a science, the AI group needed to gain the cooperation of the premier participants in this art-form. Unfortunately these extraordinary folks were determined not to part with their knowledge. They felt it was what made them unique and marketable, not an unusual position for an expert to take. Since the AI folks couldn't get the cooperation they needed, they turned to textbooks as substitute mentors. Textbooks contain the rules and procedures but

BRILLIANT	*INTEREST RATE FORECASTING*	*MANY HIGH LEVEL OUTSIDE EXPERTS*
EXPERT	*MORTGAGE PROCESSING*	*MULTIPLE EXPERTS MOST INSIDE, SOME OUTSIDE*
EXTREMELY KNOWLEDGEABLE	*PENSION CHECK PROCESSING*	*MULTIPLE INSIDE EXPERTS*
SMART	*CREDIT CARD AUTHORIZATION*	*SINGLE EXPERT*
CONVENTIONAL	*PAYROLL*	*LITTLE EXPERTISE*

FIGURE 5-1. Expertise-Required Continuum.

not the gut instincts and rules of thumb that make an expert special. So what was actually developed? It was touted as an expert system, but at great risk to those who relied upon it. Had this company marketed this extra special system to its customers they would have placed themselves at extraordinary risk. For what they eventually developed was nothing more than a very smart system.

Expert systems are hard to develop. Unfortunately many have overlooked the fundamental assessment of the expertise available or required for the more technical considerations. It is very easy to confuse the tools of the product with the product itself. Many get caught up in the high-tech world of Sun or DEC workstations and LISP programming languages. They sound so exotic. Clever technical people are throwing these high-tech platforms at senior managements who somehow are led to believe that the mere use of the tools of AI begets an AI system. This is no more true than the purchase of oil paints, sable brush, and canvas make a Picasso out of a graffiti artist. The core of the expert system is the expertise itself.

As the expertise-required continuum shows in Figure 5-1, there are many gradations of expert-type systems, from the smarter than conventional systems to the very brilliant systems. In each of these systems a certain level of expertise is required. If these systems are to be built, management should not look askance at the technology but should take an active interest in its success. The way this can be done is to become involved at the point where the actual level of expertise is selected. This selection, which can appear trivial, is fraught with risk for those that take a laissez-faire attitude. The continuum clearly shows that some systems are so complex and require as input the analysis of so many far-reaching variables, that default to in-house staff as a total solution is not realistic. For these systems, which often reside in key areas of the company such as security trading and portfolio management, including outside experts to gain a broader perspective is heartily endorsed.

There are very few brilliant systems. Some, like Interest Rate Insight, are marketed and are commercially available.

The Theory of Uncertainty conjures up a world in chaos. Compared to the decades of relative stability we lived through right up into the late seventies, it is indeed chaos. One casualty of this new age of economics was most certainly the savings and loan institutions. Not since the Great Depression have so many savings banks shut their doors on long lines of angry and scared depositors. In 1988 alone, the Federal

Savings and Loan Insurance Corporation bailed out 223 thrifts to the tune of nearly $40 billion. How could this have happened? Where were the bank examiners?

A bank is a financial entity like all others. Would it have been possible to apply some expert system here to determine whether or not the bank carried a risky portfolio? The answer is a resounding YES. Unfortunately, to date, no company has been clever enough to apply this methodology to this problem. In case they'd like to try I'll provide them with one solution in the form of one system that's ready, willing, and able.

Syntelligence Inc. is another of those sun-belt, high-tech artificial intelligence companies. Based in Sunnyvale, California the founders of Syntelligence brought together a team of world-class experts in banking. The Lending Advisor is touted by Syntelligence as acting as a "safety net" for the bank wise enough to use the product. This expert credit management system concentrates on maintaining a strong loan portfolio by monitoring risk exposure. Performing a plethora of functions, it provides a rigorous and consistent analysis for pinpointing potential trouble spots.

One of the marketing techniques that Syntelligence uses on prospective purchasers is to run that bank's loans through the Lending Advisor. The results have surprised some people. In fact, at one bank Syntelligence was requested not to show the results to the bank's president as he was not as yet informed about one loan that had gone south. Loans going south and other risky investments are at the root of the S&L crisis. Wouldn't it be interesting to run the portfolios of the 223 banks that failed in 1988 through the Lending Advisor? Wouldn't it be even more interesting to run the surviving S&L portfolios through this brilliant system?

Did we get ALL of the knowledge? Once the auditor is confident that a bona-fide expert was chosen as Kimo-Sabe* a thorough analysis should be done to determine if *all* the knowledge was captured. How should this be done? One way would be to review the transcripts of the knowledge engineering sessions, but this would be extremely time-consuming. Probably the best way is to observe use of the system in practice and look for the holes. A complete expert system should leave no question unanswered and no stone unturned. So, it should account

---

* Another show from the 50s this time—"The Lone Ranger." His sidekick, an Indian named Tonto, referred to the know-it-all Lone Ranger as Kimo-Sabe.

for all situations that arise during a sample test period. For example, suppose we build a super-duper credit authorization system. During the system development process the expert worked diligently to encode all the rules of the game plus all of the expert's gut instinct in approving credit. The system is put into the credit department amid much fanfare. Sixty people come into work on a Monday morning all ready, eager, and willing to work with their new friendly, electronic credit advisor. At 9:01 A.M. the phones start ringing off the hook. Real customers. Real credit decisions. The question is, can every situation be handled? And handled correctly?

But the auditors are standing guard. A group of credit authorizers were preselected to log all instances of variances and omissions between what the system does and what they would have done manually. This variance check is then scrutinized, gone over with a fine-tooth comb. Since this process should have also been part of the original test plan, the eagle-eyed auditors should find few problems. Given the enormity of the task of capturing the whole ball of wax, it's a sure thing that the auditors will find some discrepancy.

Auditors enjoy looking for discrepancies and the most common way they find them is with an audit trail. Now audit trails are uncommon to most computer systems for a simple reason. They cost to build and they cost to run. One of the niceties of using expert system technology is that an audit trail is almost a natural part of system design. So it should be almost trivial for an auditor to perform an after-the-fact audit. Here the auditor examines a printed audit trail and compares the expert system decision to the decision a human credit authorizer would have given.

How much common sense does the expert system exhibit? Common sense is hard to expert-systematize and even harder to miss. Some experts get so caught up in the esoterics of what they do for a living, they miss the trivial common-sensibilities of their daily tasks. Wayne J. Socha (1988) described a situation in which he was involved in building a prototype expert system for determining the scope of an internal audit. The prototype worked wonderfully in predicting the scope of a loan audit for a branch bank until it ran aground at one branch that *did not have any loans.*

Does the expert system make mistakes? What happens if the system becomes confused? No kidding, this can happen. Not to worry, our fearless auditor has a technique to pinpoint this problem and it's right out of Sigmund Freud's procedure manual. In the field of psychology, a confusion matrix is built to determine the ratios between correct responses and those responses that were close, but not quite correct. We can use this same technique to determine just how right (or wrong) a system is. Let's look at an example. We've just built an expert system to determine the type of disease based on what we say are our patient's symptoms. Our list of possible diseases is: the flu, a cold, and the black plague. Sitting in one room is a medical expert who examines several patients and makes diagnoses. Across the hall is our friendly computer who also makes diagnoses. Figure 5-2 shows a confusion matrix for the differences between our human doctor's diagnosis and our expert system's. Remember that in each instance the information given to the doctor was the same that was fed into the expert system. Presuming that our doctor is a bona-fide expert, the responses of the expert system should exactly parallel those of the doctor. You can see from the confusion matrix that this didn't happen. Each slot or entry in the matrix represents the percentage of times that the expert system differed from the human expert, which really means the percentage of times that the expert system was confused. For example, when our doctor diagnosed the flu, the expert system recommended the black plague 20 percent of the time and cold 15 percent of the time. These erroneous conclusions totalled 35 percent

	black plague	*flu*	*cold*
black plague	*n/a*	*35%*	*45%*
flu	*20%*	*n/a*	*15%*
cold	*10%*	*5%*	*n/a*

FIGURE 5-2.   Confusion Matrix.

of the time. This means that our expert system was correct only 65 percent of the time. The average of these error percentages will give us an error threshold for which each company must decide as acceptable and not. In the case of our medical expert system, the total error threshold turned out to be a mere 57 percent (i.e., the system was correct only 57 percent of the time) which would be unacceptable in anybody's medical textbook.

Is the expert system kept up to date?   By the sweat of everybody's brow, three years and 2000 hours later the system is complete. With great fanfare the system is presented to management followed by a champagne party and many press releases. While everyone is toasting each other and slapping each other on the back something terrible is happening. The expert system is becoming out of date.

You've all heard the old saw about books—as soon as it's in print it's out of date. Well the same thing's true about expert systems. Knowledge bases seldom stay static. They grow and expand beyond the developer's wildest dreams. One of the systems you'll read about later, the Loan Probe, began life at 2000 rules and wound up at 9000 rules.

How do they grow? This is the question that the auditor should ask. Which department has responsibility for entering new tidbits of knowledge? Is it the computer department? The user group?

And the auditor should be on the lookout for adolescent sloppiness. When the system is a babe in the woods there's usually adequate money, time, and enthusiasm to do the job right. After the fanfare is over and the glare of the spotlight fades, the system matures into an adolescent. Gradually the heavy hitters move away from the system to something a bit more exciting leaving our little system alone and forlorn. When a change has to be made to the system to add a choice tidbit of knowledge, it is made during (oh dread!) maintenance mode rather than development mode. For those of you who are familiar with all things computer, the term maintenance conjures up images of jailbirds in a chain gang.

Maintenance is not your most interesting work. And those who are assigned to it usually manage to work up the same level of enthusiasm as for a weekend trip to the dentist. Changes made in this manner are usually sloppy, or if you're really lucky, just careless. The meticulousness exhibited during the development stage, when the team wanted everything to be just so, is usually never replicated. So the auditor would be wise to take a look at procedures put into place to handle addition of new rules to the knowledge base as well as linkages to new databases or files.

Will the users actually use the expert system? You say you spent $10 million on your expert system and you're not sure anyone uses it? Once a decision is made, what happens then? Most expert systems are used in an advisory capacity. This means that a real live human being will read the decision and do one of two things. Use it or ignore it. A well-designed system will track the adherence factor, which can then be used by the auditor to track whether the system is being used effectively. Of course, it's a pretty good idea for management to use this feature, too.

The adherence factor is actually an audit trail of the system's recommendations. For each consultation the system keeps track of the conclusion. This conclusion can then be compared to the one that the staff actually made. To simplify the process some use an on-line justification program that permits the user of the system to enter what was actually done. Those who would serve as auditors will most likely place this high on their list of features to consider. Having it means "never having to say you're sorry."*

AN AUDIT PLAN

Most people think of auditing as a necessary evil. Systems folks don't think kindly of EDP auditors. No wonder EDP auditors take a fine-tooth comb to every facet of the development process. From file design to job control language to documentation to user manuals. They're omnipresent and omnipainful. Expert system auditing is just a little wrinkle in the otherwise superbly organized world of these denizens of the data dictionary. In addition to the questions we've covered above, the expert system smart EDP auditor will question the following:

---

*From the early 1970's movie "Love Story." Those of you who remember it— congratulations, those of you who don't—you didn't miss anything.

- Can you re-create an expert system consultation?
- Is the data captured during the consultation edited or verified in any way?
- When an error is detected, which users receive immediate notification?
- If an error is detected, does the knowledge base flag the error?
- How rigorously are the answer fields constrained?
- Are new releases of the knowledge base tracked?
- What were the test cases used to verify the system?
- After the system is altered, are new test cases used to verify the system?
- Is the expert system treated like any other production system? Are new releases quality-assured? Are new releases endorsed by the expert?
- How are differences between the system and a human expert handled?
- Is an English language version of the rules maintained as documentation?

MANAGED EXPERT SYSTEMS

To ward off the terror of the EDP audit, one should practice safe expert systems. That is, manage the *development* of the expert system process such that the completed system is beyond reproach.

This requires a wide array of skills from the development manager. This hearty soul must simultaneously be cheerleader, strategic visionary, technical guru, cajoler of users and managers, and all-around great pal.

This visionary must have eyes on both the front and back of the head. The better to see the technical complexity of the project before the process begins. The better to see how users and management fit into the overall picture.

Marc Meyer and Kathleen Curley (1989), both professors at the College of Business Administration at Northeastern University in Boston, studied many successful systems and the management tactics used in achieving these systems. Their goal was to identify these attributes and attempt to develop a usable methodology.

The first attribute that they looked at was the complexity of the knowledge to be encoded into the system. The second attribute was complexity of the chosen technology. Other factors examined were level of expertise as determined by education or experience level of expert, amount and certainty of information, duration of typical session, and accuracy required of system's conclusion. Other attributes factored into this equation included numbers of different computers or operating systems that the expert system would operate, and types of database.

The Northeastern team looked at twelve expert systems in these terms and found that they really boiled down to four different types.

A *knowledge-intensive* system is knowledge-bound but uses a simple computing environment and usually acts in an advisory capacity. The other extreme is the *technology-intensive* system, which contains limited knowledge or knowledge in a limited domain, but requires advanced computing prowess. This sort of system can usually be found in areas where improvement in organizational productivity is envisioned. The most exotic sort of expert system is a *strategic impact* system where not only complex knowledge is encoded but the system is technically complex. On the low end of the totem pole are *personal productivity* systems where limited amounts of knowledge as well as simple technology are the characteristics. The high end is exemplified by a foreign exchange trading system where advanced workstations are used, massive data feeds are integrated, and complex rules of knowledge are encoded. The low end is exemplified by an expert system that is in use by a dental company to forecast when false choppers would be ready. Run on a PC, with a very small number of rules, hundreds of patients are chewing happily today as a result of this system.

Why should it make a difference how the expert system is classified; how would this knowledge make an impact on management methodology? The answer is really quite simple. If you know up front just what you're dealing with, you can prepare. Preparation is the hallmark of good management. To illustrate, let's say you're developing a system that you predict will be knowledge and technology rich. You would need to gather 'round you a team that was composed of heavy hitters as both knowledge engineers as well as techno-gurus. You would also have to cajole a bona-fide expert to leave the line and join your team. This is easier said than done. To accomplish this feat requires selling the concept to both the expert and the expert's manager. All these things need to be taken care of up front and in successfully executed systems, they are.

CONCLUSION

There's a whole new world of technology out there. As you will soon see, expert systems are popping up all over. In banking. In insurance. In trading. They're being used for foreign exchange, for interest-swing prediction, for pension fund processing, for just about everything in the financial services arena. Let's step back from the adulation of this technology for a few seconds and take stock of what we're really doing. We're building a system, albeit an expert system, but still a system. And all systems must be made accountable, especially in financial services.

The systems with the best track record are those that start out well-planned. The manager takes into account the nuances of the area to be automated, the personalities involved, and the technology required. With this in hand, the ballgame is half won. The last several innings revolve around developing a system that is auditable; that is, can you use it and prove it.

Maybe we're presuming more than we should about certain factors that, if not addressed, could negate the auditing process. First and foremost is the experience level of the auditor. We spent some time in the beginning of this book on how to develop an expert system. One key point is the proper training of staff. This is equally true for an auditor since an auditor cannot audit what is not understood.

Once trained, the auditor can't put on those running shoes, run over, and audit the first expert system available. There's the experience factor and it must be dealt with carefully. The auditor cannot become a naysayer until some notches are scratched on the old auditing belt.

Then we know that the auditor is up to the challenge.

6 | AI on Wall Street

OVERVIEW

QLW ONSDY XWDNIVT QN QLW WIWSVWQMC
—SKDHL OKDYN WZWSTNI

It's a cryptogram. Buried in this puzzle is a quotation from a famous author. What Wzwstni is telling us applies especially to that rare breed that lives on Wall Street. They live for the enigma. They adore unravelling the threads of mystery surrounding market performance; *they* won't find the answer at the end of the chapter. But that's where *you'll* find the answer to the cryptogram.

Oh, the joy of it all. To be on the floor of the New York Stock Exchange is to be at the center of the universe. The roar of the crowd, the scent of a fresh kill quickens the pulse and flushes the cheeks. But let's exit through the side door and walk down any street. Look, over there, in that tall, gray limestone building, that's where all the real action is.

Behind locked doors, a blinking, whirring gray box chugs away uninterrupted. A few feet away, a shirt-sleeved denizen of the Wall Street canyon stands watching this magic box perform its magnum opus. Suddenly the printer begins its dance and the Wall Street trading fiend scrambles to rip the report, ink still wet, from the printer. Running to the phone, our intrepid but frazzled ivy league investment banker screams into the phone, "Buy Disney!"

Oh, the joy of it all. To have a computer that is expert. Balderdash you say? An expert computer can't beat the system? Well, in rebuttal to this rebuff, let's hop a plane to sunny Orinda, California and visit some with Barr Rosenberg of Institutional Equity Management. In two out of the last three years Rosenberg's not so little expert system, which picks stock portfolios all by its little self, has beaten the market at its own game. That is, Rosenberg's total return in 1988 was 23.1 percent versus a paltry 16.6 percent for Standard and Poor's 500 Stock Index. Around the same time he opened his company, Barr Rosenberg started working away on his expert computer system. It now works with over two hundred factors such as book values and price-to-earnings ratios to spot undervalued companies. Rosenberg's systems have figured in every conceivable factor that makes the market tick, including economics, psychological factors, short-term technical market patterns, and maybe even the kitchen sink.

In October 1987 even the kitchen sink was in jeopardy as the market dropped over five hundred points in the largest one-day decline in Wall Street's history. And now that the shock wave is behind it, Wall Street has revved up spending on computers and the software that goes in them. All in an often frustrating attempt to deal with market volatility, increasing globalization, and the proliferation of products that litter the market. So its no wonder that some formerly heretic disbelievers are increasingly turning to artificial intelligence to get the upper hand. "Expert system applications not only will be used but will be necessary to respond to the enormous amount of data generated by changes in the European financial markets," predicts Joel Kaplan, a principal in the proprietary trading group at Morgan Stanley & Company, who's a big believer. In an otherwise normally secretive Wall Street atmosphere, Kaplan is unusually candid about the system he uses. Perhaps because Expert Tick is an unqualified success.

Expert Tick is used on Morgan's profit and loss desk. And it solves what had been a costly dilemma. When a trader is busy, often the time can't be taken to review the real-time ticker and make sure that the trade just made is quoted. One of the best known expert systems on the Street, Expert Tick's goal in life is to look at all the information and figure out the likelihood that the trade hit the ticker.

Perhaps the best applications for expert systems are on the other side of the ticker. Almost every Wall Street firm has one or more projects underway to provide the trader with a tool set that will provide real-time insights and a Wall Street-type of expertise. Larry Geisel, president of Intelligent Technology based in Pittsburgh, Pennsylvania talks of the chaotic world we live in and insists, "computers and automation of investing, hedging, and tracking will yield strategic leverage."

To do this, firms large and small are investing in a combination of expert systems and advanced workstation technology. Prudential Bache's head of computer systems, William H. Anderson, calculates, "most of your analytics folks are looking for fifty to one hundred MIPS (millions of instructions per second)." Combining artificial intelligence and the speed of workstation technology gives the trading room a heady combination. Citicorp Investment Bank in New York ordered 3,000 DEC workstations. The purpose of this grand scheme is to tie its traders into a global network. This network provides each Citicorp trader with the ability to see prices on several markets. It also performs instantaneous portfolio analysis and even automatically executes orders. Yes, the integrated, AI workstation approach is a potent weapon with everyone up and down the block clamoring to get a piece of the pie. Paine Webber's Hedging Assistant prototype made use of this strategy as does the Chicago Board of Trade's Aurora system.

Perhaps the best use of AI would be as an embedded component in a quantitative investment algorithm. This could, in fact, change the face of the Street. And this change is starting to take place now. Larry Geisel's Intelligent Technology Group has developed a model that does just this and it appears to be extraordinarily powerful.

Fourteen years ago Charles Dym pioneered a new quantitative investment theory that butted heads with the three theories most widely held: the Modern Portfolio Theory, the Efficient Market theory, and the Random Walk theory. Dym's approach combined pattern recognition and probability theory. A pilot test of this theory did so well that it ranked in the second percentile of the annual Becker rankings. Fourteen years later Dym joined Larry Geisel with the goal of taking this fourteen-year-old theory and adding two additional components: the experience of the last decade and the ITG expert system.

Not every Wall Street expert system needs to run on a workstation or needs the power of Charles Dym's theories. The most widely used expert systems are those that come off-the-shelf; many of them run on PCs. Steward Pahn, a Thomson McKinnon broker who has over $350,000 in assets under management, uses a product aptly called the Intelligent Trading System. Marketed by Providence Research in San Mateo California, this product works within the level of risk agreed to by each investor and defines good investment opportunities. The ITS comes in two parts. The first is based on 42 expert rules to arrive at a buy-and-sell decision by examining the stock price information fed to it each day. The second part of this expert system scrutinizes how much of the investor's money will be spent in executing the trade.

Brooks Martin, a stockbroker with Rodman and Renshaw, says that he too "can't live without" his expert system. He uses a trio of products from AIQ systems, based in Incline, Nevada. While we'll talk at length about StockExpert; the company markets two other expert products, IndexExpert and MarketExpert, which Martin raves about.

And the list goes on. As early as 1987, Coopers & Lybrand worked with Drexel Burnham to develop an expert system that would have the capability of recognizing patterns in auditing trading data. Another innovator, Manning and Napier Advisors out of Rochester, New York, found a novel way to handle their ever-increasing trading volumes. Their novel approach includes use of the Wang VS computer to build a rule-based system that guides the trader through the process of determining how many shares to buy and for which accounts. The system tracks many variables including market value, position size, and objectives of the account. Not only does the system permit Manning to take "advantage of smaller commissions and reduced commission rates" but it's much faster than the old way of doing business. They like to quote the statistic of the new 1.5-hour program versus the old 7.5 hours to complete a trading program. Even venerable old Merrill Lynch uses TradeCenter, an off-the-shelf expert trading package, to assist in making buy/sell recommendations.

There's great potential here. From front office to back office, the expert system is being used to stem the information crunch in the same way the computer itself was used to stem the great paper crush of the early 1970s. Perhaps the most exotic use of all is on the floor of a stock exchange.

A SMART TRADING FLOOR*

The future of American capitalism and the free-enterprise system rests on the pillars of the many and diverse exchanges scattered across the globe. Where once traders, wearing the visor and using the quill pen made markets in securities and commodities, they

---

*This section originally appeared in a column that I wrote for *Expert Systems* journal. I thank Auerbach publishers for permitting me to refresh "A Smart Trading Floor," originally published in the Winter 1990 issue. Reprinted from *Expert Systems* (New York: Auerbach Publishers).©1990 Warren, Gorham & Lamont Inc. Used with permission.

are relying more and more on automated assistance. The Chicago Board of Trade has taken an innovative AI approach to opening up the market to worldwide 24-hour trading. But have they gone far enough? How else can AI be used to provide a more accessible and equitable marketplace? Let's take a look-see.

7:20 A.M. The opening bell rings. Pulses quicken. Noise levels crescendo. The fury of the auction trading market begins. All day long, throngs of traders are making markets in the pits of the Chicago Board of Trade. Buys and sells are screamed out by arm-waving, card-carrying members of the Exchange. Passions rise, fortunes fall, it's all in a day's work at the largest commodities market in the world. When the closing bell rings late in the day, the victors and the losers of the largest and longest shell game hang up their badges and go home to a fitful night's sleep. When the sun rises in Tokyo, the CBOT trading floor is still, an eerie silence surrounding the pits. Fortunes are being made and lost while the Chicago traders sleep.

But wait, coming up over the horizon is "the dawn of a new age in international trading." The Chicago Board of Trade (CBOT) calls it AURORA. It's a high-tech, computerized, off-floor, trading system that is geared to provide the benefits of the auction market to users in all time zones.

The First Step—AURORA

In 1848 when 82 Chicago businessmen founded the CBOT, they had no idea that their auction market would grow from local to worldwide popularity, from low-tech telegraph to report on prices to satellite relay. Indeed, 142 years ago, those 82 men could not have conceived of computers, much less computerized trading. CBOT's Board of Directors have taken an exciting, high-tech approach to a pressing problem that is facing all markets whether the market be in equities or commodities or futures or options. The demand for trading is exceeding capacity and quite literally, time is running out.

The recipe for AURORA was equal pinches of Texas Instruments, CBOT, and Apple Computer. Using the AI methodology of rapid proto-typing, the knowledge engineers from Texas Instruments mimicked the trading floor on the screen of a Micro Explorer. The Micro Explorer joins the Apple Macintosh II with Texas Instruments' Explorer microprocessor to give a low-cost but extremely powerful AI workstation. Using the Mac's Apple graphics they managed to simulate a typical trading pit at the CBOT. No, little people icons do not "Pac-Man" their way around the screen, but little red ovals and blue boxes do. The red ovals represent the *offering* icon and display the member's badge number or acronym and the number of contracts he or she is offering. The blue box represents the opposite side of the trade, the member *bidding* box containing the member's acronym and the number of contracts he or she is bidding for. The screen is filled with red offers and blue bids for the one active contract that is placed in the trading area of the screen. Bordering the trading area are iconized displays for other contracts, pit trade summary box, personal trade summary box, and other trading information. These are all carefully prototyped to convey huge amounts of information to the off-floor trader and to imitate the visual trading cues that the trader has historically relied upon. Traders can see who is in the pit, whether they are buying or selling, what they bid or offer. The full informational flow, now available on the actual trading floor, is simulated within AURORA. Once a trade is initiated either through the real floor or the AURORA floor, it is passed to the behind-the-scenes Electronic Order Delivery System (EOS). EOS was written to maintain real-time status on all pending orders received during a 24-hour day.

AURORA is the beginning of smart trading. Although meant to be utilized within a brokerage environment after-hours, it is easy to picture a member of the CBOT, clad in pajamas, struggle to awake to his 3:00 A.M. alarm. He shuts off the loud ring, rubs the sleep from his eyes, shuffles to his den, and turns on his Micro Explorer. Instantly he's bidding on 40 contracts of Treasury Bonds with another somnolent trader from Chicago, a more alert trader in London, and a gang of bidders from Tokyo. The glow of the Mac's screen fills the darkened den. Our trader, who goes by the trading acronym JIM, somewhat akin to having a CB handle, decides to bid for 40 March bond contracts. Using his keyboard he indicates his bid to the system. Instantly a small blue box appears on the screen. Inside the box appears the acronym JIM and the number 40. The human trader now becomes his computerized icon and can make a trade with one of the many red offering icons that represent other traders interested in the same contract. Quite simple, really. A buyer meets a seller. In this case, however, the buyer is a blue box and the seller is a red oval and the auction market is a video screen as shown in Figure 6-1.

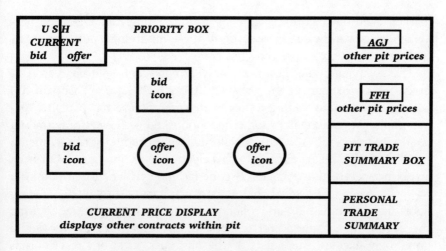

FIGURE 6-1.   AURORA Simulation.

Before JIM bid for his 40 contracts he quickly glanced at the upper left-hand corner of his screen where he took note of the current bid and offering prices as well as the number of contracts available. He sees the acronym USH, which he knows to be industry parlance for the March U.S. Treasury Bond contract. As JIM is trading, he keeps a constant eye on the lower right-hand corner of his screen where two displays are crucial to him. One is his Personal Trade Summary Box where the system keeps track of his position. The second is the Pit Trade Summary Box where the most recent trades in the current contract are displayed. Trade completed, JIM decides to call up another contract within U.S. Treasuries. He looks to the bottom of the screen and finds the acronym for April U.S. Treasuries. Using his trusty keyboard, JIM now makes the April contract the current pit and proceeds to make an offer of 45 contracts. Should JIM be inspired to deal in something other than U.S. Treasuries, he need only look to the right of the screen, where other contracts are listed by acronym with bid and offer prices and quantities. *All* JIM needs to know. At the tip of his finger.

There are cries of consternation from some brokerage houses as they foresee hiring second and third shifts of brokers in order to keep pace with the 24-hour day. There are warnings from such well-known economists as Pace University's William Freund, who forecasts disorderly markets, without technological cooperation among exchanges and brokerage firms worldwide. In spite of all these misgivings, automated off-trading is a notion whose time has come.

The exchanges are becoming increasingly more automated. The Tokyo Stock Exchange, the Swedish Stock Exchange, even Spain has gone the electronic trading route. Even Paris' Bourse has plans to "dematerialize" its trading floor sometime soon. And with electronic trading comes information. A wealth of information, accurate to the moment.

AURORA is an AI entry into this electronic trading frenzy. But from an AI perspective has AURORA gone far enough? The Micro Explorer has the power to do much more than graphically display the trading floor and generate bids and offers at the request of the trader using the device. It has the power to be a trading expert and the power to unfailingly execute the orders of the customer. One of the criticisms of 24-hour trading is the prediction that the individual investor will lose much sleep while nervously agonizing over the possibility of stocks plummeting while sleeping. Go to bed a millionaire, wake up a pauper.

The Next Step—Expert Traders

For a chocoholic on a binge, one Hershey bar is never enough. For a brokerage firm, the simulation of the pit will not be enough. Brokerage houses large and small will be hard-pressed to hire enough talent after midnight to provide the same quality service to their investors as obtained during the day. Add to this equation our somnolent trader who blearily makes his bids and offers from his den in the middle of the night. The next logical step is to couple the graphical trading pit with an expert system that can add the logic of an experienced trader to the Micro Explorer. The automated trader's knowledge base can be either of a global variety (i.e., the general rules and regulations of trading as they pertain to a particular firm) or it can be specific to an individual trader. In this way, our sleepy trader can rest comfortably while his automated alter-ego is watching the floor bidding and offering, constrained by the rules contained in the expert system. Since the "rules of thumb" or heuristics of a star trader are often proprietary to the trader, the expert system could be built with the knowledge base 80 percent filled with the general rules of the game. The other twenty percent, the "gut trading instincts" of the trader can be encoded by the trader himself.

On the flip side of the coin, we have the nervous small investors. These are the people who could possibly see their life savings go down the tube in a trading frenzy thousands of miles away and time zones apart. The addition of intelligence to the AURORA workstation could serve here as well. This could take the form of a stop-loss order system that would protect the small investor from rapid drops in prices overnight.

A Side Benefit—A Better Audit Trail

For those of you just waking up from a deep sleep or returning from a trip abroad to a country without newspapers, the issue of insider trading and a fair and equitable marketplace are daily front-page news items. The hot button is the audit trail that would serve to reconstruct the trade. Many of the exchanges have been the targets of covert FBI action on the trading floor. In all instances, at all exchanges, audit trail systems are being scrutinized as never before. An automated trading system, by definition, captures all parties to a trade—hence a real-time audit trail one hundred percent accurate, one hundred percent of the time.

Why Not Daytime, Too?

The CBOT AURORA system will be used after-hours only. The Directors of the CBOT maintain that the "live" auction market is still the best way to ensure a fair and orderly market. The American exchanges are hesitant to follow the lead of the Tokyo and London exchanges, which are totally automated and not considered auction markets. AURORA is an auction market. And one that is not only possessed of a built-in audit trail that could serve to restore the confidence of the small investor, which was lost one warm day in October 1987; it can also trade faster and more accurately than its human counterpart.

The 1975 Securities Act mandated the creation of a national market system. Fourteen years later AURORA can be seen as a seedling in the growth of an international market system. It starts with a system that simulates the trading pit or floor, provides for an automatic audit trail that can reconstruct trades across the globe or across the street.

Add to this the intelligence of a trading knowledge base and a customer stop-loss system and we have the ingredients of magic.

"The rules of the game are about to change. You can't stop the technology from taking over," forecasts Thomas Livingston, a senior vice president at the brokerage firm of McGinn, Smith and Company. And so, AURORA is indeed the dawn of a new age.

TAKING THE PAIN OUT OF REGULATION

Although the trading floor is most certainly the most visible part of a stock or commodity exchange, perhaps the one with the most drama (at least of late) is the regulatory department.

A primary function of all stock exchanges, in addition to providing a marketplace for the buying and selling of securities, is the regulation and surveillance of all its member organizations. This has a two-fold purpose: to make sure members are financially and operationally able to fulfill their obligations to their customers and to each other, and to uphold standards of high-quality service to investors. And in the overheated 1980s, the era of The Crash, Boesky and Milken, there is no more important function within an exchange.

The American Stock Exchange

The American Stock Exchange recognizes the value of expert systems, too. Their Market Surveillance Expert is used in assisting AMEX analysts to decide about whether or not to open an insider trading investigation.

Using the PC-based EXSYS expert system shell, the system ingests data from either LOTUS 1-2-3 spreadsheets or mainframe downloads. Added are rules that pattern the investigators' judgmental processes.

These processes consist of applications of SEC and AMEX rules as well as the gut-level instincts of the most senior investigators. Each of these rules is assigned a probability and it is the combination of these probabilities, or the sum score, that assists the investigator in making the decision about whether or not to open a case.

The New York Stock Exchange

No industry in the United States regulates itself as extensively as the securities industry. And don't be misled, this regulation affects all of us. From the investing public to financial institutions that use the market-place to companies whose shares are traded to insurers who underwrite business to lenders who extend credit.

Using Expert Systems. Nowhere is it done bigger than at the Big Board—the New York Stock Exchange. On the Sherlock Holmes side of Boesky-busting, the Market Surveillance department is using a expert system dubbed ICAS, which stands for Integrated Computer-Assisted Surveillance. Using workstation technology, the surveillance investigator no longer has to research the dusty pages of countless books but can flick a switch and see this assistant come to life. Expert systems are being used to monitor the financial performance of the member firms as well. In fact, expert systems are cropping up all over.

ICAS. The system first wakes up as it traps an aberrant trade. Market Surveillance always applied rules to spot trades that fall outside the realm of the acceptable. What better than to codify these rules into an expert system? This the team did and they became the first ICAS component. The next step in ICAS is quite interesting. The Exchange purchases huge databases containing much esoteric information—club memberships, corporate staff information, address information, and so on. The system now delves into these databases looking for connections between people who seemed to know a thing or two about a stock a wee bit too early. To do this, human investigative expertise had to be codified. Rules take the form of: IF X is suspicious AND Y knows X THEN Y is suspicious. Guilty by association!

ICAS handles an extraordinary amount of name and address data from diverse sources. This textual data is often hard to handle; and it was no different for ICAS. The team was required to build a natural language parser to be able to distinguish the name *Lois Lane* from the address *Lois Lane*.

FORCE-ESP. Across the alley, the back offices of the brokerage firms get their share of scrutiny, too. And this is harder than it sounds. Complaints. Advertising. Credit extensions. Financial reports such as profit loss; et cetera and et cetera. All of these things must be looked at and analyzed.

The idea is to provide some consistency in reviewing this enormous amount of data and to provide a level of tutorial for the various financial analysts who will use the system. The regulators and technology team have embarked upon implementing a project that has been quite successful in prototype mode.

The FOCUS (Financial, Operational, Combined, Uniform, Single Form) report is the bane of the brokerage community. Filling in a report that has some seven hundred blank lines is never a joy. No matter how bad it is for the firms, it's far worse for the regulators. With some seven hundred firms each seven-hundred-line report becomes a hurdle.

With a multitude of staff, all with varying degrees of expertise, it became clear that something new and clever was needed. In the early 1980s a computerized, rule-based exception system was developed that took some of the pain out of this process. One of the first mainframe, knowledge-based systems, it reviewed each of the FOCUS reports and applied a set of over two hundred rules to each of these seven-hundred-line reports. And then spit out an on-line exception report. Each rule would carry a lot of functionality. The rules can be compared to miniprograms since each was very computation-intensive. Unfortunately, this system left out something very important that a new expert system was just the thing for.

Wouldn't it be nice to have the computer tell you what to do? That was the goal in FOCUS review. Have the system analyze the report, spit out the exceptions and then proceed to prioritize these exceptions. Have it associate these exceptions with one another and then give the users a script with which they can resolve the problem.

The system, FORCE/ESP as it came to be known, was programmed to do just that. In a series of intensive knowledge-engineering sessions, the team lifted the expertise from some of the most experienced regulators around. For the prototype, the top three related exceptions were chosen since they were representative of all the exceptions. And creating a prototype using these three would truly represent the entire spectrum.

Over the course of six weeks, the team created a sort of decision tree as to what the exception required the user to do. This included going to a database and finding out which official in the brokerage firm to call, what to ask when a call was made, whether to believe the information, assigning confidence levels to each factor, and a host of other items.

The goal was to provide an embedded expert system that would attach to the preexisting analytical system. The users would turn on the tube each morning and do their customary routines. But there would be an extra added something. This something would be a screen that informed the user of the priority levels of the exceptions that had occurred from the review of the FOCUS report. Let's say that AAA Brokerage had ten items excepted upon review of their report. By the way, excepted items are not exactly like edits. Exceptions are subjective in nature and mean there *may* be a problem, not that there *is* a problem. Taken in combination with other exceptions, and after a thorough review of past historical performance, a good investigator may uncover a problem that even the firm knows nothing about. This is called financial analysis and the folks at the Exchange are very, very good at it. And FORCE/ESP makes them even better. A screen pops up for AAA Brokerage that prioritizes these exceptions, the advisor indicates whom to call and the questions to ask: it's a sort of script assisting the user in investigating the problem.

Using Natural Languages.   With over four hundred people plying the regulatory trade, the access to the dozens of databases and gigabytes of data became something akin to climbing Mount Rushmore while on stilts. It was hard and there was a lot of backward movement before any real progress was made.

This "gang" of 400 is made up of accountants, lawyers, and examiners. They spend their days, and many nights, monitoring the compliance of the hundreds of members of the New York Stock Exchange to the various and sundry Exchange and SEC rules. These regulators use thirty computer systems, including thousands of programs, to ply their trade. Unfortunately, it was found that some plied their trade better than others. The major difference was in computer literacy, or for some, computer comfort.

Before the computer, there was paper. Regulatory staff members were inundated and could not perform their mandated regulatory goals in a timely or effective fashion. Third-generation computer tools certainly helped in the storage and preformatted retrieval of huge amounts of data. It became something of a challenge to attempt to write a retrieval program for every variation of a request. Staff programmers even created forerunners of fourth-generation languages. Something, however, was missing.

The gang of 400 found it difficult, if not impossible, to react in a timely fashion to changes in the marketplace. In the work of the regulators, the marketplace is carefully monitored and the impact on the financial condition of the members of the New York Stock Exchange is assessed. For example, if a civil war in South Africa should affect the price of certain commodities, they would want to determine who would be affected adversely by analyzing position holdings.

So, early in 1983, the Exchange embarked on a study to determine whether or not it was feasible to bring in a tool that would negate the use of expensive programmers for ad hoc inquiries to the multitudinous databases. The study concluded that it was indeed a good idea to pursue this lofty goal of programmerless programming. So they went about searching for the right tool. The tool RAMIS ENGLISH was selected. At that time the product was supported by a small but intensely research-oriented company located in Princeton, New Jersey. Since then, Mathematica Products Group was taken over by Martin Marietta, which in turn, sold the division to On Line Software, which now supports the product. At the time, it was one of the first mainframe, natural language products available.

There were really two products. One, RAMIS, was what is called a fourth-generation language—used by both programmer and end-user as productivity tools. They are a lot easier to use than traditional programming tools so users take to them as ducks take to water. For example, if we wanted to write a program listing all names and addresses on the Human Resource file it might take a hundred-line program. Using a 4GL would cut this down to just a few lines. In RAMIS, this inquiry would look like:

```
TABLE
FILE PERSONNEL
PRINT NAME AND ADDRESS
END
```

Some users found even this quasi-programming language too syntactically rigid to use. RAMIS ENGLISH was the ultimate end-user tool. The user could type in nearly free-form English to access data that was needed.

The real power of a natural language product, other than its syntactic and semantic parsing capabilities, is the ability to recreate business lingo during the user/computer session. This is usually done through a dictionary (called a File Specific Dictionary in the RAMIS ENGLISH product). It enables the definition of one-word or many-worded synonyms for a field definition (the names for which are often "Greek" to users of the system). So instead of having to use the technical name, GL-TOTAL-ASSETS, the term "total assets" can be substituted.

RAMIS ENGLISH uses four internal dictionaries:

- a root dictionary of over five thousand root words that is hidden from view. This is the base dictionary.
- user file-specific dictionaries
- a dynamic dictionary used for the duration of the user session to store knowledge collected by RAMIS ENGLISH during a dialogue. Usually this would be a result of the user creating a new variable such as TOTAL ASSETS. The user merely issued the command LET TOTAL ASSETS = ASSETS A + ASSETS B.
- RAMASTER, which is the internal dictionary that describes the live database being used.

Despite intensive dictionary usage, ENGLISH's strategy is much more complex than keyword search and match. The basic mechanism revolves around the natural language device of using an internal knowledge base consisting of rules of grammar to dissect or decompose the inquiry sentence into its different parts.

The secret to the Exchange's success resolved around an intensive period of eliciting knowledge so that dictionaries could be built. This was no mean feat. On some regulatory files, each record is composed of no less than 1,000 entries. Each entry could go by many names, some formal, some colloquial. These all had to be entered into the dictionary to make ENGLISH "regulatory-smart."

A good dictionary includes all the possible variations. For example, New York Stock Exchange firms are encoded within a rather cryptic five-digit number. Very few users relate number 12345 with Merrill Lynch. More frequently they use the firm name or, what's worse, an abbreviation such as "Merrill," "MLPFS," or "Merrill Lynch." They wanted to give the user the illusion that the computer understands, so great pains were taken to create a user dictionary that would be user-friendly.

The dictionary-building process for ENGLISH can be compared to building a thesaurus. And this is what took all that time. Input and output forms were analyzed, phone conversations were listened in on, many conversations were had with many users, brainstorming sessions were held, and even a contest was sponsored. By the time this dictionary-building process was over, the users were so excited that too many entries were obtained. To be exact, over two thousand entries were created in a little less than two months.

The dictionary-creation process enables the adding of phrases, verbs, reference file names and semantic categories. The most intensive effort was in the word/phrase section, the heart of the dictionary. This specification permits you to enter easily synonyms, selectors, values, and new fields for the file. The Exchange used the synonym and selector components extensively.

CMD: _____

WORD/PHRASE SPECIFICATION

Enter Word/Phrase or exit: total assets_____

Check definition types desired and fill in relevant information:

__Synonym for: _____

__Value for RAMIS II field named: _____

__Group Field: _____ _____ _____ _____

_____ _____ _____ _____

__Defined Field Named t1 ____**with format = d13.2 and defintion of I0540 + I0740** _____

__Library Preposition of _____ **With Groupname** __

__Selector If _____

FIGURE 6-2.   Simulation of ENGLISH Define Field Feature.

For instance, to define "Merrill" as a firm, "Merrill" was entered as a word/phrase. Under selector, the statement IF NUM EQUALS 12345 was coded where NUM is the RAMIS field definition for firm number and 12345 is the value of the firm number for Merrill Lynch. This can be done any number of times for the same selector, so you could enter an infinite number of variations. The synonym feature was used to great advantage by capturing the different ways of saying the same thing.

As another example, let's look at the FOCUS report and its items of financial information. Each item has a description and an item number. For example, cash is item 200 on the report. RAMIS and the users know this item as I0200. Under ENGLISH, a synonym was created for this rather hard to remember name and it was called CASH.

The define-field feature is also beneficial because it permits the creation of new fields from existing fields without adding anything to the rather large databases. Figure 6-2 shows an example of the definition of a new field called TOTAL ASSETS by specifying its formula as the sum of items 540 and 740. TOTAL ASSETS is now accessible as is any other field.

Figure 6-3 shows the powerful verb component that permits you to enter filler-type words so the user can speak to the computer in complete sentences without ENGLISH questioning a particular word. This feature permits you to tailor the session to the specific user domain by capturing user terminology.

Once the dictionaries are completed they pass through a verification process that checks for ambiguity and other syntactic problems.

After logging into RAMIS, a user may choose between ENGLISH and RAMIS. The user enters ENGLISH by simply typing "English." At this point, ENGLISH asks for the name of the file to be accessed. After this is done, the user is now free to converse with the computer in natural English.

When an ENGLISH request is entered, it is interpreted syntactically and semantically. Next a database inquiry is generated and a report is formatted. One of the regulatory systems processes complaints submitted to the New York Stock Exchange against a broker or a firm. The Exchange processes thousands of these complaints each year from two discrete systems. One processes complaints sent directly to the Exchange by the public and the other system processes complaints sent to the Exchange by the member firms themselves. Much analysis is done on these

```
CMD: _____

   FILE-SPECIFIC DICTIONARY MAINTENANCE
   VERB SPECIFICATION

Enter each verb on a separate line. To exit, do not enter any data.
Simply press enter.

Verb

bought _____

sold _____

traded _____

       _____

       _____


   PF 5 = Exit  9 = PFKeys    12 = Help
```

FIGURE 6-3. Simulation of ENGLISH Verb Feature.

files to pinpoint problems in the industry as a whole or in a particular firm. A complaint record consists of, among other things, type of problem, broker, location of problem, and resolution.

The ENGLISH request "How many complainants were there in 1989?" produces a response of "2026" from the system. The next user request, "list them," produces a listing of the the names of the complainants. More importantly, "list them" demonstrates the powerful feature of referring back using the pronoun "them."

After several years ENGLISH has become part of the landscape at the Exchange although the RAMIS component is much more popular. The reason—ENGLISH misinterprets much like a person. And when a crisis is at hand, users opt for the safe route to their data rather than the smart route.

THE SEC'S FINANCIAL STATEMENT ANALYZER*

Poison pills. Golden parachutes. No safe route here. In the hostile world of high finance, the savvy investor burns the midnight oil to ferret out the healthy from the ailing, the stars from the merely profitable. Calculator in hand, financial statements are poured over searching for the true meaning behind the numbers. Footnotes are read and re-read looking for the subtle "truth." Success comes slowly when one pair of human eyes must absorb extraordinary amounts of minutia. Finally, in the wee hours of the morning, eyes red and weary our investor says, "Eureka."

No two financial statements are exactly alike. For starters, page layout is different from firm to firm. To make matters worse, most firms make heavy use of parenthetical remarks and footnotes. And, to hammer in the final nail of the proverbial coffin, captions or labels are often "creatively" defined. Our intrepid investor better not turn off the coffee pot just yet, as analysis of more than just a few of these financial statements can be coma-inducing.

There really must be a better way! This must have been the war cry of our friends at the Securities and Exchange Commission several years back. Like our dauntless investor, analysts at the SEC are charged with analyzing financial statements. Instead of a few at a time, thousands need scrutinizing. In fact the SEC receives well over 10 million pages of written material a year. For those of you clever souls with calculators, just figure out how many pages a day that is. If the SEC staff were to work 365 days a year, they would have to read merely 27,397 a day. So what's a poor SEC regulator to do?

Enter EDGAR. No, not a he but an it. EDGAR stands for Electronic Data Gathering Analysis and Retrieval system and it's pretty high-tech for a government agency not known for it's technological fortitude. The concept was, and remains, brilliant. Firms would file their data

*This section originally appeared in a column that I wrote for *Expert Systems* journal. I thank again Auerbach Publishers for permitting me to refresh "An Intelligent Financial Statement Analyzer," originally published in the Summer 1990 issue. Reprinted from *Expert Systems*(New York: Auerbach Publishers).© 1990 Warren, Gorham & Lamont Inc. Used with permission.

electronically via an on-line EDGAR terminal, magnetic tape, or floppy disk. EDGAR speaks fluid word-processing, up to 85 different dialects. It's not EDGAR's voracious appetite for documents, but its super-sleuth prowess, that makes jaded AI aficionados sit up and take notice.

Sadly, EDGAR is going forward out of the pilot stage without its AI progeny. ELOISE (English Language Oriented Indexing System) and FSA (Financial Statement Analyzer) "were impressive... but the cost and time scale was prohibitive," so laments David Copenhafer who is the Deputy Director of EDGAR management at the SEC. Joe Carter, head of the Arthur Andersen Artificial Intelligence consulting practice, insists it was leftover Reaganomics that burst the AI bubble.

The bubble is impressive. Combining the cream of the crop of AI concepts, FSA takes the narrow domain of financial statement data and turns it into knowledge. The world of financial analysis is necessarily limited to such nonesoteric concepts such as CURRENT ASSETS, ACCOUNTS RECEIVABLE, LIABILITIES, AND STOCKHOLDERS' EQUITY. If this sounds eerily like Accounting 101, good, you're catching on. Financial concepts form a natural hierarchy permitting the expert a hand in structuring the knowledge base. This hierarchical structure is also a natural AI network enabling logical inheritance from the account level (ASSETS) to the subaccount (CURRENT ASSETS) level. Figure 6-4 shows a simplified version of the hierarchy called ASSETS.

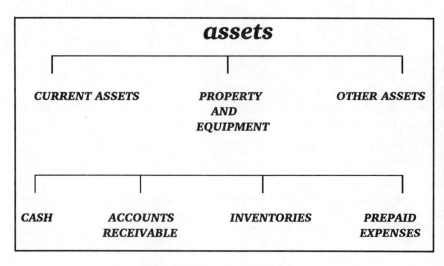

FIGURE 6-4.   Assets Hierarchy.

AI's object-oriented coding fits the hierarchical FSA structure like a glove fits a hand. Using Intellicorp's KEE software tool, each accounting concept within the chosen prototype domains of Balance Sheet and Income Statement was defined as an object. ASSETS is an object, as are its children CURRENT ASSETS, PROPERTY AND EQUIPMENT AND OTHER ASSETS. Each FSA object has one function and one function only—FIND YOURSELF. Higher level objects are able to decompose themselves by passing a message to a lower level object. And what's this message? You guessed it—FIND YOURSELF. This is done recursively until all components of one level of decomposition have found themselves. According to Bruce B. Johnson, partner at Arthur Andersen, which is the consulting firm whose AI expertise was enlisted for the prototype, the FIND YOURSELF function is done by looking through the input document and intelligently analyzing the captions or labels that it finds. A text analyzer was developed to parse the free-form footnotes. Once all values are found, they are passed back up to the highest level object where ratios can then be calculated.

Before these ratios can be calculated, the data has to make its circuitous way from the filing firm to the AI workstation. Financial statements come from a company's 10K and 10Q forms, which are customarily filed with the SEC in a paper format. About fifteen hundred firms are associated with the pilot and are using automated means to transmit their data. And each and every one of them seems to be tickled pink with the facility that EDGAR gives them in transmitting their reporting requirements. Once transmitted to the pilot IBM 4381 computers, it is possible for the SEC to download data to the Symbolics 3600 LISP machine on which Arthur Andersen runs the AI prototype.

Once on the LISP machine, FSA offers the financial analyst an interactive session. After choosing a company and a year to work on, the system can display any of the firm's documents on the workstation screen. At this point, the analyst can invoke the ratio calculations. Several ratio calculations are available. The *quick ratio* is used to measure a firm's ability to satisfy short-term obligations without resorting to inventory sale. The *debt-to-equity ratio* is another popular ratio, which is a common measure used to determine how much of a firm has been financed by short-term debt.

To perform these calculations, FSA must interpret line item captions even though they may be listed many different ways. FSA understands the caption within the contextual meaning of a section of the state-

ment. For example, a caption like OTHER may be recognized to mean
OTHER RECEIVABLES or OTHER CURRENT ASSETS. If a particular caption cannot be found, FSA is smart enough to take alternative
measures. If CURRENT ASSETS is not found, FSA sums its component
subaccounts: CASH AND CASH EQUIVALENTS, ACCOUNTS RE-
CEIVABLES, INVENTORIES AND PREPAID EXPENSES. Using the
natural language parser, FSA understands highly detailed footnotes and
parenthetical notes. For example, a company shows an ASSET total for
the year 1990 of $97,061,000. A parenthetical note of the form: (in-
cludes temporary cash investments: 1990—$69,712) is examined. The
FSA shows the adjusted CASH figure to be $27,349,000.

The FSA workstation screen shows a facsimile of the financial statement on the left half of the screen, while the right half is reserved for
FSA ratio display and commentary. Figure 6-5 shows Arthur Andersen-
generated examples of the facsimile and ratio commentary.

The commentary displays not only ratios but also the results of expert
system techniques. These more deeply analyze the statement to pinpoint
companies with ratios outside of the norm, companies with aberrant

Company Information	Statement Options	Values found:
The Dun & Bradstreet Corp	Balance Sheet	
SIC Code: 7399	Income Statement	Section current assets has
Document Type: B/S	Footnotes	been accounted for.
Ending Date: Dec 31, 1989	Change Years	
		Cash $27,755,000
1		Short term marketable
2 Consolidated Statement of Financial Position		securities $124,738,000
3 _____		
4 December 31 1988 1989		
5		
6 ASSETS		Quick Assets $426,680,000
7		Total Current Liabilities
8 Current ASSETS		$285,896,000
9		
10 Cash and Cash Equivalents 37,470,000 27,755,000		
11 Marketable Securities 245,908,000 124,736,000		
12		
13		Interaction Pane
SEC Financial Statement Analyzer		Main Options Select Company Initialize System Set Parameters Record Session

FIGURE 6-5.   Financial Statement Analyzer.

historical increases or decreases, and companies with unusual balances in any line item.

And there seem to be some unusual goings-on recently. Had FSA been "live," it would have caught a rather unsavory case of financial statement doctoring. MiniScribe Corporation, a computer disk-drive maker based in Colorado, was caught with their fingers in the "balance sheet" cookie jar. "The balance sheet was scary," says MiniScribe director William Hambrecht of the sudden jump in receivables to a whopping $173 million from $109 million. Inventories were similarly doctored from $93 million to $173 million. This spectacular sales gain had, in fact, been fabricated. And worse, the company didn't know if it could produce accurate financial statements for the prior three years. And no one, not the Board of Directors nor their accounting firm nor any of the various regulators, noticed anything wrong until early in 1989. Given the free-form nature of a financial statement, it's no wonder that MiniScribe's "cooking of the books," as the Wall Street Journal so succinctly put it, was not uncovered until it was too late. But suppose FSA had been turned loose? What would have happened then?

FSA would have applied its robust AI techniques in decomposing this free-form statement into its balance sheet components. Then the expert system would have taken over searching for anomalies. It would have pinpointed the run-ups in receivables and the bloated inventories as outside the norm, raising a red flag for all to see. In other words, FSA would have nailed them.

And in doing so it would perhaps prove to the weary and timid investors that the white hats do win sometimes. "It would be a shame if the government cannot figure out a way to make EDGAR happen. The general public is beginning to question how safe it is to put its money in the market. I think something like EDGAR can start building confidence again," argues Arthur Andersen's Carter.

The SEC white hats have another super-sleuth tool in their AI arsenal. The ELOISE for EDGAR is FSA's all-powerful sister. ELOISE was born out of the desire to analyze the electronically stored EDGAR filings to find items of interest to the SEC examiners.

ELOISE is a heavy duty, natural language processor whose prototype domain is limited to proxy statements. Keyword searches lack the sophistication to understand the nuances of a sentence. ELOISE can be taught to understand a concept. This information is then stored in the knowledge base along with knowledge about financial vocabulary used, as well as general information about the English language.

Proxy statements are written in free-form narrative and are often obtuse in nature. The concept knowledge base permits ELOISE to find a given concept with alternative wording. The staff at Arthur Andersen uses the following example that clearly shows two sentences, taken from two different financial statements, discussing the same concept:

1. "A proposal to amend the Company's Restated Articles of Incorporation to increase the number of authorized shares of Series Preferred Stock from 150,000 to 10,000,000 and to make certain changes in the terms of the Series Preferred Stock."

2. "Proposed Charter amendment 2 would increase the authorized Common Stock from 6,000,000 to 20,000,000 shares."

Both sentences have to do with anti-takeover measures. ELOISE recognized this and brought them to the attention of SEC staffers who had requested examples of anti-takeover techniques.

Where are EDGAR, FSA, and ELOISE? The SEC has awarded a contract to BDM corporation, which is a subsidiary of Ford Motor Company. With BDM in the lead, Mead Data Central of NEXIS LEXIS keyword searching fame, was enlisted for information retrieval software. For now the AI component is dead, killed by prohibitive costs. Alas, Arthur Andersen is waiting in the wings for the day EDGAR is on its feet and ready to run.

TRADING THEORIES TAKE ON A NEW ALLY—AI

"Computers Challenge Stock Market Gurus"
"Bold New Theory Could Make Investors' Day"

These are headlines in the trades. Everybody, from the chairman on down to the janitor who dabbles in securities on the side, is waiting for smart trading systems to take their bow.

Our friend Charles Dym was a pioneer fourteen years ago and he's a pioneer today at the Pittsburgh-based Intelligent Technology Group. With his AI-analytic approach to trading that seems to outperform the S&P 500, AI is getting a really good name on the Street.

Dym is your atypical Wall Street quant. He talks theory. About the Modern Portfolio theory, which is the wont of the Street. Here, it is stated there is reason for everything. Even though there's reason and rationale to all things, these reasons may not be easily seen or understood. On the other extreme is the Random Walk theory, which insists that everything that happens is at random. Dym's novel theory falls somewhere in between. His approach is to first establish the odds and then utilize a consistent investment strategy.

"Human judgement is a wild card in my theory," Dym explains. "My method works like a casino. It plays the odds and plays a consistent game, and the odds work progressively in the house's favor."

Dym's model works with the information that's readily available, no secret stuff here. The model decides rather than advises, which is somewhat of an anomaly in an era of advisor systems. The model buys groups of stocks and follows them consistently. It uses a buy-and-hold strategy, making recommendations quarterly. Dym's model also works with readily available hardware and software. Running on a DEC PDP-10 minicomputer, it is written in Fortran IV with the Oliver Database Management system for the expert system front-end. Sporting a rule base of thirty rules, it works with down-loaded information each night to bring up the answers bright and early in the morning.

Dym's theory defines risk as a function of the decision-making methodology used by the model. Choices are based on the probability that their portfolios will exceed the S&P 500 a certain percentage of the time. In certain portfolios, the performance is expected to exceed the S&P 500 ninety-seven percent of the time. Dym believes that risk and reward are inversely proportional to each other and not symmetrical as other theories tend to predict. Risk is based on a "probabilistic analog in which a continuous, consistent strategy is played and to which the advantage steadily accrues." Although the behavior of one individual stock may be random, the behavior of groups of stocks are considered by Dym to be probabilistic rather than random. This will produce stable behavior and this model's logic understands this behavior. His model also understands the three major groups of players in the market. The fundamentalists, the technical analysts, and the modern portfolio theorists all collectively represent stable behaviors probabilistically.

The Intelligent Portfolio Manager (IPM) is being used exclusively by the Starwood Group, an investment firm with over $1 billion in assets under management.

Since Dym's expert system-infused trading strategy works like a charm, and because it is so radically different from the way traditional fundamental research and technical analysis is done, this is one expert system that could forever change the face of the Street.

TO HEDGE OR NOT TO HEDGE

There they sit. The gamblers. Eyes glued to the gaming table. Millions are lost and won in the flicker of an eyelash. Beads of perspiration quickly wiped aside with damp handkerchiefs. Knots in the stomach. Eyes red with fatigue. Minds calculating the odds. Making quick decisions to hedge their bets. This game is not played out in Atlantic City, it's played out twenty stories above Wall Street. And the gaming table is the block trading desk.

Traders have to have strong stomachs and nerves of steel. After all, they're putting their firm's capital on the line in the name of institutional trading. The smart ones hedge. Think of a seesaw. Little Joe jumps on but unless his little friend hops onto the other end, Little Joe will stay firmly planted on the ground. Once Little Nell is enthroned they both giggle happily, balanced perfectly. A shrewd trader will try to counterbalance a large block trade with a combination of products such as options and index futures. This lessens risk and protects the block desks from the erratic movement of the markets.

The trader is only human. Just making it through the tumult of a typical trading day is cause for celebration. To ask a trader to perform complex statistical calculations in rapid fire-time amid all this furor is to ask the impossible.

The smarter brokerage firms recognize the value of hedging but also see the impracticability of asking their already harried traders to perform the necessary calculations to arrive at a hedging decision. The more innovative firms are at least trying. And at least one of them made the grand attempt to install something a bit elegant.

In late September 1987 the Capital Market systems group at Paine Webber in New York decided to expert-systematize the art of choosing a hedging strategy. There is no single strategy but an array to choose from. Selecting among these alternatives is a process involving complex quantitative analytical methodologies.

The head of the Capital Market systems group at the time, W. Leo Hoarty, was presented with a two-fold problem. One part of the problem involved the necessity of "cleaning up" the typically crammed desks of the traders. Traders need instant access to data that typically is displayed on various and diverse terminals. So good idea number one was to integrate all these services under one roof. For the prototype they voted for the Unix-based Sun workstation. This decided, the second problem necessitated making a difficult decision: how to turn the often judgmental knowledge of the art of hedging into a coherent and working system. A development tool was needed that would be easy to work with, easy to change, and would accommodate this sort of specialized knowledge. Paine Webber decided against conventional coding languages, forecasting a nightmare in maintenance and long lead times for development.

Instead they opted for an expert system. Since they had little or no expertise in the building of rule-based systems, they opted to speed up to the top of the learning curve by hiring an outside consulting firm. Los Angeles-based Integrated Analytics was chosen to do the hard part — the knowledge engineering.

Within two months a working prototype was built and within eight months the system was fielded out for beta testing. Paine Webber chose a narrow domain, only one trader handling up to eight stocks. And this most certainly had a lot to do with the speed of prototype development. In addition, however, the ease of use of the expert system tool, permitting rapid insertion, deletion, or change of rules, also accounted for the speed of development.

Paine Webber shrouded this project in mystery. They believed that the use of expert system methodology would most certainly add an extra edge to the competitive sword they carried. So they were necessarily vague about the details of the Hedging Assistant. However, Integrated Analytics published a paper on "Intelligent Trading Systems," which although it discusses an anonymous firm some might deduce Paine Webber ownership.

This paper describes a network of workstations on which traders state the symbol and size of the block they wish to hedge. The system processes through a series of alternative, evaluative algorithms and selects up to four alternatives that reflect the current market as well as adhere to the trader's stated preferences. This is all done in under four seconds, which is the absolute maximum response time for a system in a high-pressure trading environment.

And high pressure it is, especially after the crash of 1987 and the corrections of 1989. We're talking $25 million in losses for the year for the typical big-league firm. So it's no wonder that wise brokerage managements are looking for a better way to handle something as imprecise and inconsistent as individual hedging strategies.

After the initial flurry of activity and publicity surrounding the Hedging Assistant, the system appears to have been put out to the AI pasture waiting to be resurrected during the next market boom.

THE WATCHDOG

Washington Square Advisors manages over $6 billion. With a client asset base of such magnitude this subsidiary of Northwestern National Life Insurance Company decided to use an AI solution to the problem of analyzing the bond market to minimize losses and maximize revenues.

Before the decision was made in 1987 to proceed with development of the system, which was dubbed the Watchdog, two senior financial analysts were given a seemingly impossible task. This was to screen voluminous and quite complex financial data on individual companies of interest. This process required the use of some fifteen ratios to be applied. These analysts searched out increases and decreases of these ratios in an attempt to predict future performance. They attempted to discover causes for ratio fluctuations. They then used this information in their evaluations for each company, which then lead to Buy/Sell recommendations. The financial analysts really needed some tool to help them do this process faster and better. As one WSA analyst put it, "We just cannot process all of this information in our heads!"

Since this was the first endeavor into AI, project manager Chris Evers, wanted to build a system that was not only cost-effective but that would also serve as a base for future AI development efforts. Toward this end, an outside AI company was chosen both for their experience at knowledge engineering and for their AI tool set.

In October of 1987, a notable date for the world's securities and bond markets, a PC-based investment watchdog system that would keep an eye on current and potential holdings was given the go-ahead. Only with the caveat that it had to be complete and show demonstrable value by the end of the year. And that was only three months away.

Apparently PEAKSolutions, based in Minneapolis, Minnesota was up to the challenge. Using the KEYSTONE Expert System Development Environment from Technology Applications, the team managed to pull together an elegant solution that belies its short time frame. The system was developed to act as an assistant to the not very computer-literate financial analysts. It had to be able to access external files such as a commercially available database containing current information on over seven thousand companies. It needed to have a robust form of knowledge representation and inferencing mechanisms to perform the type of financial ratio analysis that was now being done by the expert analysts.

The PC-based KEYSTONE product appeared to have provided all of the above and more. KEYSTONE provides many of the capabilities of the tool sets that traditionally have run on workstations or minis. These include object orientation, use of production rules, mouse-driven graphic displays, and an underlying LISP environment that the programmer has access to.

It was envisioned that the Watchdog would have the capability of real-time access to the corporate financial data of those seven thousand companies. For each company, the user would have the option of selecting different time periods to narrow the financial analysis. At this point, the Watchdog would analyze the performance of each company using the same methodology that the human analysts had been performing for years. This in-depth financial analysis is coupled with the subjective judgment of the human analysts. This was obtained during the knowledge engineering sessions performed by PEAKSolutions. In addition, the knowledge base was made even smarter by loading in the determined causes of previous ratio fluctuations. The system's output is a screening report that shows changes in performance of each company in various sort categories as well as more detailed reporting on each specific company.

PEAKSolutions configured the system into five integrated knowledge bases. Three of the five knowledge bases contain explicit information on how the financial analysis is performed. The fourth and fifth, WDUSER and Watchdog, control the user interface and the current state of the entire system, respectively.

The WDCREDIT knowledge base contains information about the companies that are to be analyzed. Since KEYSTONE is an object-oriented system, objects are used to great advantage here by defining each company as an instance object. Each company object contains both financial and human judgment about the company.

The WDDATA knowledge base contains the specifics of the methodology of financial analysis. Showing its well-integrated nature, WD-DATA is able to access WDCREDIT in order to access financial data about a particular company. Once obtained, the financial analysis of the company can be performed. Here, demons are employed to activate the actual calculation of the financial ratios.

Upon completion of financial analysis, the results need to be analyzed to determine a company's financial performance over time and projection of financial performance into the future. This normally human, subjective analysis is performed by employing another knowledge base. WDRULES use production IF . . . THEN rules to approximate the formerly manual judgment applied by the human experts.

The WSA team spent under $100,000 and less than three months in creating a system that had immediate and enormous payback. A human analyst takes over one hundred hours to perform this set of procedures for eighty companies. Watchdog takes under one hour, proving the point that a little money and a lot of expertise and creativity can go a long way.

CONCLUSION

Wall Street is doing more than just dabbling in the area of artificial intelligence. The greatest attention seems to be in the area of trading strategies. According to Bohdan Szuprowicz, a director of knowledge-based systems for Deloitte & Touche, sixty-eight percent of the Street's executives plan to increase their investment in trading technologies. Of this same group fully forty-two percent of the largest firms admitted to using AI techniques.

For the most part, the systems deployed on the Street have been developed out-of-house. They've been consultant-developed, purchased off-the-shelf, or have been developed by smaller investment houses where the head of the company is also the head trader as well as the head of the expert system development project.

Trading theories are quite complex and require a multitude of staff with expertise to carry these systems through to completion. Traders traditionally have kept their expertise to themselves, making it difficult to siphon this knowledge into an expert system. The trend towards utilization of off-the-shelf products seems to support this theory. Off-the-shelf vendors, many of whom we'll meet in Chapter 10, have managed to corral a goodly number of experts to achieve this end.

Still, Wall Street needs to move toward artificially intelligent systems to remain competitive. In an era in which the exchanges are increasingly moving toward off-the-floor trading and where the Big Banks are elbowing for more room, the broker becomes less important as the investor will be able to trade independently. With smaller commissions, brokerage firms will have to look toward increased efficiencies and more intelligent trading.

And Now for the Answer (or at Least the Key)

Cryptograms are unravelled by figuring out the key. Our key appears below, use it to figure out the quote and its author.

a	K	n	I
b	X	o	N
c	C	p	H
d	Y	q	G
e	W	r	S
f	J	s	T
g	V	t	Q
h	L	u	B
i	M	v	P
j	U	w	O
k	A	x	E
l	D	y	R
m	Z	z	F

7

Banks Bank on Artificial Intelligence

OVERVIEW

$\mathbf{T}$ake two dice, one red and one green; give them to a member of your unwitting audience. While you're turning around have this person roll the dice. You're going to perform magic and tell this person just which numbers were rolled. But first a bit of mathematics. Tell the person to multiply the red by 5 and add this number to the number on the green die. Now tell your victim to double the total and add the secret ingredient—the number 11. Now tell this confused chap to subtract the number on the green die and tell you the number. Immediately you know the answer. It's all in the numbers.

Nowhere are numbers used more than in the banking industry, and I say this without hesitation. There's also a great deal of judgment that needs to be applied to these numbers. So it's little wonder that the banking industry has become the leader within the financial services industry in application of expert systems.

From Citibank's natural language money-transfer system to Chase Lincoln's financial planning system, to credit analysis to real estate appraisal to mortgage loan analysis, the depth and breadth of these applications are staggering. That's probably because the type of work that banks do and the numbers of transactions that flitter through their systems are staggering, too.

A survey from the National Council of Savings Institutions displays some pretty interesting statistics. This survey looked into the back offices of 409 member institutions with assets between $50 million and $5 billion. It showed that the banking industry is, and has always been, very reliant on computer technology to service their vast information needs. More than 65 percent of these banks use automated teller machines. And a whopping 79 percent have automated their platform areas showing a banking emphasis of placing smart technology within a customer's reach. Fred White, a vice president of Furash and Company, which performs consulting to banks and thrifts on technology topics, says that even the most technophobic CEO knows that the computer is the lifeblood of the operation.

John Diesem, a senior manager in the Financial Services Consulting Group of Peat Marwick Main in New York, speaks of the new banking buzzword of *competitive advantage* and the necessity for banking institutions to reach for higher and higher levels of technology.

In today's hostile banking environment, banks are no longer assured of the profits of the past and are faced with regulatory changes, competition, and unending mergers and acquisitions. Technology is needed for more than just competitive advantage—it's needed for survival.

Banks need to push away from the tactical data processing of the past. Here the emphasis is on pushing reams of paper through the bank. They need to look to strategic computing. Clark and Wolfarth (1989) make recommendations to apply technology in the areas of managing customer information, developing asset quality tracking, and in the area of expense control. Perhaps tracking asset quality will provide the biggest bang for the buck in application of technology. Here the overriding concern is to control risks and evaluate asset alternatives. Using technology for competitive advantage can also be applied in evaluating asset alternatives, monitoring nonperformance and in performing impact analyses on customer activities.

Knowing how to perform our magic trick puts you at a competitive advantage. The trick relies on a mathematical formula. Whatever number the guinea pig from your audience came up with subtract 1 from the first digit to get the number on the red die and 1 from the second digit to get the number shown on the green die. Let's take a quick run through. Suppose the guinea pig threw a red 2 and a green 5. Multiply the red by 5 giving us a 10, which we add to the green 5 giving us a grand total of 15. Double this 15 giving us 30 and then add the secret ingredient of 11. We now get the total of 41, from which we subtract 5 to get the final answer of 36. Subtract a 1 from the 3 and a 1 from the 6 and we get a red 2 and a green 5. It's magic and so are these banking systems you're going to read about.

AN EXPERT FOREIGN EXCHANGE SYSTEM

Money. A delightful topic. Walking about a foreign exchange trading room and hearing the babble of the trading . . . 50 million in deutsche marks, 100 million yen . . . makes a visitor tingle with anticipation. The amounts are so astronomical and the pace so rapid-fire, the uninitiated get the distinct impression that this is just so much monopoly money.

The Foreign Exchange Environment

For the foreign exchange trader this is serious business. The world of the trader is small. A lot of people are crammed into, very often, small dealing rooms. Shoulder-to-shoulder they sit, stand, and sometimes jump up and down acting and reacting to people and blinking equipment. A stressful environment, this. Sometimes six screens are simultaneously flashing information on currency rates and other market data. Pages upon pages of information streaming by. Under the glow of these displays are the trader's connection to the outside world. Oftentimes 120-line telephone boards are not even enough, so the dedicated trader installs yet new outside lines to reach clients quickly.

And it is quickly that these traders must react, for they cannot afford the luxury of deep analysis. In the bat of an eyelash they must scan and understand volumes of data, assess the historical trend of this data, discard unnecessary information, and finally reach a simple yes or no answer. To sell, to buy.

No equanimity here. Traders have been known to skip lunch, glued to their displays, eyes red and bulging, waiting for an opportunity. And when it comes they seize it and are pleased with being correct somewhere around 60 percent of the time. It's the other 40 percent that's the killer, however. Traders have been known to go out for an innocent lunch to find, upon their return, that the market did a turnaround and a large amount of money was lost. So many telephones have been ripped out in trading rooms by furious traders that Ma Bell has a franchise on the trading floor.

It was to this environment that Manufacturers Hanover Trust decided to look for technical innovation. The development of the TARA system (Technical Analysis and Reasoning Assistant) is a case study in how to do everything right in building an AI-based system.

Foreign exchange trading is a prime profit center for banking. It's a legal form of gambling in which you try to forecast which way the price of a particular currency is going. Forecasting is a tricky process. Traders have two techniques that they use to peer into the crystal ball. Using fundamental analysis, such esoteric factors as the world economy, political events, and even market psychology are studied to predict the supply and demand for a particular currency. On the flip side, technical analysis uses the techniques of charting and statistical methodologies to forecast based upon historical trend analysis. Neither method is practiced to the exclusion of the other by the trader; neither approach has any set formula and often rely on the experience and gut instinct of the individual.

It's these gut instincts that Manny Hanny wanted desperately to capture. So a team of heavy hitters was established that could bring the dream TARA to life.

HOW AI INFILTRATED THE TRADING ROOM

Back in early 1987, the trading room management team took Tom Campfield off the line. Tom, a vice president in the investment banking sector, was one of the more senior traders at the bank. His goal was to seek out innovative technological solutions to the problem of enhancing the trading process. This one act—taking Tom off the line—set Manny Hanny up for the success it ultimately achieved. Tom represented the highest level of knowledge in the trading area. He was a most valuable resource with his "hands-on" experience plus his academic credentials in international finance and electrical engineering.

A few miles away, the technology department at Manny Hanny offered a position to Elizabeth Byrnes. With her doctorate in clinical psychology the bank bought itself an expert in eliciting knowledge from human confusion. The successful development of TARA began with the joining of forces of the trading and technology departments.

The newly formed TARA team decided to do an experiment. They knew that expert systems had been developed successfully before. They had some, but not all, of the ingredients of success. They did have a recognized and willing expert in Tom. The area of knowledge they wished to capture was limited to foreign exchange trading, which was a nice narrow domain. And they possessed substantial documentation on the process of trading. What they didn't have was a manageably-sized database. With live data-feeds of thousands of pages of data a day, the problem of data access within a reasonable window of time became the *cause célèbre* within the team. And what they had too much of was fuzziness. In the world of trading, no two experts agree, each relying on intuition. In fact many traders are so superstitious that the dealing room is filled with furry bears, Gumbys and the like that are rubbed, patted, or tossed into the air for luck.

So sifting through this haze of superstition, gut instincts, and inarticulate traders was stupendously hard.

Trader A: "Why did you *sell* deutsche marks?"

Trader B: "Because I had the feeling it was going to depreciate."

Trader A: "Why did you feel it was going to depreciate?"

Trader B: "Well, I just spoke to my friend Joe at Solomon Brothers and he said . . . and then I spoke to my friend Mary at Chemical who does a lot of dealings with deutsche marks and we just got this feeling that the DM was going to go down."

The Prototype

The fearless TARA team spent three months in interviewing the traders. Three months of pulling methods out of the words of the traders. By June of 1987 a working prototype was presented to management. In 1987 the foreign exchange trading department had a comfortable income of $161 million. Management decided that if the system could have an impact of as little as a one percent increase to this income, TARA could survive. Manny Hanny also knew that virtually every foreign exchange dealing room on the street was looking into AI. So they decided to pursue TARA for two simple reasons, honest greed and competitive advantage.

The TARA team set about looking to enhance the prototype to boost the deal success rate of the trader from the level where it hovered at sixty percent. Their team motto was, "Maximize good trades and minimize bad trades." But the team had a problem. Impatient management. They needed to install a working system by December of 1988. A very short time frame indeed. To accomplish a very complex undertaking in a very short amount of time they needed to make quick decisions and sometimes compromise with solutions that were less than perfect.

Luck was on their side, however, during the initial prototype period. They did make the correct decisions. They had selected a powerful and expensive Symbolics workstation. With its 19-inch monitor, TARA is able to process all of that streaming trading data in as many as 50 windows at a time. That's a lot of machine power. The psychological and technical considerations were overwhelming. Data is coming into the system in video form. Previously this data was display only. Now it had to be captured and stored in the appropriate window so the trader could activate the screen on whim. The data also had made to be accessible to the expert programs that used these feeds as input to the "smart forecaster" that was the core of the TARA system. And all of this had to be done in a span of less than three seconds.

To accomplish this end, the team used heavy duty software. While most of TARA was written in LISP, Intellicorp's KEE was used for inferencing and knowledge representation. The knowledge representation scheme used was the rule. At the outset of the project this knowledge base consisted of some three hundred fifty rules, of which about half were related specifically to currency trading. The rules analyze both technical and economic factors. The technical factors can be considered the *dos* and *don'ts* of trading while economic factors use modeling algorithms. It is only after both analyses, both technical and economic, are completed that a trading recommendation is made. KEE's ability to both backward and forward chain through the rule base is used to great advantage when the trader wants to review the rationale behind the expert system recommendation.

And sandwiched between the knock-your-socks-off workstation display and the state-of-the-art software was the trader. All dealers have their own styles. Some use the Gumby approach to trading, some use analytical methods. So TARA had to be flexible enough to open all sorts of doors and windows so the dealer could use the system in many different ways.

A Working System

Using a rich graphical interface to simulate the foreign exchange trading environment, TARA currently is a deployed real-time system. It can be used in two modes: as a skilled assistant and as an experienced colleague. With its knowledge base of both technical and fundamental trading strategies TARA can assist in evaluating any of the thirty-odd technical trading models stored in its innards. It tracks multiple currency, bond, and interest rates, runs algorithms and fires rules to interpret these models. To sum it up, TARA makes recommendations whether to buy, sell, or hold a particular market position. As the price of a currency changes, TARA is instantly made aware of it through the diligent monitoring of the live data feed. Appropriate rules and algorithms are triggered and recommendations and alerts are flashed across the workstation display.

Like a game of tic tac toe, a technical model of any particular currency is composed of Xs and Os. The Xs representing increases in price and the Os, decreases. The model filters out insignificant price movements to permit the trader to zero in on the beginning and end of the trend. Each X or O represents a unit of price. In keeping with the idea of trader-friendly systems, this unit measure may be specified. In Figure 7-1 the British pound is modeled in a point and figure chart. The different columns of Xs and Os represent movement in price displayed according to the box reversal rule. This rule mandates that a new column is started only when the price jumps three boxes. In our example the trader set the unit price at 100 points so each new column was started when the price jumped by 300 points.

Manny Hanny didn't want to spend huge sums of money on just mimicking currently existing technical charting programs. They wanted to lay a foundation of knowledgeable analysis of this data by encoding technical trading rules that know how to use these charts to trigger a buy/sell/hold recommendation.

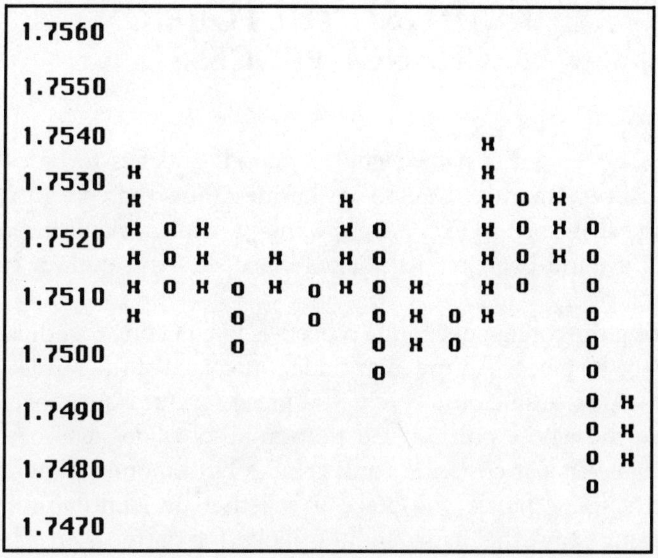

```
1.7560

1.7550

1.7540                                        H

1.7530  H                                     H
        H                          H          H  O  H

1.7520  H  O  H                    H  O       H  O  H  O
        H  O  H        H           H  O       H  O  H  O

1.7510  H  O  H  O  H  O  H  O  H  H  O        O
        H        O        O        O  H  O  H  O

1.7500           O                 O  H  O           O
                                   O                 O

1.7490                                               O  H
                                                     O  H

1.7480                                               O  H
                                                     O

1.7470
```

Source: Manufacturer's Hanover Trust.

FIGURE 7-1.   TARA British Point and Figure Chart.

TARA does not capture all of the instinct of fundamental analysis. It does not yet contain all of the rules necessary to handle the unforeseen economic, business, and political problems that make the market so volatile and mesmerizing. But it has been successful. Unveiled to the traders in May of 1988, at first they were wary of this large, blinking and talkative box. When recommendations TARA made proved to be accurate, the traders passed it off as so much beginner's luck. Gradually one and then another trader began to sidle over to the workstation and sneak a peek. These peeks turned into glances and the glances into steady use of the system.

TARA is at Manny Hanny to stay. It successfully achieved its goal of increasing the bottom line by one percent. In fact the real increase, although secret, was intimated to be considerably more. With its success came a clamoring for more. TARA is an example of expert-systematizing the front line of foreign exchange processing. Let's now take a walk over to Chemical Bank in New York to see an expert system with a slightly different slant on foreign exchange trading.

AUDITING THE FOREIGN
EXCHANGE PROCESS

What weighs 10 pounds and has to be consumed each and every month? Due to its business line that does over $750 billion a year in foreign exchange trading, Chemical Bank in New York generates a mind-boggling 10 pounds of paper. And quite a headache for its auditors!

Auditing the foreign exchange process is like putting together a jigsaw puzzle piece by piece. An irregular trade, one piece of the puzzle, by itself may not appear suspicious. When you piece several trades together you get to see the whole puzzle. And that group of trades may be irregular to the degree that it costs the bank great gobs of money. When you put together a jigsaw puzzle you piece it together by identifying patterns. In the same way, the bank auditor looks for patterns in identifying problems. Unlike a jigsaw puzzle, the number of pieces here is in the thousands.

Before the Expert

Before FXAA (Foreign Exchange Auditing Assistant) was developed the auditing staff had to use the printouts generated from the electronic trade-recording system. This system kept track of such details as date, time, price, amount, currency traded, broker, and branch.

Using this heap of data were the auditors who performed their task every 18 months. This was a manual process in which the manual entries were reviewed and spot-checked in an attempt to identify suspect trades. Due to the sheer volume of this information, there was no way that these auditors could spot all problems. You'd need an army for that. And Chemical ran the risk of letting these problem trades slip by unnoticed. So FXAA was born.

An Expert Auditor Is Built

Chemical Bank bought the expertise of Inference Corp. Their knowledge engineering skills as well as their ART (Automated Reasoning

Tool) tool were added to the Chemical Bank team to create an expert tool with these features:

- to operate as a decision-support system for human auditors
- to be easily extended to track audit policy and provide in-depth analyses of suspect trades
- to be capable of detecting and analyzing off-market transactions (defined as those transactions made at rates greater than the specified deviation from the average)
- to audit trades well enough so that the human auditors can focus on problematic trades
- to find patterns for off-market transactions
- to provide instruction for less-experienced personnel

This dream was realized when FXAA went into pilot mode. Management also got its secret wish of recovering its investment. It was reported that this investment was recovered after using the pilot version of FXAA on the very first audit.

Where once the human auditors could provide an audit every 18 months, FXAA generates exception reports on a monthly basis. These exception reports now dictate the audit schedule. If no exceptions are reported then the audit is delayed. However, if some serious variances are noted then the audit process is implemented immediately. In other words the expert system points the way.

Don't get the idea that FXAA is a total batch system. It can be that, or it can be run on-line in a more interactive mode. The on-line version displays each day's foreign exchange transactions plotted against average and closing prices. Off-market trades are clearly highlighted. The user can pick one of these transactions and zero in on it. FXAA will respond by displaying the details behind the transaction on the lower part of the screen. FXAA will also provide expertly generated explanations of why the transaction was targeted as off-market. Was it part of a swap? A retail trade? Whatever the reason, the auditor can look to these explanations to search for activity patterns. FXAA can also act in an advisory capacity by recommending items for further research.

Bottom line: the use of this audit expert has permitted Chemical to expand the scope of the audit by an astonishing factor of 30. That's a lot of "bang for the yen."

THE CITIBANK MONEY
TRANSFER PARSER

Yen. Dollars. Pesos. What a nice ring to these words. And sometimes words have a way of getting all jumbled up on messages. Do you remember the movie *Close Encounters of a Third Kind?* In this classic Sci-Fi the skies were darkened by the enormity of an alien spacecraft. It was kind of common as spacecraft go. You know, oval with blinking lights. What was different was its attempt to communicate with us lowly earthlings. The aliens, which turned out to be skinny little bald creatures, attempted to speak to us via blinking lights and music. This message was a sort of an intergalactic Morse code. Well the humans on the ground looked up at this monster spaceship in awe and scratched their heads trying to figure out just what the aliens were getting at.

Getting at the Gist

Getting at the gist of the message was terribly important to our Sci-Fi crowd for it meant world peace and galactic harmony. Back on Earth getting to the gist of the message means money to hundreds of banks that wire billions of dollars in the thousands of funds transfer messages that are telexed or SWIFTed criss-cross the globe each day.

At Citibank the crew in the Institutional Bank International Service Management department would have done marvelously well in interpreting the musical message of our little alien visitors. Each person in this unusual entourage seems to have a musical alter ego. The lead ego plays keyboards and acts while the rest of the group either acts, sings, or plays the harp. This isn't as unusual as it sounds.

Expertise in the natural languages branch of artificial intelligence requires a unique perspective. After all, what kinds of people like to sit and look at a word and say to themselves, "I know that this word means these two different things in these two contexts. What are all the other contexts?"

The precision of musicianship coupled with the love of the fluidity of the human language make for fireworks in the application of natural language. Why is natural language needed for funds transfer? In a word the answer is marketing. A second word here is customers. Bank customers like to take the easy way out. They're paying big bucks to the banks to move money from one account to another. They want to do this transfer as easily and quickly as possible. They do not want to be encumbered with rigid formats and procedures. They just want to type an English message on a telex and press GO.

"Pay through Chase for the account of San Juan Bank to the account of John Doe."

"Pay to John Doe of San Juan Bank through Chase."

There are as many ways for a message to be written as there are tentacles on aliens from Mars. Conventional programming systems, those that do Accounts Payable and Human Resources, can't cope with the irregularities of the English language. When the study of AI opened the door for use of natural languages in business, the big banks did a jump-start and forged into the heady world of international funds transfer.

Citibank jumped into the deep end of the pool in the institutional banking area about five years ago. The forward-thinking Citibank management decided that natural languages could be the answer to the question of how to process the thousands of garbled fund transfer messages received by the group each day. They wanted to develop a smart system that could determine whom to debit, whom to credit, which reference numbers to use, which account numbers to use and all within a short period of time.

So an AI project was funded. As was the way in the mid-1980s, Citibank did a search of outside consulting firms who could do the project. At that time AI was surrounded by a cloud of mysticism. AI was unique, sexy, and couldn't possibly be done by your every-day programming Joe. Citibank fell into the trap that so many commercial houses had already fallen into. The "Can't possibly do it unless you have a Ph.D from MIT" trap.

When Dr. Expert was finally hired he was held in such high esteem that the everyday ordinary practicalities of system management were discarded, or at least overlooked. No systems planning. No documentation. They flailed and Citibank failed.

Like the mythological Phoenix, Citibank resurrected itself. Resurrection came in the form of one young natural language expert transplanted to New York from California. Greg Parkinson is a guru. An expert in LISP and one mean keyboard player. He also likes to talk in his own

disarming way about the events leading up to the successful implementation of his series of natural language systems. Greg was hired to pull
Citibank out of a hole. Citibank had spent a goodly sum and had little
to show for it.

When our hero arrived he was told, "There's a lot of people here
who believe that it's only possible to do AI with a Ph.D. And no one
with a Ph.D, who's smart enough, would want to work for the bank. So
that's why we have to go to these consulting companies. But, we don't
believe in this. We believe that, properly managed, these systems can
be successful and that someone who knows what they're doing and has
a fair amount of experience can achieve as much or more than a person
who has a Ph.D from MIT. And the way we're going to prove this is by
getting the system done in three months." Quite a mouthful.

Well Greg walked right into it, didn't he. Evidently he's made of the
right stuff because he achieved success, but not without a few sleepless
nights. The first problem was the AI tool that was at Citibank at the
time. A good natural language tool is many things. At a minimum you
would want to have the ability to put in word definitions and patterns.
The tool that they had was your very basic pattern matcher. Greg and
friends worked long and hard at giving the tool more intelligence. They
gave it the ability to do contextual understanding. They gave it the
ability to do generalization.

Alpha Searching

Greg found that a lot of mythology had been built up around the
tools that had been provided by the consulting companies. Part of this
excess baggage was what is known as the Alphasearch interface. This
slightly smart program was written to compensate for the often nebulous
manner in which bank customers write the name of the sending or
receiving bank in the message. For example a bank in Tokyo would
send a money transfer to Joe at Citibank New York. Which Citibank?
Operators at the receiving end spent much time in looking up the left
out information. The original Alphasearch was left untouched for two
years. The users, however, compiled a list of over two hundred items
that were wrong with it.

Now rewritten, this smarter version of the Alphasearch hits the right
button between 80 to 95 percent of the time. Not your ordinary name-

lookup function, it uses natural language methodologies to do spelling corrections, expand abbreviations, understand synonyms. It knows that the Commercial Bank of Ghana is the same as Banque Commerciale de Ghana. It knows that Manufacturers is short for Manufacturers Hanover Trust. It also knows that Security Pacific is not enough information. Is it Security Pacific National Bank or Security Pacific Asian Bank?

Picking out the right city in a message is even more difficult than figuring out the right bank name. The secret of a successful money transfer is the interpretation of both bank name and city. You get a message, "Swiss Bank Zurich Pay through Chase New York." A person viewing this message would immediately interpret the message as pay through the Chase New York bank, which is a bank name.

For the computer, it's not so easy. Remember it's looking for two banks and two cities. In this case it could interpret New York as a designation rather than as part of the bank name. And then there's the problem of messages that contain complete addresses and the street names within these addresses that contain cities. How about New York Avenue, Chicago, Illinois. As in all things automated there is a danger that this smart system is too smart and will correct these addresses into something totally different from what they're supposed to be. To compensate for this, Citibank provides human staff members to verify each one.

Structured versus Unstructured Messages

An average money transfer message is one page long. All messages that are routed over the telex are unstructured, free-form English of approximately one page in length. SWIFT is another method of sending instructions across the wire. The SWIFT service forces a structure on messages sent across the wire. Given the structured SWIFT format and the unstructured telex format, bank customers sometimes garble the two. So what you get is pseudo-structure typed into the telex. Since the SWIFT format is a bit like Morse code, there is a great potential for system confusion. So the team wrote what they call a shunt program to determine which format the message is in and pass it to the appropriate processing program.

With all this expertise in money transfer message deciphering it's no wonder that the bank decided to expand their horizons and use natural language technology in reimbursement claims message understanding. Here the system analyzes a rather free-form message of the ilk "I didn't get my money." The system determines whether or not this claim is a new one or old one and then routes the message to the appropriate human staff member at Citibank.

The User's Reaction

And what do these humans at Citibank think of their AI smart computer systems? As Parkinson so delicately puts it, "Some users understand, some users don't." Some users did understand that this was a fuzzy process. No such thing as 100 percent accuracy. You're always dealing in percentages. Many users are quite uncomfortable with this notion. They were born and bred in an era of—the computer is always right. It takes time to make them understand that if you have less than 100 percent accuracy it doesn't mean that it's broken. Still, many distrusted the system to the point of backing out a release of the system when a very large error was made. The problem was, whose mistake was it—people's, machine's, or both?

At the same time that this particular release of the AI system went in, the bank began receiving messages from a new bank customer. This customer had a whole new way of sending in messages, complete with uniquely formatted dates. A whole slew of payments were incorrectly sent out by Citibank on the wrong date because of the way these messages were interpreted by the system. Well, the head of the department blew a gasket and the system was sent to the corner with a dunce cap. Upon careful investigation they found that the system was making the same mistakes as the human operators. So our little dunce was called back from the corner and forgiven.

What Citibank Learned

What did Citibank learn from its foray into the wild and wooly world of natural language-based systems? Right off the bat they learned that the best idea was to manage consultants yourself. Don't let them run wild and bypass normal systems control just because the comfort level with the technology is low or because everyone is in awe of the sheepskin diplomas owned by the guru that was hired. Manage. Manage. Manage.

Brace the staff to handle less than perfect results. In natural language systems you're always dealing in percentages. Greg Parkinson recommends determining up front just what the minimally acceptable percentage is so that you have an adequate return on investment.

Using natural language techniques in deciphering money transfer messages will become a standard in the financial services industry and, of course, any AI-laden trading system is also bound to become the norm. However, it is in the area of credit analysis that the banking community will find AI techniques to offer the power punch.

AND NOW FOR THE MOST POPULAR EXPERT SYSTEM IDEA— CREDIT ANALYSIS

A man strode into a bank and asked to borrow $100,000.

The loan officer, handing him an application said, "Certainly, sir. Can you give me a statement?"

"Yes," said the man. "And you can quote me. I'm very optimistic!"

From Gerald F. Lieberman, an actual teacher of humour who has taught the likes of Jackie Gleason.

Ah, the smell of money! Or nowadays, plastic. Open any wallet and out will fall two American Express cards, one personal and one corporate, two Visa cards, two Mastercards and a slew of various department store charges. Americans have taken to buying things on credit like an oinker takes to a mudbath. We revel in it.

$613 billion. That's how many dollars we owed to banks, finance companies, and assorted other credit grantors in 1987. And quite a large portion of this debt can be considered . . . er, deadbeat. So what's a poor financial company to do?

Banks, finance companies, and the like are in a tight bottleneck in their race to compete for mortgage, credit card, business . . . ad infinitum . . . credit dollars. The bottleneck occurs when the loan goes out for credit review. While these credit institutions really do want to grant you the loan, they need to be extra cautious just whom they grant credit to.

The art and science of projecting the credit worthiness of individuals and investors is called credit analysis. Here the underwriter attempts to piece together a financial puzzle consisting of many, many pieces. If it's a mortgage you're after, the underwriter looks at such things as your income and debts as well as the type of neighborhood the house or apartment is in. If you're a business, the underwriter looks at revenue, assets, liabilities, cash flow, and a host of other minutia. The object here is to grant the maximum number of loans with the minimum percentage of bad debt.

This takes time and experience to accomplish. There have always been automated credit analysis systems. But now there are expert credit analysis systems.

Several vendors have jumped on the expert system bandwagon knowing a good opportunity when they see one. First Security Bank of Idaho in beautiful downtown Boise has been innovatively using Financial Proformas' FAST credit analysis software for years. Financial Proformas, based in Walnut Creek, California built a system revolving around 550 proprietary rules in its goal to create a system that produces historical analyses and forecast assumptions. Another California company, which we will meet intimately in chapter 10, assists loan officers and credit analysts in assessing risk. Syntelligence's Lending Advisor was written to combat the experience void. David LaFluer, vice president of marketing, explains that 50 percent of the people making loans today have under five years of experience. Using expert products gives these five-year and under babes in the woods the experience level of 30-year veterans and speeds up the process by 30 to 50 percent to boot.

How do these systems work? The secret inner workings of an expert, corporate credit management system were unveiled by two professors who developed a prototype credit granting system for a nameless Fortune 500 company.

Venkat Srinivasan is the Joseph G. Reisman Research Professor at Northeastern University. Yong H. Kim is a CBA Fellow Professor of Finance at the University of Cincinnati. Srinivasan and Kim (1988) set out in the middle 1980s to develop a robust, working expert credit grantor. Prototypes of this nature are often more interesting than ones in the industrial segment since academic models tend to involve leading-edge ideas. In addition, the mix of individuals involved and the numbers of reviews that this project was subjected to ensure the viability and completeness of the finished system.

Development of the system was divided into two segments. As in most expert system development projects, the first step is to elicit the knowledge from a base of one or more experts. In this case our two academics had the cooperation of a participating financial entity. A multitude of in-depth interviews of credit management staff were performed over a period of time. To ensure that they obtained all viewpoints of the credit granting process, the team made sure that they had interviewed diverse staff members across the management hierarchy. They also did a detailed analysis of the actual decisions that were made.

Credit Granting Defined

Their analysis, which was necessarily iterative, found that the credit granting process was composed of two different processes. The granting institution must first determine a line of credit. Second, it must be reviewed on an annual basis. There are always exceptions to the rule and these must be handled to the satisfaction of both the customer and the credit institution. In the Fortune 500 company that participated in the prototype, the rule was that all major credit lines, which are defined as greater than $20,000, are reviewed once a year. Upon review, credit limits can be increased pending analysis of updated information on the customer. The exceptions to this rule are for new customers and customers who have exceeded their credit limits (join the club!).

Procedural rules for the granting of credit are heavily dependent upon the amount requested. At our friendly Fortune 500 company requests for less than $5000 are quickly approved after a cursory review of the application form, while requests for credit up to $20,000 include review of bank references. And when more than $20,000 is requested, then watch out for that Dun and Bradstreet report.

There are so many subjective decisions to be made that it's a wonder any credit is granted at all. Let's say you stop by the friendly Moolah National Bank for a $30,000 line of credit for your new business. You sit down opposite someone in horn-rimmed glasses who grills you for over an hour, interrogating you on such things as "What's the growth potential of your business?" "How are others doing in your location?" "How good is your management prowess?" "What are your bank references?" "What's your market position?" "What is your order schedule like?" "What about the other products that you market?" "What's your payment record like?" "How long have you been in business and have you ever filed for bankruptcy?" and on and on until your shirt is as wet as a sponge and your nerves turn to jelly.

The Prototype

The Srinivasan-Kim system was designed around two phases. The first is a customer evaluation phase where all of the information collected in our little scenario above would be evaluated. This entails the design of both a database and knowledge base to support this grand plan. Once evaluated, a credit limit determination model would be deployed in phase two.

Even though the overall design of the system is interesting and quite insightful, since it is rare to find such a complete specification of an expert-type system; it is the rule base that we are most interested in.

The rule base for both the customer evaluation component and the credit line determination component is really a series of interconnected rule bases. Using 11 different classifications such as financial trend rules, business potential rules, and liquidity rules, the large rule base was able to be logically segmented, which was quite innovative for an expert system built in the middle 1980s. Each segment contained rules specifically for that category. The academics shared several of their rules, which are presented in Figure 7-2.

The judgmental conclusion of rule evaluation is ultimately passed into the credit limit model. Toward this end, what is known as the AHP-based model was chosen to assist in making this all-important financial decision. The AHP (Analytic Hierarchy Process) model had been used in the past in areas such as predicting oil prices, planning, and marketing. AHP, based on the concept of tradeoff, works in the following way. First, the problem is broken down into a hierarchy composed of a set of elements and subelements. The very bottom level of this hierarchy is composed of the specific courses of action or conclusions that are under consideration. Each element is assigned a relative weight using a 9-point measurement scale with 9 being of absolute importance and 1 being of equal importance. You will note that the rules in Figure 7-2 make frequent mention of the word excellent. For the purposes of this prototype an excellent rating was assigned a value of 9 on the 9-point measurement scale. A weight of 3 indicates weak importance of one over another, 5 indicates essential importance and 7 indicates demonstrated importance. The in-between numbers of 2, 4, 6 and 8 are just that—intermediate values between two adjacent judgments. These pairwise comparisons are then evaluated such that global priority levels or weights are determined. In other words the decision making system

Profitability
If sales trend is improving
And customer's net profit margin is greater than 5%
And customer's net profit margin trend is improving
And customer's gross margin is greater than 12%
And customer's gross profit margin trend is improving
Then customer's profitability is excellent

Liquidity
If sales trend is improving
And customer's current ratio is greater than 1.50
And customer's current ratio trend is increasing
And customer's quick ratio is greater than .80
And customer's quick ratio trend is increasing
Then customer's liquidity is excellent

Debt Management
If sales trend is improving
And customer's debt to net worth ratio is less than .30
And customer's debt to net worth ratio trend is decreasing
*And customer's short-term debt to total debt is less
    than .40*
*And customer's short-term debt to total debt trend
    is decreasing*
And customer's interest coverage is greater than 4.0
Then customer's debt exposure is excellent

Overall Financial Health
If customer's profitability is excellent
And customer's liquidity is excellent
And customer's debt exposure is excellent
Then customer's financial health is excellent

Source: Srinivasan and Kim (1989).

FIGURE 7-2. Credit Granting Customer-Evaluation Rules.

is required to respond to such questions as "What is the relative importance of customer background over pay habits?" What this all boils down to is a decision to either grant or deny credit.

In comparison to the non-expert system mode of credit approval, the prototype developed in this academic exercise was deemed to be correct 97 percent of the time, which is quite impressive. Although the prototype omitted many other credit granting components such as keeping track of collateral maturities, it provided an interesting insight into the way an expert system is developed in an area of great complexity. Here, a detailed rule base was gleaned from expert users and associated with a statistical model to achieve the desired goal of accurately and consistently granting maximum credit with minimum losses.

AMERICAN EXPRESS—NO BANK BUT STILL A GREAT EXAMPLE OF CREDIT ANALYSIS

Another company that lives by the maxim, "Max credit, Min losses" is American Express. It's hard to categorize American Express in any of the three slots that describe the financial services industry. What is American Express anyway? It's not banking, insurance, or securities. But it is the ticket to exotic places. Tahiti. Paris. China. It is better known for its unique type of credit card that is low on the credit (since you can't really carry over a balance unless you have a line of credit with an associated bank) and high on the niceties such as no preset credit limit on the gold card, which can get a body into scads of trouble in a duty-free port such as St. Thomas in the Virgin Islands, a town virtually littered with jewelry stores.

Why Expert Systems

Since American Express provides the most popular and prestigious of the credit cards, the gang at the home office is always on the prowl searching out the new and better.

One of the new and better tools that they discovered was a technology tool. They knew that they had a problem. This problem was not unique to the industry. Banks have dealt with this for centuries. It's called bad debt and fraud. In American Express' case, with their huge number of cardholders, it's easy to understand why their losses from bad credit authorizations and fraud would be substantial. Since conventional computer systems didn't make much of a dent in reducing this problem, the idea of an expert system became more and more appealing.

American Express began development of their expert system, to be called Authorizer's Assistant, in the early days of commercial expert system acceptance. Since few companies tread where American Express dared to go, they developed new techniques which, years later, many other financial companies have endorsed in their own journeys into expert systems.

One of these strategies was to create a corporate group that would coordinate this new technology among its several subsidiaries. These subsidiaries were already tackling other expert system projects in such diverse areas as trading, customer service, back-office support, and insurance underwriting. These reflect the wide variety of American Express business interests.

The Authorizer's Assistant was destined to become the *pièce de résistance* of the American Express company and perhaps the single most visible expert system anywhere in the annals of financial services.

In a nutshell, the system assists operators in granting credit to cardholders based on a review of the customer's records. Since there is no preset credit limit, this process can be a bit tricky. The authorizer usually is called into the picture if the customer is making a purchase outside of the limits governed by the normal computerized system. This means that small purchases can be approved by using the ubiquitous telephone, automatic approval device. Here the store clerk slides your card through a slot that picks up your card number, enters the amount, and waits for an approval code. It's when the amount is over a certain level, which is different for each store, that Authorizer's Assistant goes into play.

Developing the Prototype

In developing the system, American Express chose the path of utilizing an outside consulting firm. In this case the firm was the vendor of the product that they chose to use during prototype mode. Inference Corporation sells a heavy-duty expert system shell called ART or

Automated Reasoning Tool. They also sell their services as knowledge engineers. American Express took the package deal.

The goal was to build a system that would assist, but not replace, the human credit authorizer. Using the five best senior American Express credit authorizers, Inference Corp's knowledge engineers went to work at eliciting their knowledge. Their knowledge allowed them to determine whether a current transaction should be approved.

In making this determination the senior credit authorizers reviewed many items such as customer's outstanding charges, payment history, and (my favorite) buying habits. You see, the American Express philosophy is that you can charge anything as long as you pay your bills on time. Gradually, over the years that you have your credit card, you can build up the amount that you spend on your card until one day they permit you to charge a Mercedes on it. Some people have.

The system required about four and a half months to prototype and consisted of about 520 decision rules. It ran on a stand-alone Symbolic workstation. Using a forward-chaining inferencing strategy, the system permitted the authorizers to speed up their review of the customer's files to grant that request faster. This assistant has the capability of guiding the authorizer through phone dialogues with merchants and cardholders. If the situation warrants, it prompts the authorizer for an appropriate inquiry to make of the customer. In addition, as is the forte of expert systems, the system can display its line of reasoning, which is marvelous in the training of new authorizers.

While the prototype contained 520 rules the pilot contained over 800 rules. When it came time for American Express management to review this pilot and provide a yea or a nay for wholesale deployment, they reviewed astonishing statistics. They found a 76 percent reduction in bad credit authorizations. They also found the system to be accurate 96.5 percent of the time as compared to the human rate of 85 percent. Management gave the nod and the team started to plan for deployment of this system to the 300-odd authorizers.

In order to make this system work, the expert system had to be connected to the mainframe as a co-processor. The system also had the constraint that the hardware currently used could not be changed. The authorizer workbench consisted of a 327X IBM terminal connected to an IBM mainframe. Since American Express already made a huge investment in this hardware, it was decided to keep it and embed the expert system. In embedable expert systems, the expert system component is called by the conventional mainline processor. It's not obvious to users that this is an expert system, they just notice that extra ingredient of intelligence.

RESRA: SECURITY PACIFIC BANK'S SMART REAL ESTATE APPRAISER

Perhaps the most difficult credit decision of all is the one in which a bank evaluates thousands of minutia to determine whether or not a mortgage will be granted to an applicant. Dead center in this web of complexity is the real estate appraisal requirement.

Why Expert Systems?

The movie star needed a mortgage. An appraiser was sent from a nearby bank. When the appraiser's beat-up old Volkswagen chugged its way to the top of the hill, its weary little engine finally conked out. Frowning, our appraiser grabbed his briefcase and headed down the road, eyes blinded by the magnificent Pacific coast sunset. All around were tall pines. Nestled here and there were homes hidden in the hills. Our appraiser finally made it to Number 32, which sat atop a hill overlooking the ocean. The buzzer already rung, our appraiser felt a bit uncomfortable in his polyester sports jacket. After what seemed an interminable wait, the door was opened upon an entrance hall the size of a movie theatre. Which, of course, was apropos.

The movie star, dressed in silks, graciously greeted the appraiser with the ubiquitous "Dahling," a catch-all phrase used to greet whomever ambles in—from producer to gardener.

The blonde-tressed and diamond-studded thespian showed the appraiser the indoor/outdoor pool, the tennis courts, the bowling alley, the six bedrooms, the summer kitchen, the winter kitchen, and let's not forget the private movie theatre. All through the tour our appraiser gaped and gasped, oh'd and ah'd.

Scribbling madly the appraiser noted every detail down to the Italian marble on the floor of the two-story doghouse.

Two hours and twenty pages of notes later, our appraiser returned to the now dead Volkswagen. A couple jogging by overheard our appraiser grumble, "I hate her movies—mortgage denied!" And so the bitter appraiser sat in the Volkswagen filling out the Uniform Residential Appraisal Report (URAR) with, shall we say, somewhat erroneous answers.

Foolish little story. But people are only human; envy and greed figure into decisions made each day. When our appraiser got back to the bank, the mortgage was indeed declined. The movie star tried again and again, never knowing that it was her personality and not her property that was doing her in.

Of course, this would never really occur. Still, appraisal is more akin to art than to science. And it was this truism that drove Security Pacific National Bank into the arms of artificial intelligence. Checks and balances. A system to force-feed a bit of scientific consistency into an area deep into human idiosyncrasies.

They first tried commercial real estate appraisal but found out quickly that this task was far too complex for their first jump into the realm of expert systems. They then turned to the residential side and made the decision to develop an expert system that would review the results of that appraisal task.

The Prototype

What would have been the result of the movie star's mortgage application had the appraiser worked for Security Pacific? Let's see. Our now Volkswagenless appraiser returns from a long, long hike. The appraisal report is keyed into the system. Within minutes the personal computer-based RESRA (Residential Real Estate Appraiser, if you haven't already guessed) spits out a log of inconsistencies. After all, how could a $20-million-dollar mansion in a very good neighborhood, with an ocean view no less, be a bad risk?

The form the appraisers fill out, the Uniform Residential Appraisal Report, is logically broken down into sections. The appraiser walks through and makes judgments on such things as neighborhood, site, room, improvements to the property, interior, cost, market, and finally value. Each section of the report has its own set of policies and procedures that an appraiser would know or look up when forming the final evaluation. These policies and procedures can be turned into expert system rules.

RESRA is used by all Security Pacific appraisers in the state of California. Back in 1986 it was only a dream. Security Pacific owns an automation subsidiary aptly named Security Pacific Automation Company. Deep within the recesses of this group there is an AI Technology group in which the multitudinous programmers speak Prolog and C. A Prolog guru was called in who spent a lot of time with two managers of the appraisal process. These were the experts. Within four months a working prototype was created. It worked so well, and was so well-received that the prototype became a permanent part of the scenery.

Security Pacific decided to use this smart new tool for appraisal review and for training. Since mortgages are the bread and butter of any bank it was important not to let the system take over and be the final word. The human appraiser could choose not to use the system at all. And if the system was used and it made a mistake, the human appraiser takes the responsibility; giving the impetus to observe carefully the prowess of the system. The human appraisers found this system so beneficial they gladly took responsibility for it; after all, it reduced the review process considerably. In some cases the review time was cut down from an hour to less than one half hour.

The appraisal process is more complicated than it seems. They look at such things as too many houses in the neighborhood to nearby garbage dump locations to quality of schools to you name it and it's included. So it's no wonder that the appraisers took to RESRA like a fish to water.

Rewrite for Portability

Richard Clements, Vice President and manager of the AI Technology group was always uncomfortable with leaving a system that was built as a prototype in a production mode. Initially that's exactly what happened as the system worked perfectly the first time out. In spite of its success, Clements knew that prototype systems are often built quickly and the eye to efficiency is usually closed. He was also aware that since not too many programmers actually can code in the Prolog language there was a risk to the company of long-term nonmaintainability of the system. Also, he always hated the front end. It was so inelegant.

So Clements' staff rewrote the system in the C language, which is more and more becoming, *ipso facto*, the standard in expert system languages. The front end was entirely reworked with a smarter data entry component so that the appraisal form could be edited as it would come into the system. In doing this he modularized the system, separating the data entry component from the actual expert system. He trimmed the system into a lean, mean dynamic tool, whittling down the number of extra rules used to handle data processing. The rules now in the system reflect only the expertise needed to review the appraisal. The number sits at 650, although Clements' staff is continuing to add, change, and delete rules as the bank's policies change and as the crow flies.

Why did Clements decide to buck popular tradition and reinvent the wheel? There's a whole bunch of prewritten expert system products out there that are touted to do everything and anything your little heart desires. According to Clements, that was the problem. Either the product did too much or it did too little. Too much and it used up too much juice in the computer and gave him an overhead headache. Too little and he had to try to get into the package to do his own tuning; he compared this process to trying to get into Fort Knox.

So RESRA was born of expert appraisal skills and expert programming skills. And the next time our movie star went for a mortgage loan she made sure the RESRA system was used.

MAI: A USER'S VERSION OF A REAL ESTATE APPRAISER

RESRA was created by one of California's "big banks." However, the profession of real estate appraisal is filled with independent agents with some real solid experience behind them. Here's a story of one of them with a novel expert system idea.

No matter how complicated the mortgage process is, real estate appraisal is trickier. The reason in one word—judgment. The art of appraisal comes from the judgments formed from years of experience. This is one business where the use of heuristics is rampant.

Heuristics is not quite enough. Any AI real estate appraisal system worth its salt should have the capability of recognizing plain English. In this way the appraiser can have a detailed conversation with a smart, computerized colleague.

This is, in a nutshell, what one certified appraiser suggested to his peers. Brent J. Dreyer has been an appraiser since 1978. And he's now hard at work on joining his appraisal expertise to his computer expertise by building an expert real estate appraiser.

So Dreyer has some pretty good insight as to just what would constitute a good expert appraisal system. First on the list is the computer's ability to understand ambiguities in an appraisal lexicon that is filled to the brim with ambiguity. For example, if asked to list all apartment sales where the unit rates are greater than $50,000, the system should inherently understand that what is being asked for are the sales of apartments that sold for greater than $50,000.

An intelligent dialogue between the appraiser and the computer would sound something like:

Appraiser: Start the appraisal session.

Computer: How tall is the building in feet?

Appraiser: 60.

Computer: Is this a clear height or is the measurement to the roof line?

Appraiser: I don't know what you mean. Please explain.

Computer: The roof line is measured from the floor to the surface of the roof while clear height is generally less than the roof line height. Clear height is measured to the bottom of the joist or ceiling surface.

Appraiser: This measurement is a clear height.

Computer: The building has 60-foot ceiling heights; it is likely that this is a special-purpose building with craneways. Does this building have cranes?

Appraiser: I don't think so.

Computer: Is there a R-41c format requirement for the report?

Appraiser: No.

Computer: Good. The status of R-41c is in limbo. Do you wish a cost approach?

Appraiser: Answer a question for me.

Computer: Yes.

Appraiser: Were there any vacant industrial land sales in the area recently?

Computer: Wait. I'll search my records . . .

Note that Brent Dreyer's dream appraiser, discussed in the January issue of *The Appraisal Journal* (1989), includes some very strong features. Not only is this an expert system with a natural language front end, but it's an integrated one. It can access external databases to find just what has been sold in the area, it answers questions, it deals with ambiguity and it speaks a pretty good version of English. Trust a user to come up with something and the user usually does.

THE CITIBANK PENSION EXPERT*

It's not the ides of March that scare us but the ides of April. The specter of taxes causes weak knees and fits of despair in the strongest of us. We spend the days before April 15th mired in a cocoon of pencils, calculators, and self-help tax books. Fortunately, April 15th comes but once a year for the mere mortal; but the processors of those giant pension funds are not so lucky. For these banking institutions, withholding taxes need to be calculated on a daily basis for hundreds of thousands of pensioners. For them, this is taxes with a twist.

Citibank is one of the largest banks in the world. Its parent Citicorp boggles the mind with 90,000 employees, over 3000 offices and $200 billion in assets. Their data processing functions were decentralized long ago. In fact, they have more data centers and more dollars invested in technology than a fair to middling-sized foreign country. Citibank is segmented into three major business lines: Individual Banking, Investment Banking, and Institutional Banking. A common thread among these three diverse areas is the Corporate Technology group. It is these gurus who set the standards and make recommendations; but, it was the hot shots in the line area that really got expert systems heated up.

Citibank-IBM Joint Effort

Abhik Dasgupta is a quiet man with a burning passion for expert system technology. When a joint IBM-Citibank study was initiated in November 1987 to determine a flagship project for expert systems, Abhik

---

*This section originally appeared as an article in the June 1989 *AI Expert*. I would like to thank *AI Expert* for their courtesy in permitting me to reprint it here. Reprinted from *AI Expert*, June 1989; Copyright 1989 Miller Freeman Publications.

jumped at the chance to get involved. IBM and Citibank looked at three very diverse possibilities in the many far-flung areas of the bank. The first possibility was a Statement System. The goal of an expert system here would be to process prior period corrections of security transactions—a sort of retrofitting of transactions. Another possible system would be in the stock and bond area where the system would identify dividends in a complex world of stock splits and interest declarations. Last but not least was the system finally chosen. Pensions are big business to any bank. Hundreds of thousands of checks are processed and mailed to retirees every working day. What sounds like a simple process is complicated by the complex structure of the differing tax laws in our country. The Feds are one thing, but each state and local government is different. Any pension system must be able to process a check with the correct deductions depending on where Joe actually lives and how many exemptions he takes. If Joe lives in New York with a wife and three kids, his pension check will look different than had he moved to Kalamazoo, Michigan.

In 1986 Peter J. Coughlin found that he had a problem. Peter, who's a Vice President at Citibank, was handed the news that California had passed a new tax law that was to have a profound effect on his then COBOL-based pension processing system. This COBOL system had only the capability of processing federal taxes. The specter of adding the differing, and quite, complex state tax laws was quite unnerving. The COBOL system was dutifully modified in early 1987. It was a 120-labor/day effort for the state of California alone. The estimation for adding the remainder of the states to the system made Peter think there had to be a better way.

When IBM and Citibank began looking at the pension processing system as a possibility, Peter and Abhik pushed hard. Their efforts paid off, as DOLS (Disbursement Online System) took flight. And none too soon, as the user demanded that the final system be implemented no later than June of 1988 and it was already January.

The Prototype

Lesser men (and women) would be mortified at having to learn a new tool and new techniques as well as implement a real, not a prototype, system in a six-month effort. The Citibank-IBM team was apparently up to the job. Citibank had one constraint, the system must be developed on their IBM 3084 MVS/XA system, forcing the developers into the untried domain of mainframe expert system shells. Around this time, the majority of expert systems were being deployed on AI workstations or personal computers. Given the hundreds of thousands of transactions and the very large databases filled with tax and pensioner information, the mainframe platform was the only game in town. The IBM mainframe expert system shell, Knowledgetool, was selected as it exhibited the richness of tool set that was necessary for the system. Using a consulting paradigm, Knowledgetool employed forward and backward chaining as it processed each DOLS transaction by residence of the pensioner.

The Knowledgetool inference engine, written in PL/I, is touted to be a high-performance expert system shell. It uses a very efficient, but proprietary, algorithm for pattern matching. Astute users of the tool do well to employ the OS PL/I optimizing compiler on their applications as this serves to increase throughput. Citibank found that use of this tool actually enhanced the performance of the system over the more conventional COBOL approach. Remember, they already had a good benchmark completed with the COBOL system only recently redesigned for the state of California. In fact they determined that they had a decrease of 14.3 percent in clock time in the running of the expert system version of California.

How do the guts of Knowledgetool work? It processes a knowledge application in a *recognize-act* cycle (or for you conventional programmers, loop). As shown in Figure 7-3, the inference engine matches rule conditions to existing class members and updates the conflict set with the instantiations recognized. We now have a set of rules ready to fire. This is the heart of the process and Knowledgetool uses an IBM version of the OPS5 algorithm, one of the fastest available. During the second step of this process the inference engine attempts to resolve the conflict set. Here it chooses which rule, among many, to fire next. Citibank took the option of controlling or predetermining the order of rules, which is a Knowledgetool feature. In the last step of the cycle, the rule selected is executed, or to use expert system parlance, fired. The rule fired is procedural and might add, change, or delete class members or might even fire a nested recognize-act cycle for a nested block of rules.

Like most large MIS shops, Citibank's programming language of choice was COBOL. In fact, only one staffer had ever used PL/I. Knowledgetool, written in PL/I, had structured its development environment using a syntax similar to PL/I as shown in Figure 7-4. So when the project was begun, Citibank was far behind the eightball. They were

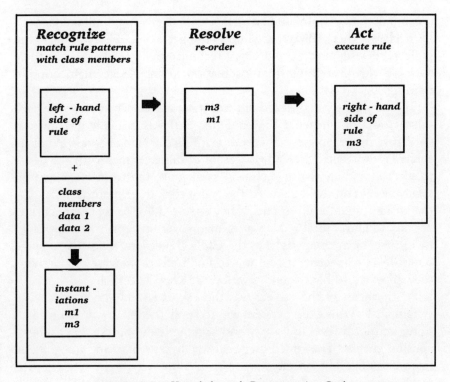

FIGURE 7-3. Knowledgetool. Recognize-Act Cycle.

```
Spend_Cash:

    WHEN (i=>item (i=>owner not = 'me')     /*when we have an item*/
                                             /*whose owner isn't me */
      & m=>money (m=>cash > i=>price        /*and I have more cash */
            )                                /*than the price of the */
    BEGIN;                                   /*item then buy it.     */
      m=>cash = m=>cash - i=>price;          /*Take its price from   */
      i=>owner = 'me';                       /*cash and make me it  */
                                             /*owner.                */
      CALL INFLATE;                          /*Recognize inflation  */
    END;
```

FIGURE 7-4. PL/I syntax of Knowledgetool.

unfamiliar with AI, unfamiliar with Knowledgetool and unfamiliar with PL/I. Here's where IBM stepped up to the gate. Since this was a flagship project, they supplied large doses of technical help. IBM was right there to assist with everything from installation to knowledge engineering to training.

The project team consisted of three full-time staff members, one consultant, and one intrepid IBMer. Since PL/I was virtually unknown at Citibank, the group spent one week learning the fundamentals. Another three days was spent in Knowledgetool training. Armed with the desire to succeed and all of this technical know-how, the team spent two intensive weeks on the design. At the end it took three months to develop the entire system, soup to nuts. They averaged five to six complex rules per day to find a total reduction of manpower usage in the range of 12 to 13 percent in comparison to the COBOL version. Since the original senior-level management goal was to find tools to increase productivity, they appeared to have found a winner in Knowledgetool.

At the heart of the project was the expert and his knowledge. The system goal of this expert system was to apply the tax law at the federal, state, and local level uniformly and accurately during the processing of pension checks. The stated user goal was to automate and integrate all tax processing. The unstated goal was to eliminate the System's department interference and let the business unit run with the ball. Walter Feldman, Vice President for Pension Disbursement at Citibank, acted as disseminator of tax information. It was Walter who created the rules, based on information from the Tax Department. And it was Walter who was heavily involved in testing the accuracy of a system that would need to pass muster with the auditors.

Since this system would deal with disbursements of millions of dollars, each evening the team tested and tested and tested some more. A case history approach to validation of the system was used. This is a tried and true method of testing for expert systems as it permits a parallel test of the expert system versus the current system or the manual method, whichever is applicable. In this case, the team jointly worked on a representative sampling of test cases. Each test case was run through the expert system and then compared with the results arrived at manually. The user painstakingly compared all test results. After all, one misguided rule could result in Grampa John in St. Petersburg receiving a surprising windfall. Testing completed, the user department gladly signed off with a flourish.

DOLS

The DOLS knowledge or rule base contains over one hundred rules. Since some of these rules were generic, that is, they apply to all states, the total knowledge base can be considered to contain over two hundred rules. The team, practicing the "art of structured design" and having learned from the much publicized mistakes of several of our forerunner expert systems such as DEC's XCON, organized the rules by state of residence or jurisdiction. This method provides for easy maintenance. In the case of DEC's XCON, the system which assists in the configuration of DEC's one-of-a-kind computers, the knowledge base was composed of more than ten thousand rules. Rules were entered into the system in no particular order, making it a nightmare when a rule needed to be modified or erased. The new and enhanced version of XCON now contains such structure, but DEC paid dearly to have it enhanced. Fortunately for Citibank, the design team combined their conventional data processing experience, which is characterized by a love for the organized, with the new mysterious art of expert system design to create a structured knowledge base.

DOLS can be considered a two-tier system. On the front lines is the user interface, or "Chinese menu," permitting users to modify the tax parameters in the knowledge base. Bringing up the rear is the overnight processor. Issuing hundreds of thousands of checks is by no means a real-time application. In the dead of night the conventional component of DOLS performs mundane processing routines. On ready standby is the DOLS expert system, carefully embedded into the system architecture, eager to make decisions about withholding amounts for these complex check disbursements. Pension data is stored on a standard IBM VSAM file. One of Knowledgetool's fortes is the ability to integrate easily into the standard IBM VM or MVS batch or on-line environment. Interfaces exist for the IMS/VS, DB2, and SQL/DS databases as well as "hooks" for the PL/I, COBOL, FORTRAN, Pascal, and Assembler languages. This permits Knowledgetool to integrate fluidly with any existing application through one of the interfaces or hooks, as was the case with Citibank. In effect, the expert system acts similarly to any other called application, the only difference being in the sophistication of the processing.

Right on target, the first week of June 1988 saw the unveiling of the most sophisticated pension processor on the street. And the only one to use an expert system at its center.

CHASE LINCOLN'S FINANCIAL PLANNER

People have always depended upon banks for advice. With the addition of new regulations and new products it's not as simple anymore to give this advice.

Nowhere do they feel the pinch more keenly than in the United Kingdom. With the impending formation of the European market in 1992, the roar of complexity crescendos. According to Mike Pickup, a manager with the London-based company of Sema Group Business Strategy Advisors, this has forced U.K. firms to jump both feet first into the pool of expert systems for financial planning.

Although there is a large profession of independent financial advisors, bankers have long since realized the necessity of providing this service. Not only has it commonly been done, since the days of yore when Grandma Annie Oakley requested her bank manager to plan her investments for her, but it has the potential of becoming a profitable business line as more and more people become more and more confused about their financial options.

Joining the traditional financial planning system to an expert system opens new vistas. Obviously it permits people with more limited skill to utilize the functionality of the system. This would open up the floodgates to provide financial planning services at a local branch level. Come in off the street to make a quick deposit and get a quick financial plan. And it is definitely a money maker. Pickup's research has shown that people would gladly fork over from fifty to two hundred dollars to be able to walk out with a comprehensive financial plan.

And what a boon to the bank's information banks then to have all of that financial data on its customers on its computers. This data could most certainly be used to market other banking products, providing the banks with a most valuable competitive weapon.

One bank that has taken this advice to heart is Chase Lincoln Bank located in Rochester, New York. Their system, the Chase Personal Financial Planning System, is so innovative that it actually won an award from the American Association for Artificial Intelligence. Now, that's quite a feather in their cap.

With the help of Arthur D. Little consulting experts, the Chase Lincoln team worked for five long years to develop a system that takes the tedium out of working with 30,000 pieces of financial data. Geared to customers earning from $25,000 to $125,000 a year, this expert system handles more than 60 different investment options. The net result of the system is the publication of a 75- to 150-page plan, laser-printed, replete with graphics, tailored specifically to the user. These statistics are mind-boggling when one puts the figure at about $10,000, which is the cost of a very complicated financial plan that would consider many of these 30,000 variables.

Now with the use of this expert planner Chase Lincoln's financial planning department is no longer losing money but making money.

EXPERT SYSTEMS AND THE SAVINGS AND LOAN CRISIS

The problem with the savings and loan was too many bad loans losing money and not enough scrutiny. If we had an automated system that analyzed these loans in the same way as a most senior reviewer, what do you think the result would be? So, could the S&Ls have been saved by an expert system? I hazard a *yes!*

I am in esteemed company. Peter J. Elmer and David Borowski think so, too. Elmer just happens to be the Director for Investor Analysis at Fannie Mae and Borowski is the Risk Management Analyst at Freddie Mac. And Fannie and Freddie are very knowledgeable about just this sort of thing.

Elmer and Borowski (1988) developed an expert system prototype that analyzes the financial health of a savings and loan institution. They discovered that expert systems are a useful predictive tool; their prototype tested out as superior to more traditional tools in its performance 7 to 12 and 13 to 18 months prior to bankruptcy.

S&L System Design

The primary knowledge source of the Elmer/Borowski system came from the Federal Home Loan Bank Board's (FHLBB) *Examination Objectives and Procedures Manual*. Additional sources of knowledge were expert, industry analysts and others with extensive S&L experience.

These rules, which form a risk matrix, act upon S&L financial conditions by using publicly available financial data to produce a single index ranking of financial health.

To produce this ranked index, a series of financial ratios and other statistics are first applied to the available data to determine whether an S&L is a traditional or nontraditional S&L. From the knowledge sources Elmer and Borowski developed some 27 significant ratios, a sample of which is shown in Figure 7-5.

It is important to make this distinction since two different automated support systems were built to deal with these differences. A traditional S&L, which is the more common of the two types of S&Ls, is one whose principal business is originating mortgages through the use of bank deposits. A nontraditional S&L, on the other hand, is variant in that it has some unique features that makes standard analysis of it impossible. Here an automated expert support module segments these S&Ls and ships them out for further review by a human analyst.

This expert support module recognizes three types of nontraditional S&Ls through use of ratio analysis. The first type are mortgage bankers who rely on fee income rather than the traditional spread between deposits as liabilities and mortgages as assets. The second type of nontraditional bank is known as a *conduit*. These typically possess very large amounts of liquid assets for the purpose, most typically, of generating arbitrage income. The last nontraditional S&L is one that owns one or more subsidiaries. These are given the nontraditional label due to the FHLBB not requiring consolidation of subsidiary financials with their parent.

GNW/TA	*GAAP NET WORTH/TOTAL ASSETS*
GW/GNW	*GOODWILL/GAAP NET WORTH*
RL/TL	*HIGH-RISK LOANS/TOTAL LOANS*
ORA/TA	*OTHER RISKY ASSETS/TOTAL ASSETS*
ARM/TA	*AJUSTABLE RATE MORTGAGES/TOTAL ASSETS*
VL/TA	*VOLATILE LIABILITIES/TOTAL ASSETS*
MBS/TA	*MORTGAGE-BACKED SECURITIES/TOTAL ASSETS*

FIGURE 7-5.   S&L Bankruptcy Ratios.

Traditional S&Ls

Some 90 percent of savings and loan institutions are traditional. For these Elmer and Borowski used the widely recognized CAEL model for analysis.

CAEL is an acronym for capital, assets, earnings, and liquidity. And it is all of these factors that the model must effectively evaluate. CAEL is composed of a series of ratios that lead to a final weighted-average score that ranges from 1 to 5. The weights themselves were taken from a poll of S&L presidents while the ratios were analyzed using asset-sized segmentation into peer groups. Rules built into the expert system permitted the override of the ratio thresholds set by this peer group comparative analysis. For example, in the liquidity evaluation three analyses are performed: Interest Bearing Liabilities compared to Earnings Assets, Volatile Liabilities to Total Assets, and Liquid Assets to Total Assets. Coupled to these is a rule that states: If stock is exchange-traded and total assets are greater than or equal to $20 million and total CAEL score is less than or equal to 4.5, then add 0.5 to total CAEL score.

The CAEL expert system effectively mimics human analysis. Because of the integer nature of its ranking mechanism (i.e., increment or decrement score) the system adapts readily to the changing environment.

Testing the Expert System

Elmer and Borowski tested their expert S&L predictor by performing an analysis of S&Ls for the 1986 time period. It then used these results to attempt to predict 1987 first-half failures.

Two other bank failure models were used to correlate results. The researchers found that their model outperformed either of its competitors in predictive performance.

Elmer and Borowski praise the use of an expert system as a more robust tool for use in distress-prediction models. They stress that models that are based solely on historical correlations are not adaptive to the new environments that the S&L industry finds itself in.

A DUO OF CHASE MANHATTAN BANK SYSTEMS

What's the link between credit card fraud and trade products message-processing? At Chase Manhattan Bank in New York, they're both AI systems.

Chase's Technical Research Department is charged with evaluating key technologies and products, with an eye toward using them in the wide and diverse business units. Because of the acceptance of AI into the mainstream of technology at Chase, the Technical Research Department is one of the more successful R&D groups in the financial services industry.

Neural Networks and Credit Card Fraud

Chase Manhattan is the second largest issuer of credit cards in the world. With over seven million cardholders, the potential for fraud is great.

Detecting fraud is an almost impossible task, but there are some rules of thumb. Depending on type of fraud it may take up to 45 days for a customer to report the problem. When a card is stolen, the average fraudulent use of it is between five to seven days. Add to this the newest twist where your card is not even stolen, just the number is. And so we have an industry-wide problem where losses run into the hundreds of millions of dollars.

Since the goal of an analyst in this area is to search out patterns of fraud, the Technical Research Department opted for a neural network approach. The project was officially kicked-off in June of 1988. Using NeuralWare's NeuralWorks the team, which was composed of staff from the Technical Research Department and members of the Fraud Operations Department, achieved positive results a scant three months later.

Neural nets come in many flavors. Chase chose the cumulative back-propagation algorithm to develop a relatively simple network consisting of 12 elements.

The Fraud Operations Department cooperated in getting the test-bed set up so the net could be trained. This consisted of 2,000 transactions:

1,000 fraudulent and 1,000 good. The net was able to pick through these examples and develop the patterns for determining possible fraudulent uses of credit.

Trade Products Message-Processing System

Like Citibank, Chase chose a natural language approach to interpreting free-form messages. Like Citibank, Chase was inundated with a large volume of free-form messages that had to be read, classified, and physically separated into separate bins for further processing. One of these processes requires messages that are printed to be reformatted and keyed into a system for transaction processing. This was, to say the least, a labor-intensive task that required special training.

For this project, the Technical Research Department enlisted the assistance of Cognitive Systems Inc. to provide a combination natural language and case-based reasoning approach.

The project was started in the fourth quarter of 1988 but had to be modified due to major hardware and software changes taking place in the area at the time. The project was redefined to concentrate on areas with a larger payback. The scope was reduced to two phases: bank-to-bank reimbursement message formatting and routing of all messages. Phase one was installed in August of 1989.

Chase represents the avant-garde of the old guard in the banking industry. They're not afraid to delve into new technologies. And they're finding that these technologies are affording them with opportunities that traditional data processing never could.

8

AI in Insurance

OVERVIEW

You can take one die of a pair of dice and spin it on its corner like a top with absolutely no problem. The magic is in balancing one die on its corner while standing still.

The insurance industry is caught up in their very own balancing act. It must balance an enormous outflow of cash as it pays claims, against an inflow of premium dollars. Industry buzzwords such as cost-containment and loss-control are the caveats by which these firms, large and small, operate. And there are problems. In Massachusetts the auto insurance sector is in turmoil because the state's insurance commissioner capped the permissible insurance rate rise. As auto rates nationally rose 40.3 percent in the years between 1984 and 1987, the rates in Massachusetts rose only a paltry 11.3 percent.

To make matters worse, a 1988 study by the Insurance Accounting and Systems Association found that the automated systems in use did not meet the needs of the industry. Top insurance honchos are asking for more sophisticated analytics. With rising claims, increased regulation, and inadequate system support we need something dramatic here. So it's with no surprise that these firms are turning to smarter automated systems to keep balanced.

Milwaukee Insurance

"Joe" is your average driver. A couple of near misses, two bent fenders, one speeding ticket. He's twenty-six years old and drives a 1979 Toyota. Joe needs some car insurance. If Joe lives in Milwaukee, he may meet up with your smarter than average insurance agent. This agent may be an expert system.

Using Neuron Data's Nexpert Object, an expert system shell, Milwaukee Insurance has developed the next best thing to an underwriter. Running on a DEC VAX host using a relational database, the Nexpert expert system uses data from the driver's application and information from the Department of Motor Vehicles computer files. Its goal is to reach a conclusion about whether to issue a policy or refer the applicant to a human underwriter for further consideration.

Nexpert is an object-oriented system. In this sort of system, items such as type of auto, age of driver, and past driving infractions are defined as objects. Then they are reasoned about by the standard underwriting policies encoded in a rule format. This encoded knowledge reflects the methodology that a human underwriter would use to reach a conclusion about a prospect.

The introduction of this automated underwriter has permitted an expansion of business without the burden of hiring additional staff. It's also made a great dent in controlling the inevitable insurance paper mountain.

Why AI Is Essential to Insurers

Milwaukee's foray into the world of expert systems is reflective of the rest of the insurance industry. According to John J. Smith, a senior manager for Ernst & Young in Cleveland, two-thirds of the nation's insurers are using or developing expert systems. And three-quarters consider expert systems as essential to their future progress. There are three major issues that are now besieging the insurance industry that can be addressed rather nicely and neatly by expert system methodology.

1. Companies need to increase the productivity and consistency of the average nonclerical worker by making use of the knowledge of experienced professionals.
2. Companies are looking for consistent performance that will reduce risks and improve customer satisfaction while minimizing the impact of turnover in highly specialized functions.
3. Companies want to maximize management decision support and to gain a competitive or strategic advantage in the markets.

Keeping these issues in mind, industry observers see virtually an un-limited potential for the use of AI systems. And while the majority of the current crop of "smart tools" has gravitated around codifying under-writing expertise there's plenty of great ideas out there.

Paula Johanson, a DecisionLink principal consultant, envisions using the AI-brand of systems in insurance marketing. In the past, "when you needed a better response from a list you bought more names." Using this old-fashioned method saw all data treated the same—from group applicants to claimants to customers. When the expert system switch is turned on it will be possible to break down these populations to sub-groups with independent characteristics. The sky's the limit here with the ability to sub-group by such things as age, sex, and geographic lo-cation with the goal as determining likely sales. She goes on to suggest the use of expert systems to define the agent attributes that are the most profitable. And then to use this knowledge base to help in agent selec-tion as well as target marketing new insurance products. And that's not all. She predicts use of this technology to fine-tune premium calculation in the group area by looking at plan attributes, individuals within that plan, and the resultant claims. Dr. F. N. Burt, president of Cogensys, goes even farther down the road of "big brother." He suggests that in the future, systems should be able to detect previous policyholder medical conditions as well as misrepresentation by a policyholder.

Many of these dreams are quickly becoming reality. Even Ernst & Young's John J. Smith predicts invasion in those sacrosanct areas such as strategic business issues. Here insurers can build systems to assist in such creative activities as product development, investment analysis, telemarketing, client profiling, reinsurance, and executive decision sup-port.

Fireman's Fund

The insurance industry is hot and heavy into expert systems. Fireman's Fund's Donald Stratton describes an expert system as an underpinning of the company's auto insurance lines. As the insurance application glows on the CRT screen, the expert system works with the underwriter to make determinations that will help the system decide whether to accept the business and underwrite the policy. Questions are of the ilk "is the vehicle standard or nonstandard?" The underwriter and the system work in tandem each coming up with a decision. The expert system not only suggests a decision. It also displays the elements of risk it has uncovered and compares this risk to the company's "ideal risk profile." Using this system, Fireman's Fund reduced its loss ratio by a resounding five percent.

CIGNA

CIGNA, one of the largest insurers, uses an expert system to help their clients keep track of proliferation of employee health care claims. With the huge numbers of medical claims and the ever-increasing costs to industry, more and more companies are looking for help in controlling what some say is a crisis in health-care costs. CIGNA's Medical Management Information System smartly reviews client health-care coverage. It reports and highlights areas of concern and suggests possible solutions.

Hartford Steam Boiler Inspection and Insurance

While cost-containment is certainly a hot ticket and certainly CIGNA's ticket to success, loss-control represents even a hotter ticket for the insurance industry. One Connecticut insurer takes the loss-control issue so seriously that it has developed an expert system that it offers free-of-charge to its policyholders. Hartford Steam Boiler Inspection and Insurance Company is looking to its TURBOMAC and TOGA expert systems to save it millions of dollars. TOGA, or Transformer-Oil Gas Analyst, reflects the expertise of Dick Lowe. Dick has an imposing 30 years experience in the area of electrical insulation and transformer problem diagnosis. TOGA's goal is to determine the health of a transformer by analyzing the mineral oil used to cool and insulate it. Transformers are used by electric companies to convert the high voltage produced by power plants to a level more usable by homes and businesses.

To reach a conclusion TOGA performs a two-step process. First, an oil sample is drawn and then sent to a lab for chromatograph analysis, which determines the percentages of various gases within the oil. The results are then entered into the expert system, which ponders the significance of the results. The way in which the system ponders mimics the way Dick

Lowe would normally analyze the concentration of these gases. Using about 250 to 300 rules the system successfully agrees with Lowe 100 percent of the time in determining whether there is actually a problem. And it agrees with Lowe 90 to 95 percent of the time as to what caused the particular problem.

TOGA's big brother, with over 9,000 rules, is TURBOMAC, which is also a diagnostic expert system. This system detects problems in turbines and other rotating equipment. Costing up to $500,000 each time a turbine is taken out of commission, TURBOMAC is an important cog in the wheel of loss-control. Because of the complexity of the turbine engine as compared to a transformer, TURBOMAC does not come up with a definitive answer but a series of answers ranked by probability of likelihood.

Superagent

TOGA and TURBOMAC represent perhaps the most innovative use of expert systems in the insurance industry. Perhaps more mundane, but to the policyholder as important, is the ability to pump up the agent to the level of superagent in knowledge about different policies. To this end there probably are few insurers who have not implemented or at least thought about implementing smart policy manuals. Nippon Life of Japan has already succeeded at codifying their complex policies and procedures. They had to. With over forty thousand applications a year, they were swamped and needed to speed up the process. Before the expert policy manuals, a Nippon agent took five to six years to become expert. With the expert system it now takes only three months.

CoveragePro

The Dallas-based research and publishing firm of IRMI (International Risk Management Institute) agrees wholeheartedly. They are publishing a series of expert system manuals collectively called CoveragePro. Together with the firm of Intelligent Insurance Systems, they have already unveiled its first progeny—the Umbrella Analyzer. This expert manual contains a knowledge base of information on more than seventy-five umbrella policies. Not only is a smart manual used to determine the disparity between the umbrella policy and the underlying liability policy; but it also makes policy improvement recommendations.

Lincoln National Reinsurance

The perception within the insurance industry itself is that the life/health side of the industry has been quicker to adapt to expert systems than the property/casualty side. Perhaps what has aided this process is the commercial availability of some expert systems such as the one developed internally by Lincoln National Reinsurance. The Life Underwriting System or LUS is unique in that it addressed the entire scope of the underwriting process.

From soup to nuts, LUS begins at application development time and chugs along to the time the policy is either issued or declined.

Insurance Needs AI

Perhaps the newest fly in the ointment is also the most interesting. Although the neural network is still in the incubator stage, there is a lot of talk about using it in underwriting. After all, underwriting is basically the art of approving or not approving policies based on some ideal historical norm. That's exactly what neural nets do best.

Using actual underwriting decisions, the net could be "fed" these examples until a substantial network is built. Hence, any new applications for policies that come in could be passed through the net in which the substantial knowledge base of examples could be employed to make a consistent decision. On the flip side, data from the application can be used to build a net that would predict what losses an applicant would generate for the insurer.

The insurance game is no game of dice. The secret to our magic trick is in setting one of the two dice on the table with its one-spot up and setting the other one atop with the corner perched inside the one-spot. Like magic, the die will balance. But unlike the ease with which the dice were balanced, the insurance industry needs all the help it can get in balancing costs against income. Conventional automation has remained status quo and permitted the industry an unprecedented level of growth in the last decade. However, it is the expert system and other advanced technologies that will keep the firms solvent in an era of increasing claims and costs.

NERSys: A CURE-ALL FOR CLAIMS

These angels in white are indispensable not only to the nursing profession but to the insurance industry. They are used, not only inside the walls of the hospital, but outside as well. Nurses are used to advantage in the processing of the thousands upon thousands of medical claims that are kicked out of the many mainline claim processing systems at the many medical insurers across the country. And these highly experienced men and women are in very short supply.

Blue Cross of Western Pennsylvania felt this crunch. They decided to do something radical about it when four nurses left within a very short, 18-month time span. What they lost was irreplaceable. A total of scores of years of experience in reviewing the approximately twelve thousand possible diagnoses and four thousand procedures known to medical science.

Blue Cross of Western Pennsylvania had an advantage. David Gorney, now director of knowledge engineering for the company, started to delve into artificial intelligence systems years before. In the complicated world of medical insurance there were certain problems that never had adequate computer solutions. AI tickled his fancy as he began to see it as a solution to the impossible. His first system was a resounding success. Called Plan Tracker, its purpose was to review the performance of the company's diverse medical plans that it operated.

The hurrahs over Plan Tracker gave the Blue Cross management team the confidence that they needed to give Gorney the green light to develop a medical claims processing system. Using Gold Hill Computer's GoldWorks, Gorney's team built a prototype of a system soon to be dubbed NERSys or Nurse Expert Review System.

This jewel of a system uses a model of several nurse/reviewers' logic to accept, reject, or question a claim. Gorney gives an example of a claim for a routine visit to an obstetrician. Using Blue Cross' guidelines, this claim should amount to somewhere between $55 and $75. If a claim were filed for $125 it would be rejected by a conventional system.

However, NERSys noted that this patient was also given a special test in the doctor's office. Therefore, the claim is legitimately higher than the accepted standard and is paid.

The first strain of NERSys is in the pregnancy-diagnosis area. It has become so popular with the nurse/reviewers that the "expert system virus" is spreading and Gorney expects that, before long, much of the claim processing problem will be solved at Blue Cross.

ALEXANDER HAMILTON'S UNDERWRITING EXPERT

On a gray day in the year 1804, two men stood pistol to pistol on a bluff overlooking New York Harbor. A single shot rang out fatally injuring one of the greatest statesmen the infant America had ever known. A fighter in the Revolutionary War, an aide-de-camp to General Washington, he was the first and some say the best Secretary of the Treasury of the United States. Perhaps his greatest achievement was in establishing the financial policy we still largely follow today. His name was Alexander Hamilton.

His legacy was the legend of great organization and careful attention to detail. This apparently has been handed down to one of the companies that bears his name—Alexander Hamilton Insurance Company based in Farmington Hills, Michigan. As an insurer with a network of independent agents, this Alexander Hamilton uses its legacy to great advantage in developing automated tools that keep their not always loyal agents close to home.

How does an insurance agency compete for business? The independent agent has so many choices, and often among them is picking the insurer that can underwrite the policy the fastest and the most accurately. With the deluge of applications glutting the workplace, it's really easy for an insurance company to inundate its underwriters with the flood.

The Cogensys Connection

Mike Wilson, Vice President in charge of the technical area, was chosen to step in and close the floodgates. And he did this with the help of a La Jolla, California company named Cogensys.

This California firm had a good business sense. It built a great tool. And instead of putting it on the rack with the rest of the indistinguishable expert system tools, Cogensys decided to infuse itself with practical business expertise. It aptly decided that the insurance industry seemed a likely target. So it began to look for a company that would be willing to trade its time and expertise for use of the Cogensys "judgment software."

The search stopped in Farmington Hills in the executive offices of Alexander Hamilton. Always searching for ways to increase their competitive edge, Alex's management staff pretty much salivated at the opportunity to apply high-tech to their paper-crunch problem.

Mike Wilson was the perfect choice for project manager. With over twenty-five years of experience in the insurance industry his story was unusual. He had been in charge of the underwriting department before high-tailing it into the computer department. So he was really the best of all possible worlds.

Acquiring Underwriter Knowledge

He says the task was easy. Cogensys was built to soak up knowledge. It does this by what is known as induction. Most systems today use the rule-based format of knowledge entry. The problem with this is that it's time consuming and as Mike says, "experts really don't know how they make decisions." So it's a really painful process to dig in and excavate to piece together these tidbits of knowledge. The Cogensys folks recognized this, too. They also discovered that the way in which experts reach a conclusion is very similar regardless of who they are and what they do. They broke it down into four discrete steps:

- selects the data that is relevant to a particular decision
- categorizes each data element by comparing it to a set of norms or a range of possibilities
- assimilates and evaluates the entire data set in light of prior knowledge and experience, giving greatest weight to the high-priority items and last, but not least
- reaches a decision

Cogensys markets its judgment software as using the same process. With over fifty integrated modules, this PC-based product, according to Mike Wilson, is easy and powerful to use.

So Mike sat down with his expert and rolled up his sleeves. His very first question set the stage, "What do you think about?" Induction software learns the logic of its expert or mentor by observing real examples of the mentor's decision-making process. In the beginning, the system needs some ground rules. These take the form of factors that are considered to contribute greatly to the decision making in the area of choice. These factors are actually phrased as a series of questions. So Mike's universal question provoked great thought in the mind of the expert.

The answer was risk. Risk over insuring the proposed person. So now Mike had what he termed a universe called risk. Now this team broke down this huge thing called risk into logical, functional types of risk. The underwriter might be concerned about prior health, current health, current occupation, and financial ability to pay. In all, they came up with thirteen areas of risk.

Within the underwriting universe, Alexander Hamilton broke it down into thirteen planets. For each of these planets they determined the particular areas of concern. Since underwriters usually work off questionnaires, they found this process tailor-made. These concerns were stated in English. A question would look like:

	normal
Build of insured is:	skinny
	obese
	not known

It was really as simple as developing a series of questions and the list of possible responses. Notice the "not known" answer, which permits the system to handle what we like to call fuzzy logic.

These thirteen planets revolve around a fourteenth, which is set dead center. This fourteenth planet basically considers all the results occurring on the other thirteen planets, does a little work on its own, and comes up with a final conclusion. Not that the conclusion is always black or white. In other words, it didn't always come back accepted or denied; sometimes it came back with I DON'T KNOW. TEACH ME.

Have you ever seen the play or movie *Little Shop of Horrors*? Well Audrey, the man-eating plant, became famous for the line "FEED ME." This is basically what Cogensys does. Instead of blood it wants to be fed knowledge. When it doesn't know the answer, the mentor or expert gets right back on the system and supplies it with the information. This new knowledge is stored in the system and can be acted on the next time a similar situation arises. So the system grows naturally.

Even while Mike was busy feeding the system with knowledge, he was well aware that the underwriting process was choked in a bottleneck. Application forms were entered into a mainframe system and then sent to the underwriter for review. Clever devil that he is, Mike took an unusual approach to the problem. He let the data entry process make the underwriting decision, as shown in Figure 8-1.

Well, why not? Here he was building an expert system. Why not make the data entry process more intelligent, infuse it with the expertise of a senior underwriter? In this way all of the simple applications could be handled automatically while the juicier ones could be referred directly to the underwriter.

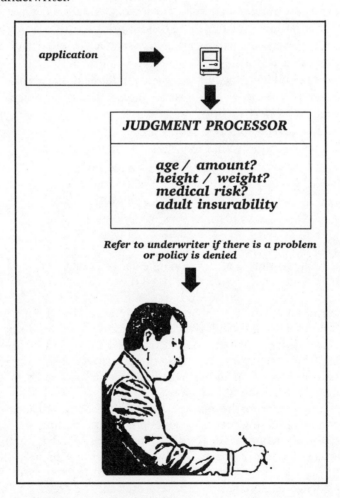

FIGURE 8-1. Alexander Hamilton's Expert Underwriter.

The Induction Model

Using the Information Manager Cogensys module, Mike was able to create electronic forms with the look and feel of the paper form the data enterer was using. A series of thirty-one personal computers were networked together and linked to the Alexander Hamilton mainframe computer so the data entry staff could enter data from the paper forms to the screen facsimile form. Now here's where the intelligence part kicks in. After the data is entered, this smart system takes off and assesses risk using the universe of fourteen problems that we've just discussed. The system comes back with one of three answers. Either yes, approve the application (in which case no underwriter is needed), or NO, or I DON'T KNOW. When NO is the answer the application is routed to a human underwriter. Alexander Hamilton will not let the system turn away any business. For this case and the I DON'T KNOW response, the system asks for help from its mentor. Since the system automatically tracks these requests for help it's easy for Mike's group to keep making sure that these requests for knowledge are being answered. The answer comes in the form of the mentor turning on his or her PC and "teaching" the system a thing or two.

As the knowledge base grows, the system learns the relative importance of each question and actually attempts to extrapolate from prior experience to make decisions about unknown situations. Growth occurs as applications are entered into the system. The Judgment module uses the application as an example. As the roster of examples grows the system becomes more sure of itself and begins to suggest tentative decisions. Eventually so many applications or examples are entered that the confidence level in the system's decision is extraordinarily high. Sounds just like human learning, doesn't it?

The Expert System on the Firing Line

The bottom line was get it in and get it approved. For Alexander Hamilton the summer of 1988 became the proving ground for the use of expert systems in underwriting. Sometime in 1988 Alexander Hamilton doubled its business virtually overnight. Gobs of application forms inundated the data entry department. Alexander Hamilton merely crossed the street to the local community college and hired a crew of smart, but untrained, college students.

Now it normally takes years of training to learn the tricks of the underwriting trade. It even takes three to six months to learn the intricacies of the old mainframe data entry system. With this expert system it took only four hours and the students were on their way. They never could have processed this new business alone. They needed help and they got it with their shiny new expert system.

In the later part of the 1700s, the man Alexander Hamilton forged ahead with his plan for the financial operation of the young country. He was the first expert in American monetary policy. Being the first and, at the time, the only expert he encountered resistance and lack of understanding around every corner between New York and Philadelphia. Think what he could have done with an expert system!

LINCOLN NATIONAL LUS

Headline—*Wall Street Journal.* 1987. The Life Insurance Industry Spends $7 Billion on New Computer Hardware. Now that's a lot of cheese and crackers. What they didn't say is that those crack life insurance folks also spent gobs and gobs on software.

Somewhere in the middle of America is a land called Indiana. It's a land where the grass grows tall and the breeze is scented with the perfume of peonies. Fort Wayne is a small town by New York standards but large when it comes to technological know-how. For smack dab in the center of town stands the building that houses Lincoln National Risk Management, and it was here that they built one of the first integrated expert systems.

Lincoln National Reinsurance created Lincoln National Risk Management for the sole purpose of creating a system that could handle extraordinary amounts of complexity in the area of risk management. This is defined as the selection, pricing, and claims adjudication of insured risks.

LUS System Design

Russ Suever's group developed a three-pronged approach. They would develop a life underwriting system, a claims management system, and a comparative analysis system. Since they felt that the underwriting system was crucial and could serve as a basis for the two remaining management systems, the Life Underwriting System, or LUS, as it came to be known, was developed first.

The project was started in 1987, and the group's search into the expert system marketplace did not come up empty. Working with Arthur Andersen consulting, the IBM mainframe-based Aion Development System (ADS) was selected as the expert system platform.

The goal was to create a system that could streamline operations and give a boost to long-term profitability. This could be done in several ways: by improving the expense to income ratio, by enhancing service to the actual agent, by coordinating risk selection with pricing and marketing, and finally, being able to leverage underwriting with that missing commodity—medical expertise.

Russ Suever, a Vice President at Lincoln, knew that the only solution that would work for them was an integrated solution. And with that as inspiration the group designed a total underwriting solution that included:

- data entry and screening
- a workflow manager
- information display
- underwriting decision assistance tools
- management system for underwriting management

all linked in one underwriter's workstation.

How LUS Works

As in all insurance systems the basic input is the application form. This and other relevant information is stored on a database so it will be ready for the decision-making process. First, the system will analyze the information and make a determination as to what type of case it is. Certain cases are routed to their administration or issue systems.

At this point an expert module takes over to do a bit more complex analysis in the realm of financial, nonphysical, and medical data available. It can also identify underwriting problems such as pre-existing medical conditions or over-insurance. Coupling its extensive rule base to the data at hand, LUS can perform the rote review an underwriter would normally do. The LUS can look at a case and accept it. Or it can recommend additional requirements be met such as a doctor's note. Or it can pass the case to a human reviewer when it is stymied.

As its name implies, the Workflow Manager provides the underwriter with a bird's eye view of the entire process, permitting adjustments and modifications to be made. It forms a sort of audit trail that greatly assists in tying up the administrative loose ends in the final processing of the case.

The part of the system that makes superagents out of agents is the Information Display. The entire Lincoln National Life Underwriting manual has been codified as well as references on medical terminology. Since expertise in these areas is scarce, this expert manual will see to the achievement of consistency in level of expertise applied, which plagues not only the insurance industry but all industry.

Perhaps the most interesting component of the LUS system is the underwriting decision assistance tool set. Using an interactive approach this tool set comes in many flavors. Underwriters use it to obtain assistance in determining how the problems on the application can be underwritten. One way of doing this is by obtaining interpretations and information contained in the expert underwriting manual. Or expert modules can be called in to play that lead an underwriter through the decision-making process by posing a series of questions. When answered, the result is a recommended debit or flat extra rating for the impairment on the application being agonized over. These ratings can be adjusted and a record of these adjustments can be made available for management review.

Management review is an important product of LUS. Of course, standard administrative reports are produced, but the system also provides the data to address strategic issues such as trending. And when some policy issue mandates a change to the logic of the system, a few quick keystrokes see to it.

MONY'S CLUES

Another underwriting system! But CLUES is different. In early 1987 Mutual of New York, or MONY as it is gamely called, installed yet another traditional IBM mainframe system to issue insurance policies. These policies were issued automatically after the data had been entered and the underwriter had given the green light.

MONY was not entirely satisfied with the new system. The missing link was the underwriter's approval, which was painstakingly obtained.

So they huddled around the campfire and decided to do a number of internal studies. They realized that the final underwriting decision was the result of a complex web of hundreds of rules and regulations. If this wasn't bad enough, they knew that the company would be adding new products at a dizzying pace and each of these products would have new rules and regulations. On top of all of this, the team wanted what every other management team in American wants. Consistency and accuracy. With more than 150,000 applications processed each year this was something that they just had to have.

What they needed, they all agreed in unison, was an expert system.

Embedding the Expert System

MONY ultimately hired Teknowledge Inc. out of Palo Alto, California and American Management Systems based in Arlington, Virginia. Teknowledge's emphasis was on the development of the knowledge base. AMA would concentrate on integrating the expert component into the IBM mainframe system.

By April of 1988 nearly all of MONY's agencies, some eighty in number, were tuned into CLUES (Comprehensive Life Underwriting Expert System).

When an application is received from one of the many local insurance companies, data is entered into the conventional mainframe component. An automated search function is then triggered with the system looking up information in such databases as the Medical Information database or the Total On-line Policyholder Database.

At this point CLUES takes over. Approximately 40 percent of the applications input can be handled by CLUES without intervention. The other 60 percent are forwarded to flesh and bones underwriters who use a CLUES review module to make the appropriate adjustments.

Not all experts agree with other experts. The same is true of an expert system. In 15 percent of the cases the human underwriter overrides the CLUES decision. This override forces a textual justification, which is then sent back to the conventional processing system.

MONY used Teknowledge's mainframe expert system shell called S.1. Shells provide robustness for the judgment process but normally do not provide the powerful processing capabilities that a conventional system offers. Nor should they. Linking the expert system to a conventional system permits the joining of judgment power and processing power. On the processing side, the expert system was embedded into the IBM IMS DB/DC transaction and database system. This integration, unusual for its foresightedness, was necessary to deliver a decision to an underwriter out in the field in a matter of hours rather than the manual system's average of three days. Tying the expert system to their NBS or New Business System permits MONY enormous functionality. Now they can perform easily such functions as searching in a variety of mainline systems for informational purposes, sending messages to the various agencies, as well as policy text printing on a high-speed laser printer.

The MONY folks had some really good ideas, didn't they? Another one was to create what they termed a model office, complete with its own floor space. (MONY must be loaded with money!) What it provided them with was the opportunity to thoroughly test this newfangled expert system, train staff, and experiment. And test they did. Teknowledge developed a method for generating test cases. With the 4,500 they developed, an intensive pilot test was performed.

This foray into another case of underwriting wasn't so bad, was it? It demonstrates the power of integrating or embedding expert system methodology into conventional methodology. And in such a seamless way that you don't know where one begins and the other one ends.

EQUITABLE'S DFT

Many people don't know it but insurance companies do a lot more than just insure Aunt Tilly's house and Uncle Elmer's old bones. More and more insurance companies are becoming involved in private placements and leveraged buy-out operations. And with the entry into this marketplace there developed a need to calculate and assess risk.

Equitable dove into this market in a big way. Their Investment Advisory Department manages a rather large portfolio of pension funds that cover a broad spectrum from ultra-conservative to wildly aggressive. To manage this broad portfolio, the Investment Strategy Committee met on a weekly basis to produce guidelines. This would serve to create a set of discretionary trading ranges for equities and fixed-income investments. Once it got down to the investment manager level, the guidelines served as a base to which they added their own gut instincts about the market.

It seems as if this process was ready-made for an expert system with the main goal of providing consistency and a second important goal of considering customer preferences. Considering customer preferences on a timely basis was a hard nut to crack without automated means. Each investment manager was responsible for quite a few client accounts ranging in size from $1 million to more than $100 million. And of course, there loomed that extra incentive of competitive advantage. It was envisioned by the crew that the expert system could act as "an active memory" for each client producing a detailed report that showed each investment and its justification for each client. Kind of an automated pat on the back for the department.

The real secret behind the system would be the automated expert guidelines, which became the core of the system. The system goes by the name DFT or Discretionary Funds Transfer. It was written in the LISP and Prolog programming languages and originally ran on a powerful Symbolics workstation. Now running on a PC, DFT functions as an investment manager's integrated workstation.

George, who is an investment manager, sits down at the DFT workstation. He selects an account to work on. Immediately a client database is accessed and George reviews the client's current position and investment preferences. George now asks DFT that all-important question. What should be done for this client?

This is where the guidelines come in. Stored in a knowledge base, these guidelines are used in conjunction with the client's information, which includes customer preferences, to come up with a suggestion. George gets his answer "this client is under-invested in equities—add to position." Not only does DFT recommend but it justifies its decision. George reviews this justification, which for this client is due to "a shift in the recommended asset mix made by the committee."

DFT itself became an asset for the Equitable.

THE PAUL REVERE INSURANCE GROUP

Like Alexander Hamilton, Paul Revere was an American hero. Revere became famous for his midnight ride, warning that "the British are coming, the British are coming!" Not to be outdone by the original Revere, the Paul Revere Insurance Group has developed an expert system that warns, "the claims are coming, the claims are coming."

Claim Processing Complexity

The Claims Administration department at Paul Revere handles a large volume of claims. Between 200 and 250 new claims are opened each week, while an average of 7,900 active claims are in process at any given time.

On top of the large volume, the diversity of the claims makes for complicated processing. Claim types include HIP, Major Medical, Family Hospital, and Residual to name a few. For each type, the claims examiner has to understand and then perform tasks that take these differences into account. In addition, several other factors have to be taken into account during this phase of claim processing. Factors such as potential liability, claim reserve, length of time that the policy is in force, claim history, and a cadre of others must be added to the claim equation.

To add to this growing complexity, the policies handled are diverse. This can depend upon policy type, geographic area, and even original company of issue. The ever-burdened claims examiner must also be cognizant of the diverse types of illnesses and diseases that are categorized within the insurance industry. If this isn't bad enough, state regulations and rulings also must be dealt with.

While the claims examiner is performing the filing review, it becomes necessary, at times, to contact various external sources such as doctors, the IRS, the claimant, and a host of others. It's obvious that the claims examiners needed a helping hand.

Enter Expert Systems

This was the atmosphere that the data processing group found themselves in when the Paul Revere Insurance Group decided to explore expert systems with the goal of enhancing quality assurance and customer service.

The reasons for building an expert system for this process were the ones that you hear in every conference room in every office building in the financial services industry. Everyone wants a system that provides for consistency across the department so Betty doesn't do the process differently from Joe. In addition, what could be better than an embedded training tool that would get a junior claims examiner up to par in a very short period of time. And just by encoding the expertise of the very top claims examiners, Paul Revere could permanently document departmental policies that had never been written down before. Finally, the system could act as an audit trail by documenting reasons for specific actions taken.

The system that was finally built was completed in a modular fashion so it would be easy to expand as the need arose. It was built as an adjunct to the existing conventional system, which the claims examiners were comfortable using.

Planning for Acceptance

Even though the users of the new system were most certainly computer-literate, the data processing department ensured the system's success by extensive planning for acceptance.

This acceptance plan incorporated the use of a claim examiner sub-committee that would have access to the prototype as it was being built. The data processing group, eager for their user's acceptance, remained open to suggestions from the committee during development mode.

Once the system was completed, an extensive six-week training program was initiated. The trainers were not only the data processors but the members of the committee as well. The system was run in optional consultation mode at the very beginning, but the users were cajoled into doing from two to ten consultations each day. Soon they began doing more as the system gained widespread acceptance.

With all of the planning and care that went into the development of the Paul Revere claims system it's no wonder that the system was a success. It was also successful from a financial perspective. The payback period was calculated to be less than a year while the internal rate of return was a very large 307.4 percent. So bring on those claims, Paul Revere can handle it.

9

The Big Eight

OVERVIEW

. . .
. . .
. . .

Does this look familiar to you? You probably played this game in school. The object here is to connect all of the dots by drawing no more than four lines and without lifting your pencil from the paper. Believe it or not, there are many solutions. From using a rather thick paint brush to cover all of the dots at the same time to folding the paper in various ways to holding the paper so that only the edge shows. You'll probably come up with creative solutions of your own.

Accounting firms are in search of creative solutions as well. There is probably no more fertile ground for the use of artificial intelligence than in an accounting practice. And although the tasks of these firms are many and diverse, a premier goal of the accounting practice is to assess the various risks associated with performing a client audit. This assessment is a complex and difficult one. It implies an understanding of the impact of the various economic and internal organizational factors on the client's accounts.

Audit Risk equals Inherent Risk times Control Risk times Detection Risk. This equation is the AICPA (American Institute of Certified Public Accountants) audit risk model and it is the basis upon which most accounting firms perform their audits.

What the audit risk model states is that total audit risk is the product of the client's accounts being susceptible to errors, the client's own internal control system not being able to catch these errors, and the

242

accounting firm's audit process not being able to detect the prior two deficiencies.

Each area of risk comes associated with its own set of procedures applied during the audit with the purpose of uncovering any deficiencies. In the area of inherent risk such things as susceptibility of assets to theft, past history of error, personnel experience level of internal accounting department, how the client's financial position may or may not motivate management to misstate an account's amount, and the effect of external economic, political, or organizational issues are just some of the many items needed to be scrutinized. Control risk is also evaluated with a scrupulous attention to detail.

It is this level of detail, and the manner in which the audit has historically been performed, that makes this industry so ripe for development of expert systems. For the most part, each component of an audit is based on a questionnaire. This questionnaire details the scope of the audit. During the planning stages of the audit the questionnaire is narrowed down some so only questions and procedures actually relevant to the client are asked and performed. There are basically three ways of handling each of the questions on the questionnaire. One can merely ask the question, "How are current assets calculated?", observe the client's staff in performing the task associated with calculating current assets, or "test" this attribute. Testing usually entails sampling accounts, performing the calculation and comparing these results to the actual results.

Even though there are thousands of accounting firms out there we'll concentrate on just the "Big Eight" since they've all made a bee-line through the door labelled artificial intelligence. So let's see how these audit-gurus use the new and exciting world of advanced technology to pump up their ever-vigilant practice of defending the honor of the numbers.

The Auditing Roundtables

At one of the Arthur Young, now Ernst & Young, sponsored roundtables, a group of academics, accounting practitioners, as well as representatives from industry and government discussed the high potential of expert systems.

Audit Planning is on top of the list with the idea of using an expert system to assist in evaluating risks. This expert audit planner would be able to tailor the scope of the audit to the specific client, prescribing appropriate questions to be asked and procedures to be taken.

Another area of concern where expert help would be appreciated is in the area of internal control analysis. When an accounting firm walks in the door of a client firm one of the things on its checklist is to oversee the internal accounting controls of that particular client. In other words, it scrutinizes the acceptability of the firm's accounting procedures and controls. This expert internal control analyst would ask the appropriate questions and perform the necessary evaluations to reach a conclusion about the operational control procedures performed by the client firm.

Expert systems could also be a great aid to the account attribute analysis phase of review. Here the accounting firms select an attribute of the client's accounting process—say, accounts receivable—and review the adequacy of the related valuation reserves.

The accounting decision assistant popped up next on the list. Here the field auditor would have a smart assistant to indicate the proper accounting procedure to be applied to complex transactions such as foreign exchange.

Tax planning is our next stop. This is similar to audit planning with only the extra added attraction of being able to cope with the complex tax laws. This is in fact what Coopers & Lybrand did in its ExperTAX system. More about ExperTAX later.

And we shouldn't forget to automate the most profitable of the Big Eight businesses, which just happens to be management consulting. Here expert systems could assist in identifying patterns and relationships, which would permit the proper matching of solutions to problems. Plant site selection and data security were offered as two examples of expert system applicability.

Last, but not least, we should not forget that all-time favorite. The use of expert systems could be a real boon to the art of training these denizens of the ledger.

Let's get a tasting of what's going on behind closed doors.

Coopers & Lybrand

Along with ExperTAX, an intelligent tax planning expert system that we'll discuss at length, a second big-scale expert system was completed, which has gained renown in the industry. ExMarine is an expert system that assists in the underwriting of marine liability umbrella insurance policies. Simply put, the system collects and analyzes information about an applicant. It then advises the insurance broker on how to underwrite the risk and even suggests a premium.

More recently the staff at Coopers is piling up the overtime on an audit risk expert system. This system will identify areas of risk for each client.

A massive project, the knowledge acquisition phase alone, where thousands of rules were generated, took over a year. The process of knowledge acquisition, some call it knowledge elicitation, is unique at Coopers. The process is data driven and much of the knowledge is obtained during simulation exercises. In this way a more accurate representation of how the data is manipulated can be obtained than in relying on how the user thinks the problem is broken down.

Once this knowledge is collected, a small prototype is built, or as they call it, a model of knowledge. Then they take a look into its inner workings and make the determination as to how the expert system should actually work for the full-blown system. What they found out about Audit Risk was that it required the use of more than one inference engine. So they developed more than one inference engine. This demonstrates the Coopers approach—they will build to suit the specific application.

This flexible approach is evidenced by Coopers integrating AI into each of its six U.S. regions and two international regions located in London and Caracas.

Peat Marwick Main

Although the biggest of the Big Eight, Peat is not one of the biggest developers of AI software. However, it does see its possibilities.

Using purchased, expert system shells, rather than building its own as did Coopers & Lybrand, Peat made the news when it created the Loan Probe. Loan Probe was created for the express purpose of assisting its banking clients to assess its commercial loan portfolios and detect probable losses.

Developed using Information Builder's Level 5, this expert system became so popular that Peat is readying it for market. And no wonder, it makes the process of loan review so easy. And it offers appropriate recommendations such as to establish a loss reserve or restructuring the terms of the loan.

Ernst & Young

With the merger of two of the largest of the Big Eight, you get the side benefit of a merger of two discrete AI departments. When Ernst and Whinney merged with Arthur Young an interesting synergy of AI talent was forged.

Rick Richardson, National Director of Technology, talks about E &Y's AY/ASQ (or at least that was the original name before AY became EY). The goal here was, again, to expert-systematize that all-important audit planning. During two years of all-nighters they created an expert system that contains thousands of rules. One that is capable of asking subsets of some forty-five thousand planning questions.

The system was based on the heuristics, or gut intelligence, of senior partners. Within one automated system the whole of auditor methodology was encoded for posterity. AY/ASQ runs on a MacIntosh and was written in the Pascal programming language. This system provides an on-line manual, enables the user to customize the rule base, and is one heck of a smart assistant in audit planning.

AY/ASQ builds a matrix of risk and recommends applicable procedures. For example it might tell you that receivables are significant and request that a particular procedure be dispatched.

What E &Y found was that using this system made the audit process much more efficient. Less time was spent on the actual planning so more time could be spent actually auditing.

Arthur Andersen & Company

Although many of the Big Eight parcel their staff out to consulting services to build expert systems for clients, probably none are as visible as Arthur Andersen. Since the early 1980s this Big Eight firm has dabbled in, dallied over, and designed some heavy-duty expert systems. Like Peat, Arthur Andersen realized early on the value of developing an expert system approach to analyzing mortgage loans. Their version of the system, called the MLA or Mortgage Loan Analyzer, was developed on the ever-popular PC. It uses the AION Development System, which is one of the more popular expert system tool sets. MLA uses some two hundred data elements to evaluate and then draw a conclusion about a particular mortgage. Acting in an advisory capacity MLA asks the loan officer questions that often require subjective answers. MLA produces a final report and the loan officer can accept or decline the advice. Whatever the outcome, the loan officer documents this decision to MLA. In this way MLA learns and grows.

Arthur Andersen probably has the broadest experience of any of the Big Eight in the area of expert systems. Its been involved in automated customer service, credit cards, oil and gas systems, and even one for the Securities and Exchange Commission.

And All the Rest

All of the Big Eight have AI groups. Deloitte, Haskins & Sells has a group that develops internal systems for use in accounting and auditing. Price Waterhouse has done the same, except adding the extra wrinkle of using this technology for consulting as well. And Touche, Ross & Co. has just reorganized to emphasize AI.

The Big Eight were probably the first in the financial services industry to recognize the value of expert systems as a strategic competitive challenge. Although not many of the potential systems described in the very beginning of this chapter have been given life, they've all been given consideration.

EXPERTAX

It's 2:00 A.M. Tomorrow is the big day. The staff is elbow deep in the tax files of ABC Credit company. Crushed cigarette butts litter the floor. Ed is curled up on the couch, eyes half closed, murmuring "Woe is me. Woe is me." Emily is on her 20th cup of coffee since midnight. It's been a long day and the guys are (not) looking forward to an even longer night.

The sun comes up over the river. Ed, Emily, and friends straighten their shirts and skirts and head out heads up, spirits down. Today's the day of the BIG TAX AUDIT.

Could this scene have been prevented? You bet. With proper planning and accounting procedures, there's no reason to fear Uncle Sam. Even the accounting firms with the best intentions at times err. And unfortunately it's the customer that pays through the nose.

One of the Big Eight accounting firms wanted to make sure that it provided the most comprehensive audit and tax planning service possible. This company just happened to be Coopers & Lybrand. Coopers just happened to be one of the first of the financial services firms to enter the big, bright, beautiful world of artificial intelligence.

In the days when the rest of the commercial world was gluing the sticker Information Center to an office door, and patting themselves on the back because they were so forward thinking, Coopers pounded the AI LAB sign on its door.

Inside this palace of wonders were machines of various makes and sizes and all manner of software. Yes, they had it all. So when the Tax department needed inspiration they went downstairs and banged on the door of Dr. David Shpilberg, head of the Decision Support Group during those heady days.

The Dreaded Questionnaire

They had a problem, they explained to Shpilberg. They were using what they called the "dreaded questionnaire." It was long, sometimes up to two hundred pages, and tedious and there was plenty of room for error. It was also quite a nuisance to change. And change it usually did as the tax code changed. On top of all of these problems was the problem of the new tax accountant. There was no way that any of these green accountants, try as they might, could make this questionnaire talk to them. They wanted explanations. They wanted enlightenment. But a piece of paper doesn't talk.

So here we have the elements of success. First, we have an idea for a product that would make Coopers premier among accounting firms. Second, it was questionnaire-oriented. If you peruse the literature of AI, you will find that almost everybody advocates these types of projects as fodder for expert-systematizing. Third, the users wanted a bigger and better questionnaire. They wanted it to explain the *why* and the *how* And last but not least, the user experts were willing to donate their time to the effort. What a perfect combination.

So our Coopers AI group sat down, took deep breaths, and began to plan. Since this was early in the annals of expert system popularity there were few tools for this group to choose from that were applicable to the financial environment. So they did what any entrepreneurial high-tech group would do—they invented their own.

FFAST

Using Gold Hill's Golden CommonLisp, these AI-techies created a finance-oriented expert systems shell that they call FFAST. Actually FFAST was not created just for ExperTAX but as a shell for the many financial applications that Coopers envisioned. And FFAST is more than just a shell. It is a whole environment consisting of the software and the procedures to perform knowledge acquisition and knowledge engineering.

During many sessions utilizing the expertise of over twenty senior tax and audit experts the "dreaded questionnaire" was dreaded no more. The ExperTAX inference engine is a forward-chaining, rule-based system incorporating a frame manager, which works with two types of frames. Question frames are those associated with questions to be asked and Issue frames represent issues to be raised by an analysis of the answers. When all was said and done, the group had come up with over a thousand frames.

The Intelligent Questionnaire

ExperTAX functions as an intelligent questionnaire acting as a guide through the information-gathering process. It is smart enough to ask only those questions that are germane to the client situation. It is more than capable of raising issues when warranted and makes frequent use of its dialog prowess to ask more questions when appropriate. For those green accountants it contains an EXPLAIN facility that can be used to explain just why a question is being asked and why the response was relevant. On top of all of this it provides an audit trail of questions asked, answers given, and user notes.

For over ten years the "dreaded questionnaire" was filled out manually. It only took several months to get the staff to use ExperTAX. Each and every tax specialist saw the utility of this expert system right away. Jerry Leener, a partner at Coopers, explains that the old way was not insightful. If you had a question about an inventory issue, you had to drag out the manual to get more information. With ExperTAX it's available at the press of a button. Another partner, Lynford E. Graham, Jr. lauds expert systems' ability to respond to change, to grow over time without having to rewrite the entire program. This theory was put to the test when ExperTAX had to be modified to incorporate the new tax laws following the Tax Reform Act of 1986.

In November of 1986 each audit and tax partner was asked to assign the use of this product to at least one engagement. It was so instantly popular that in short order all 97 offices were begging for copies.

As the sun sets in the west, our friends Emily and Ed contemplate their tax audit over sushi. "Next time, Ed, let's get an accounting firm in here that has some technological hocus-pocus that can raise us our tax issues *before* we get to the IRS."

VATIA—A DIFFERENT SORT OF TAXING PROBLEM

The very, very British arm of Ernst & Young was faced with a very inconvenient problem not so very long ago. That cumbersome practice of Europeans of collecting a value-added tax (or VAT) was developing into quite a bit of a nuisance for the E &Y auditors and professional advisors. The problem can be tied to the British introduction of a whole slew of civil penalties for noncompliance to the rigid VAT code.

Since E &Y auditors had long made it a practice to review their clients' VAT systems, a whole culture of VAT expertise had grown up at this firm. The normal modus operandi was the ubiquitous questionnaire of the audit business. Now this questionnaire took on a new significance; an error would mean heavy misdeclaration penalties.

E &Y was faced with a dilemma. VAT rules were complex and everchanging. Should they take on many more VAT specialists? Or should they try to find a way to make this specialized expertise available to anyone anytime. They decided to take on the challenge of the second option and thus they entered the new world of expert systemdom.

Christine Tindall, a senior manager in the computer development department in the United Kingdom, set out to create an expert VAT system. It was dubbed VATIA (short for VAT Intelligent Assistant). The hardware/software selection criteria were based on two all-important caveats. One was that this software had to run on a micro-based system since this was the platform of choice for other audit software. Second, the cost of the run-time system had to be reasonable since more than six hundred PCs had to be outfitted with the final product.

Tindall did a thorough search and decided upon Crystal, which is an expert tool set that is quite popular in Europe and the United Kingdom. Additional niceties that Crystal does not handle were programmed in by using the C programming language.

Tindall's team then set out to codify the essence of the VAT audit process. One former Customs inspector, now with the firm, provided the raw expertise that was fused into the system. This expert was backed up by the head of the VAT group and his group of six specialists.

Value-added tax accounting is not as simple as it sounds. It's a merger of legal, accounting, and audit expertise. Add to this a layer of Customs practices, knowledge, and a bit of commercial experience and you have one meaty knowledge requirement.

Like Coopers & Lybrand, E &Y has its very own methodology for cracking the crucial knowledge nut. Called KBM, it is a knowledge base mapping technique, which is a paper representation of human expertise. Using iterative rounds of knowledge base mapping sessions the team tuned and then fine-tuned their knowledge base.

The system finally developed and was divided into seven discrete components: registration, returns, output tax, input tax, partial exemption, records, and other. Similar to other audit expert systems, VATIA guides the user through the intricate world of VAT laws and regulations in a tailored-to-the-client manner.

A consultation with VATIA takes about two hours. At the end of the process, four typical audit reports can be generated: a management letter pointing out key issues, areas where immediate action is required, key points for the auditor to note, and general client notes.

In May of 1988 VATIA was distributed to the far reaches of the E &Y empire where it now graces the personal computer of the very proper British auditor.

THE PEAT MARWICK LOAN PROBE

Back in the good old USA, they descend in great hordes, these bow-tied and white-shirted auditors. Sometimes four or eight abreast they march in unison, ledgers in hand to stalk their quarry. Pencil nestled behind the ear, shirtsleeves rolled up past conservative wristwatches, they sit under the harsh glow of fluorescent lighting munching and crunching numbers.

They live for the chase. They seek to find the bad postings, the erroneous credit, the mistaken debit. Day after day, long night after long night these intrepid troopers pick their tortuous way through paper trails that send lesser souls screaming into the night.

Picking a Project

Phew. It's hard to be an auditor. They're forced to ascertain right or wrong, yes or no, black or white. But not everything is so easy. Especially a bank loan.

In 1981 Peat Marwick's Audit Research Group, located in Montvale, New Jersey pushed hard to get into this new fangled technology called expert systems. After all, the role of this research group was to investigate ways and means to increase efficiency and effectiveness of the audit process. Since this is the bread and butter of any accounting firm, this group had important work to do. Money found its way from the Peat Marwick Foundation to the University of Illinois, which was to be the academic research hub. For two years the academics twiddled and toyed and finally concluded that this technology seemed an appropriate match to the audit process.

In 1983 Gary Ribar, senior manager of the Audit Research group, got the green light to move full-steam ahead. It was time to take the highfa-lutin theoretical model and turn it into something a bit more practical. Gary was presented with a challenge—find a use for this technology. And find it he did. At the same time the guys from Montvale were well aware of the increasing volatility of the banking industry. Bank audits had become so complex that our white-shirted audit friends were burn-ing out real fast. Maybe expert systems would work here? Well Gary and friends voted a resounding yes and luckily the mighty higher-ups agreed.

Wouldn't it be great to create a tool for internal audit use in reviewing commercial bank loans? Not all bank loans, just the ones that were the most complicated, the ones that statistical review methods handled none too well. Loan collectibility relies heavily on subjective judgment rather than hard, cold statistics. In most cases the auditors performing manual loan evaluations completed this task in about one hour. Their methodology consisted of applying procedural and "gut instinct" rules along what essentially was a large decision tree. To those of us who know little about the behind-the-scenes work of loan evaluation, this process seems deceptively simple.

Loan Complexity

Let's go into business. We're now Rolling Stones Incorporated makers of, you guessed it, rolling stones. We've got great prospects but we need a cash infusion real fast. So we go into Rocknroll Bank of America all dressed up in our Sunday finest and fill out an application for a commercial loan. It's only after we're out the door that the work begins. And according to Gary Ribar this process turns out to be startlingly complex and utilizes a variety of types of knowledge. About fifty pieces of information, ranging from the financial to the more quirky nonfinancial, are evaluated as shown in Figure 9-1. The evaluation focuses on one main conclusion—exposure. Exposure to noncollectibility of the loan. Can Rolling Stones pay back the loan? Is there collateral? Are there multiple loans outstanding that might share legal access rights to the collateral? All this, and more!

And what if there is no collateral? Rolling Stones Inc. sure doesn't have any. Rocknroll Bank did grant our little company an unsecured loan, but it went through quite a bunch of gyrations before it did. They first took a magnifying glass to our current financial condition, which basically means looking at short-term liquidity, business risk, and finally financial risk. Short-term liquidity is easy to understand. It's how well you can pay your everyday bills with the assets you have on hand. Even so, from a bank's perspective there's a lot of factors to analyze. How else can these short term assets be used? How recent are the financial figures that are being looked at? How objective are these financials? And how to factor in all that nonfinancial information? The myriad of details is all neatly tied together with a weighting factor.

Risk, on the other hand, is much more vague. So many factors come into play that can make short-term assets inaccessible for loan repayment that the person who reviews the loan almost needs a ouija board. Maybe the demand for rolling stones will dry up. Maybe the company will experience internal fights among its owners. Maybe there will be a flurry of hostile or none-too hostile takeovers. The final two factors analyzed are cash flow prospects and loan performance history. Anyone who has ever applied for a loan or filled out an application for a credit card instinctively understands why the bank might be interested in your past loans and how you repaid them. However, the concept of cash flow prospects is much more vague. The bank looks at the money that goes in and out of the till relative to the repayment of all your debt, including

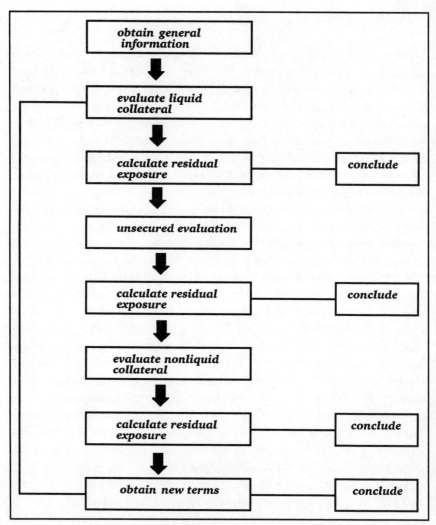

Source: KPMG Peat Marwick.

FIGURE 9-1. Loan Decision Flow.

this new loan. How much money usually is in the till? How is this amount expected to change? How certain are we that this will change?

If you were to draw a picture of all the things that are scrutinized in this review process it would look like a tree with many, many branches. Some of these branches were large and clearly defined, while many others trailed off and got lost among the leaves.

Turning the Tree into a System

Right around the same time that the Audit Research Group of Peat Marwick decided to explore the use of expert system methodology to the audit process, they were in the middle of a several-year effort to develop microcomputer-based audit support. Since auditors are forever in the field, portable or at least luggable microcomputers seemed like a natural. The expert system project was considered a logical extension of this effort. So their first constraint in building the system was to find an expert system tool that ran on a microcomputer. Their second constraint was to minimize the costs of the project.

With these constraints in mind and with the knowledge of the tree-oriented structure of the problem Gary Ribar went off on a search. It would lead him to meet and greet the multitudinous vendors that crowd the expert system tool marketplace. Each of these vendors claimed, "Me, I'm best. Try me." But Gary was smarter than that. He knew how important it was to balance the tool's salient features with cost and complexity of the tool. So what it all boiled down to was the selection of Information Builders Level 5 expert system tool. It was easy enough for the auditors to use, but complex enough to encode the often complex and judgmental process of loan evaluation.

Of course, we all know there can be no expert system without experts. In Peat's case two primary people were selected as target experts, although many, many others were used as secondary sources. Usually the knowledge engineering team spruces up for combat with the experts by studying the manuals and checklists that are the "bibles" of the department. In this case there were none. Gary began this process as a babe in the woods.

There would be some four thousand hours of interviews over a three-year period. If Gary had any advice at all for would-be expert system creators it would be, "Don't underestimate the knowledge acquisition process." It became for Gary a game of CLUE. Although each interview session was extremely well-structured, Gary found most of his golden nuggets outside of the conference room. He began to develop an ear for hints they would throw out as they walked out of the room and down the hall. He found it was all a matter of trying to deal with and understand the metaphors that the experts had to deal with on a day to day basis. One day, after their first prototype test at a bank in Miami, they were walking out of the demo room with the uneasy feeling that they hadn't quite captured the essence of cash flow. As Gary walked despondently behind two of Peat's partners, he overheard them say something that made something click in his own mind. Finally he saw the light.

In the end, the system would capture 9000 rules. It would store a checklist of over 1500 questions such as whether management has any kind of internal conflict that would distract them from the routine conduct of business.

Out of the 9000 rules on the three types of loans that the Loan Probe evaluates, an auditor would traverse only the route that had relevance to the situation of the borrower. Occasionally, along the way, one might get waylaid by a question that would seem to have a nebulous answer. The Loan Probe handles this by using what is called fuzzy sets. Questions asked in this vein are permitted answers that permit a weighing of evidence such as STRONG, MODERATE, or WEAK.

A Working System

With the knowledge part complete, the team was able to tailor the system to provide a front-end data gathering mechanism. This permits loan information to be imported automatically by the expert system. This was appealing to many who used it since it permitted the system to drive the process. This made the judgment process clear for the novices. For they were not only learning the system, but learning the auditing process as well. The more advanced users preferred to enter the input during the system's forward-chaining process.

No matter which way the system is used it successfully evaluates the commercial loan process. Gary found the measure of success of the system to be the lessening of the amount and nature of work that needed to be performed by audit reviewers during the audit process. The audit process is characterized by a team approach. The auditors on the very bottom rung perform the actual grunt work. The results are passed up successive levels of team management. Usually each level of management has a modicum of work to perform to "clean up" the evaluation. The Loan Probe appears to perform a clean evaluation from the starting gate.

Our bow-tied and white-shirted auditors have replaced their ledgers with computers. The stark glow of the fluorescent light has been replaced by the fuzzy-white glow of the video screen. What's this? Smiles on their faces? What, they're leaving at 5 P.M? Wait, someone's staying behind to work long into the night. Let's open the door and see who this workaholic is. As we open the door we can hear the printer churning and we can see the white light of the video screen. Hey, there's nobody here. Nobody but the Loan Probe working long into the night.

AUDITPLANNER—A TEXTBOOK EXAMPLE

One of the buzzwords of auditing aficionados is materiality. Materiality judgments affect every facet of the audit function. The trouble is that there are no FASB (Financial Accounting Standards Board) guidelines for making these judgments. And studies have shown there is considerable diversity and lack of consensus among auditors as to what constitutes materiality in specific instances. In fact, the studies found what we all knew innately concerning all areas of human judgment. None of us agrees on anything.

Since the judgmental process is the stuff of expert systems, Paul J. Steinbart, when an Assistant Professor of Accounting at the University of Utah, decided to take a look-see into building an expert system for making planning-stage materiality judgments (1987).

Although Dr. Steinbart is not related in any way to any of the Big Eight, his Auditplanner can give us some insight into the way the proprietary Big Eight systems already described actually work.

Modeling Judgment

In brief, Auditplanner's judgment model breaks down the materiality judgment into two separate but equal decisions: a choice of a base to calculate materiality and a choice of a percentage rate to apply to the chosen base.

While the Professor was most certainly an expert in accounting, he thought himself not expert enough for this exercise and thus went out on the prowl for practical expertise. Eleven major accounting firms were asked to participate, and it is to their credit that ten actually agreed to cooperate. The search was narrowed to the four firms that documented their planning-stage materiality judgments. From this field of four, one audit partner at one firm was finally selected to become the expert whose judgment would be emulated by the Auditplanner expert system. In spite of this emphasis on just one expert, other experts at this same firm were asked to participate in reviewing the final product and in recommending further refinements.

The Professor now had to choose his tool. And since this project took place in an academic atmosphere, what better expert system tool than the "premier" tool that opened the expert system floodgates to the world. MYCIN was one of the first expert systems ever; developed as a university research project, it concentrated on acting as a consultant in the field of infectious diseases. It was the building of this system, and several others like it, that convinced the world of the practicality of the expert system methodology. Seeing the applicability of what they had done, the creators of MYCIN emptied the system of its medical knowledge and produced the first expert system tool or shell as these tools have come to be known. Hence, empty MYCIN begat EMYCIN. The Professor chose this tool since the system he was building worked in a similar consulting capacity.

A Sample Audit Consultation

Consulting systems do just that—consult. They ask a series of applicable questions to the situation at hand:

1. What is the name of the client?
    EXAMPLE
2. What is Example's main line of business or industry classification?
    MANUFACTURING
3. Is this the first time that we have audited Example?
    NO
4. Have there been any acquisitions that either singly or in total amount to ten percent or more of the client's total assets?
    NO
5. Some of the questions that follow will ask you to input dollar amounts from the client's financial statements. Will your answers be in terms of thousands of dollars?
    YES

6. Does Example have any publicly-traded debt or equity securities?
    YES
7. What do you project retained earnings to be?
    7616
8. What is the amount of current assets?
    5822
9. What is the amount of current liabilities?
    3009
10. What do you estimate the annual income from continuing operations to be?
    3786
11. Are the financial statements going to be used in connection with a public offering of securities?
    NO
12. Are the financial statements going to be used in connection with a transfer of interests in Example?
    NO
13. Are the financial statements going to be used in connection with a contest for control of Example?
    NO
14. Are the financial statements going to be used to settle some litigation involving Example?
    NO
15. Are the financial statements being used in connection with an inquiry by a regulatory commission?
    NO
16. How much long-term debt does Example have?
    882
17. Does Example have any covenants on either its long-term debt or existing lines of credit?
    YES
18. Does Example have any debt covenants that restrict dividends to a percentage of either current earnings or cash flow?
    NO
19. Do any of Example's debt covenants require it to maintain some level of earnings?
    NO
20. Does Example have any debt covenants that require it to use part of its cash flow to retire its debt?
    NO

The overall materiality level to be used in planning the extent of audit procedures is 189,300. The reasons for materiality judgment are as follows:

The calculation of the materiality level was based on the use of income-from-continuing-operations as the base for the materiality calculation. The materiality level was calculated using a percentage rate of 0.05 (Steinbart 1987).

To develop Auditplanner, the expert and the Professor had to sift through numerous examples of audits where this sort of process took place. They reviewed a wide spectrum of business and situation types to ensure the completeness of the rule base. This included a machine-tool manufacturer where the company was involved in an acquisition of a subsidiary, several nonprofit companies, a trucking firm that was the subject of litigation, a common carrier that was the subject of a regulatory inquiry, a microcomputer retailer poised to go public, and several run-of-the-mill, no-problem companies. This diversity provided a wide spectrum of judgment issues to be encoded into the final system.

How and Why

Auditplanner was developed as a proper expert system tool—that is, it provided the facilities that set expert systems apart from conventional systems. If a user of the system disagreed or was curious about how some decision was made, Auditplanner provided *how* and *why* functionalities. For example, in the third question of the preceding list, where the user is asked whether or not this is the first time that the client has been audited, a *why* asked at this time would get: "Whether this is the first time that we have audited a client is one of the five standard parameters that identify a client. This may be useful later in the consultation. For example, it is relevant in determining whether there is a need to reduce the calculated materiality level due to the increased risk associated with an initial audit of the client and is relevant in determining the percentage rate used to determine the materiality level."

The *how* function neatly provides a user with a succinct answer to the methodology that was used to get to a conclusion. In Auditplanner the *how* might be asked as a result of a *why*. For example, a user might be asking *why* Auditplanner asked a question concerning filing with a regulatory agency in preparation for the sale of securities in the public marketplace. The *why* description concludes with the statement that: "It is definite (1.0) that the type of entity Example is private." At this point the user is confused and requests a *how* to determine how Auditplanner arrived at this determination. The system responds with a description of the rules used to arrive at this conclusion (Steinbart 1987):

It has already been established that

[4.1]   Example does not have any publicly traded debt or equity securities, and

[4.2]   Example does not have any restrictive debt covenants that are measured by or depend on financial statement amounts or ratios that involve results of operations, and

[4.3]   Example is not controlled by a public entity

Therefore
there is strongly suggestive evidence (.9) that the type of entity Example is private.
[RULE056]

This expert system contained ninety-five rules. Using the expert system capability of certainty factors, this system was able to deal with the more abstract type of reasoning found in this type of accounting problem.

All told, this academic exercise was quite successful and certainly useful for those of us in the real world by permitting us an inside look into the creation of a financial expert system.

10 Off-the-Shelf Financial Expertise

INTRODUCTION

Harry Blackstone is one of those entrepreneurial vendors of magic. He has a challenge for you. It is to take a drink from a bottle *without* removing the cork. Harry will tell you the answer at the end of this introduction, but read on to find out about the real entrepreneurs in the expert system market. They perform their own magic.

Perhaps there is no greater innovation or industriousness than in the expertise-for-pay market. Write it, can it, sell it. Now that's the approach.

It's an approach that has an interesting side-benefit. Most in-house created systems, whether they be in banking, securities, or insurance, are "quietly" developed. Perhaps the reason for this is that they are protecting some very competitive knowledge. Whatever the reason, these firms are very reluctant to talk about their endeavors. But one thing is sure. For the most part, these firms use home-grown expertise. Commercial expert systems are different.

Their driving force is in synthesizing the technology to the expertise. And their definition of expertise often calls for searching high and low for those possessors of that rare gem—wisdom. Woody Brock of Strategic Economic Decisions picked up on this early. He canvassed some 48 experts on interest rates to develop his Interest Rate Insight expert system. You'll read about Woody and his gang of 48 a bit later.

I don't know, maybe the magic is the old dollar sign. But somehow these entrepreneurs realize that the expert is the key behind the expert system and turn cartwheels to ensure that every last shred of knowledge is stuffed into their systems.

And now for our trick. Have you tried it? Impossible, isn't it? Well, no. Take one of those bottles that has a raised bottom creating a cavity under the bottle. A wine bottle will do very nicely. Turn the bottle over, fill it with water, and then drink out of it.

Like our magic trick that speaks for itself, these products can do the same. So onwards and upwards.

INTEREST RATE INSIGHT

The old bent Gypsy woman peered into the glowing crystal ball. The room was still except for the heavy breathing of the six men and women who sat, hands joined, around an ancient table. The glow of the crystal ball cast many shadows. Beads of perspiration crept across furrowed brows. Finally the old woman was ready to speak. Breathing stopped, hearts pounding, the six waited. "The interest rate will move upwards by 20 basis points. That will be twenty dollars please."

Forecasting Interest-Rate Swings

Interest-rate movement forecasting has always been difficult. And investment managers have had to resort to a bit of hocus pocus to home in on trends in a volatile marketplace. This volatility is partially caused by the large number of factors or variables that make up the marketplace. Couple this with the silent factor of uncertainty and you have an environment in which conventional methodologies of forecasting fail roundly.

Gene Lancaric, formerly of Chase Investors and now happily ensconced at Swiss Bank Corporation is one of that rare breed that understands the inherent flaws of the current econometric models of the marketplace. Gene has long recognized that most econometric models have been based on a single chain of events. Many make the leap between forecast and price without taking that intermediate step of scrutinizing how this will all affect supply and demand. All too often the effects of supply and demand can counteract each other. One can be stronger than the other under certain circumstances.

To make matters worse most econometric models today rely on the historical past to forecast the future. Everybody knows that in the past the relationships between economic variables has not always been constant. Gene gives us some examples: "During the period when the United States had a high rate of inflation the factors determining interest rates were very different from the current decade when interest rates are very low. During the period when monetary exchange rates were fixed, relative volatility of U.S. and foreign bond market were different from what it is today when exchange rates are freely floating." The point he makes is that if you take one economic variable over a long period of time and regress it against another without isolating these shifts in the underlying environment you will get a spurious relationship. This will lead you to forecast incorrectly if you assume that the future will be like the past. With economics, the past often has little or no relationship to the present, much less the future. Most economists today base their forecasts on a time slot from the end of World War II to the present. Gene points out that this period hasn't been homogeneous and not necessarily representative of the way the economy actually functions.

Today we hear a lot about the globalization of the economy. It's the current buzz word around the economic think tanks in all parts of the world. Given this trend, the slice of time economists use to forecast would tend to give false results. Gene suggests that if you really want to compare the past to the present, use the period between 1875 and 1914 as this was a period of more closely integrated world financial markets.

So what's a portfolio manager to do? The current model, which relies on past performance to forecast future activity, is imperfect and dangerously misleading. What's needed is the ability to use the economic principle of identifying the "states of the world" and assign probabilities to them. A tool is needed to recognize that environments differ, that these differences constitute changes and that these changes interact with each other. This jumble of differences and increasing volatility lends credence to a theory first espoused in 1973 by Nobel prize winner Kenneth Arrow. The concept behind the "Economics of Uncertainty" is the marketplace being wedded to the multiple possibilities of different states of the world. At long last, probability theory was wedded to the different economic laws such as the law of supply and demand. In an age when nobody can predict the future, people want the next best thing—they want the odds.

The Gang of 48

And Interest Rate Insight gives it to them. Horace "Woody" Brock practically lives at the doorstep of the hallowed halls of Artificial Intelligence research. Woody's Menlo Park, California firm specializes in research on the vagaries of interest rates. Strategic Economic Decisions Inc. provides up-to-date intelligence about interest-rate behavior in a most complex credit market. Woody's backyard forays over at Stanford University got him thinking of an expert system approach to interest-rate forecasting.

The Interest Rate Insight personal computer-based software package was born of 48 fathers. Nobel prize winners, people on the Fed, economists, people expert in risk and uncertainty, capital flow pros, trade deficit aficionados, and market experts were the bloodline that became the sires of the software. This alone is a masterful feat. Finding one expert to contribute to a project is cause for applause, finding 48 highly placed experts is cause for ovation. Woody cajoled and coaxed these experts into giving up their gems of wisdom while meeting them halfway. He recognized that if he was to be successful in squeezing the intelligence from these esteemed personages, he must meet them on their own turf.

Many said it couldn't be done. After all, many of the target contributors to his software were the visages you would see on the cover of *Business Week* and surely they wouldn't have the tolerance for the typical computer nerd. Woody wouldn't take no for an answer. "Wait a minute, they're doing this in their heads everyday at lunch." Woody realized that the secret to building an expert system was to speak to these experts in their own parlance, to dress like them, to think like them, to structure the questions carefully. No nerd talk. No jargon. No jabbering about vectral autoregression. Just plain talk, pure and simple.

Assisting the Rate Forecasting Process

And while Interest Rate Insight doesn't quite make interest-rate forecasting simple, it does make it understandable. It was designed specifically for investment managers who are confused about movements of interest rates in today's overheated, deregulated, and global environment. Interest Rate Insight actually consists of two complementary pieces of software. Rate Logic™ is an expert system tutorial infused with the intelligence of its 48 fathers. J. P. Morgan Company uses it to train staff in such esoteric topics as Fed policy, inflation, government deficits, the dollar, trade deficits, international capital flows, risk, uncertainty, and volatility. Rate Logic is a veritable "all you wanted to know about the credit market but were afraid to ask." It gives you the scuttlebutt so you can interpret the economic news that you read and usually yawn over every day. Like this 1985 tidbit from the *New York Times:*

> The Federal Reserve announced a $5.3 billion increase in the nation's basic money supply yesterday, roughly twice as large as expected. The news stunned the credit markets. Although interest rates rose only modestly after the Fed's announcement, economists and traders expressed bewilderment over the combination this week of statistics showing a lackluster economy, but robust money supply growth for the week ended August 5.

With this new found wisdom, courtesy of Rate Logic, the investment manager can use the AI-laden Rate Forecaster™ to perform *What if* analysis using the economic scenarios of choice. The net result is a series of graphic representations of the U.S. credit market. This graphic snapshot serves to explain why interest rates will change as it simulates behavior on both sides of the credit market. You can actually see the reactions of both borrowers and investors.

Before we can get to a result we must supply the system with the assumptions that will become the basis for the forecast. These assumptions will be coupled with the expertise of the 48 fathers. The goal is to predict the change in basis points of short- and long-term interest rates. Ten input variables form the basis for the forecast. The system provides you with a menu listing the ten. You are asked to specify whether market expectations of each of the ten will increase, decrease, or remain unchanged. You are also asked to determine whether any change will be slight, moderate, or large.

Figure 10-1 shows the final input for one novice market forecaster. Most of the input variables are self-explanatory. For the confused, the Rate Forecaster provides a mini-tutorial that eloquently explains the concept and definition of the term. Woody hired a novelist to de-jargonize the system such that even the "D" student in economics can readily understand it.

```
┌─────────────────────────────────────────────────────────────────────┐
│  SCENARIO MENU - - PROJECTED CHANGES IN MARKET EXPECTATIONS           │
│                                                                       │
│  A  INFLATIONARY  EXPECTATIONS            small increase(1%)          │
│  B  GNP GROWTH                            no change?                  │
│  C  FED POLICY                            slightly "easier"           │
│  D  TRADE DEFICIT                         medium increase($20B)       │
│  E  FOREIGN INVESTMENT ("CAPITAL INFLOWS")  small increase($10B)      │
│  F  GOVERNMENT DEFICIT                    small increase($15B)        │
│  G  VALUE OF THE DOLLAR                   small increase(4%)          │
│  H  CONSUMER CONFIDENCE                   up slightly                 │
│  I  BUSINESS OPTIMISM/SPENDING  PLANS     up slightly                 │
│  J  MARKET RISK PREMIUM                   up slightly                 │
│                                                                       │
│  INSTRUCTIONS: To enter your scenario, please TAP REPEATEDLY          │
│   the corresponding LETTER appearing to the left -- until satisfied. The │
│  program permits you to alter ONE to TEN variables at once. Then press │
│  RETURN to run the model.                                             │
└─────────────────────────────────────────────────────────────────────┘
```

FIGURE 10-1.   Simulation of Interest Rate Insight Selector Menu.

When the GO button is pressed, the Logic-check feature is called into action to test for internal consistency of the inputted variables. On the scenario presented to the system in Figure 10-1, the system quickly reacted with first shock, and then the warning message, STOP AND RECONSIDER YOUR SCENARIO. The inputs defied the current accepted logic of the marketplace. Not only does it tell you that you're a dummy, it even tells you specifically what the inconsistencies are. In this case it indicated that higher inflationary expectations are usually accompanied by a TIGHTER (their emphasis) Fed policy—not by an easier Fed policy. In addition, a HIGHER trade deficit is usually accompanied by higher foreign investment and a lower value of the dollar. It sums up this finger-pointing by explaining that it is in this way that trade deficits are often positively correlated with interest rates. And did I take these points into account?

After discretely modifying the inputs, the GO button was once again pressed. This time it passed the Logic-check with flying colors. An important note here is that the system in no way forces you to change your scenario. After all you may have some insight that defies the natural laws of economics, if so let it ride.

The input/output relations that are deep in the heart of the Rate Forecaster represent hundreds of rules of expert knowledge that took many labor-years of effort. In the words of the Rate Forecaster itself, "the methodology employed transcends that of standard econometric models that blithely extrapolate the past into the future. It is particularly risky to extrapolate in today's non-stationary financial market environment in which the future rarely replicates the past." The software itself is non-stationary. Updates are sent quarterly to the many subscribers to the system.

This *au courant* and very smart expert system finally arrives at its conclusion. Short-term interest rates will increase by approximately 75 basis points relative to today's rates. Long-term interest rates will increase approximately 160 basis points relative to today's rates.

The 1980s was a decade when we developed an extraordinary array of products to help people manage interest-rate risk. But there was always something missing. There was no way for a person to amass all of this information and interpret it easily. Oh you'd get experts on Fed policy, other experts on trade deficit, and other experts on the value of the dollar. You might even find some hot-shots who were experts on three of these variables all at the same time. But ten variables? Not without a crystal ball. Perhaps Woody's products don't perform crystal ball miracles. They do make peering through the crystal ball a lot less murky.

FORECAST PRO

A great thinker once said, "The trouble with our times is that the future is not what it used to be." Paul Valery, a little known, French, twentieth-century philosopher, poet, and no crystal ball gazer said quite a mouthful so long ago.

When once our great thinkers pondered and lamented over the variableness of it all, our modern day Valerys are hard at work in applying technology to figure out the key to the puzzle of the future. For many, this key is statistics and the door to be unlocked is the relationship between the economic past and future.

For most of us, statistics is the course in school that we put off until senior year. It's the stuff of memorization by rote that we conveniently wiped out of our minds the moment the final exam was over. The terms exponential smoothing, Box-Jenkins, and regression make you grab for the aspirin and retreat to the TV to catch up on the latest soap opera.

Resist as we might we really do need this type of methodology. So when a product is developed that makes it "oh so simple" we eagerly jump up on the bandwagon.

This product is Forecast Pro that uses that old black magic—artificial intelligence—to provide startlingly accurate forecasts. In a nutshell, Forecast Pro lets you enter variables. It examines these variables and then guides you through one of three statistical models. The nifty trick is that it picks the model that best suits the data. From a menu of exponential smoothing, Box-Jenkins, or regression techniques, the Pro makes the complex seem, well not quite trivial, but certainly understandable.

A Quick Statistical Tour

For those of you who never knew or for those, like me, who blotted out these details from main memory, let's take a quick tour through statisticsland. The Box-Jenkins and regression models are termed correlational methods. Here it is assumed that data can be adequately described by a normal probability distribution involving a limited and reasonable number of variables. The model fits the variables to the historical correlations and means of the data. The grand assumption here is that the future can be described by the same probability function that describes the past. Although many, including our French philosopher, dispute that the future is a direct result of the past, this model is most certainly useful for narrow period forecasts. Forecasts here span years rather than decades. In order for these methods to be useful, two criteria must be met. First, as discussed, it must be plausible that the future of the series can be described by the same probability model as the past. Second, there must be sufficient data provided to compute accurate values. If these conditions are not met, then the smoothing model should be used.

Exponential smoothing is the most popular of the forecasting models. With the market being as variable as it is, the robustness of this approach, with its facility to handle volatile data, is a perfect match for these troubled times. And, if I haven't confused you enough, there is a wide range of smoothing models. The Pro uses five: Simple one-parameter smoothing, Holt two-parameter smoothing, Winters three-parameter smoothing, Damped trend versions of Holt and Winters for more accurate long-term forecasting. These smoothing models go by the name (you guessed it) the Holt-Winters family of exponential smoothing.

Forex

So where does the expert system fit in? It comes in the form of the two heavy-hitter statisticians who founded Business Forecast Systems in Belmont, Massachusetts. Robert L. Goodrich, who holds a Ph.D. in the field, and Eric A. Stellwagen worked long and hard at infusing Forecast Pro with the knowledge of master-level forecasters.

Most of the really useful knowledge about forecasting has come to us by way of academic research comparing the accuracy of different methods. What they found is that there is no single best method (gee, I could have told them that and saved them time and money!). From their findings they deduced that the best model to use was the one that fit the data that was inputted. What works for one type of data set may not work for another. Your best shot is at trying multiple models and looking for the best fit. Sounds nice, but attempting this manually or even with a computer program is time-consuming and laborious. The Pro not only attempts to choose the best model but can also run multiple models letting you use its diagnostic component to compare and evaluate. This diagnostic facility is done graphically. So even if you don't understand what F-statistic or Ljung-Box mean you'll most certainly understand the peaks and the valleys of the graph.

Getting back to the expert system underpinnings, Forecast Pro gets its pizzazz from the concepts developed way back in the dark ages of expert systems. In 1984 Robert Goodrich presented a paper at the Fourth International Symposium on Forecasting in London. The title was *FOREX: A Time Series Forecasting Expert System*. Forecast Pro implements the rules and strategies found in the FOREX system. FOREX's forte was in matching the properties of specific time series and applications to the capabilities of forecasting methods.

How the Pro Works

The Pro first determines the properties of the data by direct statistical examination. Such esoteric items as seasonality, volatility, and correlational complexity are examined. At this point, a forward-chaining, rule-based system takes over. While these rules are proprietary to Business Forecast Systems Inc., the net result is to form a conclusion concerning the optimum forecasting method to use. These rules were assembled by study of the principal empirical research papers as well as by the brainy expertise of both Goodrich and Stellwagen. Actually the expert system component is entirely optional.

When using the Pro, the first step down the road of forecasting is to define variables. This is done rather easily through a series of pull-down menus. Once defined we eagerly pull down the Explore Data sub-menu. Here we can look at a graph of the raw data before any analysis takes place. It's at this point that the user can select the Expert System option as shown in Figure 10-2. And most will because of its penchant for efficient analysis.

Evidently this combination of expert systems and statistics is appealing to a broad range of users. The program can be used either automatically or interactively, or a combination of both methods. It is extremely useful for a novice statistician or for those of us who would rather forget everything we ever knew about statistics. For the novice, the expert system functionality of the *why* function assists in training the novice to become a skilled practitioner in a shorter amount of time.

Their user list reads like a *Who's Who*: AT&T, Bank of New Zealand, Salomon Brothers, Citicorp, and dozens of others. They use it for ev-

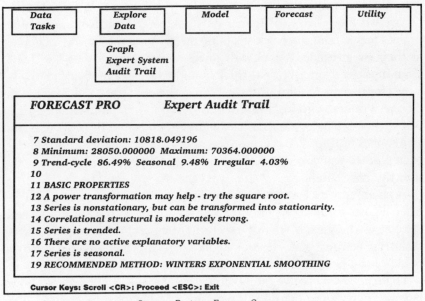

Source: Business Forecast Systems.

FIGURE 10-2.   Simulation of Forecast Pro's Expert Model Selector.

erything from corporate planning and marketing to utility forecasting. One of the largest insurers is using it for forecasting claims and inquiries. This helps them to predict staffing levels and administrative resources. This is done by actually predicting claim pay-outs. If this insurer can accurately project the number of claims, then it can staff up or down to appropriate levels. In the insurance field, where the number of claims is enormous and resultant staffing levels are equally so, accurate budgetary forecasting can save impressive sums of money. The user, a non-DP sort of guy, absolutely loves the expert system component of the Pro. He doesn't have to worry about evaluating the data to determine which model to use, he lets the Pro do it.

AIQ STOCKEXPERT OR HOW TO BECOME AN INVESTMENT GENIUS FOR UNDER $700

It's one of the hottest days of the summer of 1989. The old red, white, and blue hangs limp in front of Federal Hall in downtown New York, for there's nary a breeze. The denizens of Wall Street emerge from the black steaming pits that are the subways, dabbing at their sweat-beaded brows with linen, monogrammed handkerchiefs. Even in the early morning the thick humidity leaves everyone breathless.

A crowd starts to form near the corner of Wall Street and Broad. One by one, visitors, with brightly colored shorts and handycams slung lazily across their shoulders, queue up for the main event. By 9:30 A.M. the line snakes up Broad street, past the newsstand, past the candy vendor, even past the souvlaki stand. Finally the doors open and they are ushered into the cool building.

A small crowd of no more than ten wedges their sweating, camera-laden bodies into the elevator for the silent ride to the third floor. All is quiet as the visitors silently revel in anticipation. Finally, after what seems an eternity, the elevator doors open and they emerge into the world of the New York Stock Exchange.

High up they observe, unobserved or ignored by the raging crowd below. They watch, but do not participate. They turn to leave.

The Investing Public Has Disappeared

There's something very wrong here. Once the foundation of the stock market, the investing public seems to have disappeared. According to the *Wall Street Journal*'s "American Way of Buying" consumer survey, the public casts a wary eye on the securities industry. What's worse is that according to this same study, performed by the *Journal* with the Roper Organization and Peter D. Hart Research Associates, many don't even know *how* to buy a share of stock.

Surveying some two thousand folks about their savings and investment attitudes they found that nearly half of all consumers are ignorant of the stock market. And these weren't your average Joes. A quarter of those with incomes over $50,000 felt the same way. To make matters worse, this pattern of nonparticipation in the market is consistent even among those bright lights with professional or executive jobs.

Oh, ye of little faith! Well now they can fight back. And fight back hard because they have the "A" team (remember that TV series with the gold-chained Mr. T?) on their side. In this case the "A" team is AIQ systems based in Nevada.

"Win-Win" the Stock Market Game

Nevada is a great location for developing software that deals with the stock market. Close enough to the gaming tables of both Reno and Las Vegas to smell the money and perhaps, along the way, to develop a "win-win" philosophy of life.

Dr. J. D. Smith and Diana Kincade founded AIQ systems in 1985. Dr. Smith was long an AI-techie. Way back in the 1970s, when most of us were mere tots, he was among the first to apply artificial intelligence to those newfangled desktop personal computers. And it was in the early 1970s that Smith conceived the idea of combining the desktop computer with AI to conquer the stock market. Unfortunately, he had to wait until the power 1980s to realize his dreams.

With a degree in economics, an M.B.A. and a Ph.D. in management science Dr. Smith is surely a renaissance man of the technological 1980s. Coupled with Kincade's impressive programming skills, the dynamic duo were ready, willing, and able to take on the New York elite.

AIQ StockExpert's the name and expertise's the game. But, it's not really a game and StockExpert is deadly serious about solving the problem of making the right selections in the stock market.

I must admit I had loads of fun playing with StockExpert. With *Wall Street Journal* in hand I spent hours upon hours checking up on this expert system's track record. Yes, I must admit that I was pretty wary of the market in spite of my very close association with it. You know the old adage "familiarity breeds contempt." Well, this was most certainly true in my case. In the beginning I was a bit confused with the recommendations that StockExpert made. Gradually the light over my head started to shine brighter as I began to discern some of the rules of thumb that make up this expert system. I could barely refrain from calling my broker.

StockExpert is one heck of a usable tool. An embedded expert system, its purpose is not to instruct you on the vagaries of the stock market, but to assist you in making intelligent buy-sell decisions. It's so easy to use that you don't even realize that the "oomph" behind this program is artificial intelligence. Using a series of pull-down screens you can do everything from entering stock splits to graphing the stock you are interested in. You can even get an expert's opinion on whether to buy, sell, or hold tight, as shown in Figure 10-3.

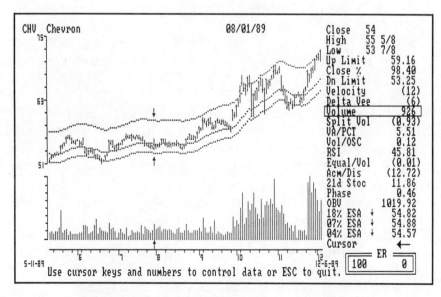

FIGURE 10–3. AIQ StockExpert's Expert Rating (ER).

Expert Ratings. The secret behind StockExpert is what is known as expert ratings (ER). These ratings are generated on every market day for every stock in the database. This database itself is composed of the stock you entered plus an entry database of the Standard and Poor 100. Using one of the many pricing services available, one needs to only use the AIQ communication feature to import these prices into the system.

The expert ratings are easy to understand. They are based on a scale of 1 to 100. An upside rating of 95 or more is considered a buy signal, and a downside expert rating of 95 or more is deemed a sell signal. The reporting option provides a report that sorts upside and downside ratings in descending order making it quick indeed to get on the horn to call your broker to buy or sell. For those of you who love to look at the undulating curves of a stock plot the AIQ graphics are probably some of the best.

The Rules. The approximately 120 rules of this expert system were gleaned from those market experts who have been making the right decisions for years. These rules include some things that the average investor wouldn't even dream of including and some things that are just too complicated to tackle. I've included several rules that AIQ supplies with their documentation. They show rather nicely the power of the rule base. Remember, the key here is the synergism of these rules when combined. One rule by itself is useful, two rules give one a heady feeling, but 120 rules are a potent weapon against program trading and "Ivan Boeskyism."

> When average price is increasing and volume is increasing, an up signal is generated. When average price is increasing but volume is decreasing, a down signal is given.
>
> A new low closing price with a positive VA PCT (Volume Accumulation Percentage) is an up signal. The reverse is also true: A new high closing price with a negative VA PCT is a down signal.
>
> An upward price trend with a downward volume accumulation trend is a down signal. A downward price trend with an upward volume accumulation is an up signal.

Inferencing. To process these rules an inferencing strategy must be selected that closely aligns with the type of knowledge to be processed. The authors wrote an inference engine that uses a forward-chaining, deductive, graph-oriented approach.

Along with these stock-guru rules are facts about daily price and volume of the different exchanges as well as information concerning over twenty-five different technical indicators. Leading these indicators is average price, which is an exponentially smoothed average, equivalent to a 21-day moving average. The system tracks volume movement or average volume as well as volume accumulation percentage. This percentage indicates buying or selling pressure. The system reviews the 21-day price stochastic, which is a percentage of the current closing price to the prior 21-day price range. And, last but not least, the system monitors on-balance volume, which shows the accumulation versus distribution action within the marketplace.

The inference engine looks at each rule to see whether it is true or false according to the current state of the technical indicators. Using a decision-tree type of knowledge representation, StockExpert views each rule as a node in a decision tree. There are three possible outcomes to this review: yes, no, or maybe. This capability of processing *maybes* or fuzzy sets as this inexactness has come to be known, is one of the features that sets an expert system apart from a more traditional software tool. The expert rating of 0 to 100 is calculated by adding up all of the values associated with the rules. Values are assigned to these rules based on regression analysis techniques governed by past performance.

Outperforms Wall Street

Perhaps the best way to demonstrate the viability of an expert stock program is to take a look at its performance. On the fifth of August in 1986 the StockExpert indicated an upside rating of 96 for United States Steel, now known as USX Corp. Taking a quick look at the stock for this period would hardly encourage action on the part of an unautomated investor. Over the prior two weeks, volume had been increasing dramatically even though the price had been decreasing. The system's VA PCT is positive. The 21-day Stochastic is greater than the previous day. This change, which moved this indicator over the 20 value, triggered a whole slew of other rules to be fired by the expert. The result was a strong up signal. If one had taken the system's advice and purchased the stock, an increase of over 67 percent would have been enjoyed over the next two months. And if some lucky devil had been smart enough to buy call options on the sixth of August and then sold them on the eighth of October, a profit of 2500 percent would have been folded neatly into a leather wallet.

For those faint of heart, StockExpert's Profit Manager component comes complete with a Stop-loss analysis report that very noticeably indicates with blinking accuracy when to sell and when to hold.

According to that same *Wall Street Journal* survey only 11 percent of respondents would trust the advice of a stockbroker. But this goes much further than honesty, even the most well-meaning and honest stockbroker cannot possibly give the type of advice for a myriad of stocks that a computer program can give. And couple that program with the intelligence of the leading "brains" of the marketplace and you have a broadsword with which the little investor can slay the Wall Street dragon.

The time is a hot, humid summer sometime in the very near future. The souvlaki stand is still standing, although long since automated, as throngs of plaid-shorted tourists jam the front of the Exchange building. But this time, instead of handycams slung over their shoulders, they have portable PCs strapped to their waists. And inside on their hard disk is smart investing software. Okay, guys, come out fighting.

THE PORTFOLIO MANAGER

If you thought just keeping track of your own stocks was a huge task, just try managing an institutional portfolio that is valued in the billions! Portfolio management is, at best, a tricky art. The goal is to recommend the best of all possible groups of stocks for individual clients. With an overwhelming number of choices and the enormous amount of detail data to process from such places as the New York and American Exchanges, this process would seem quite ripe for expert-systematizing.

Athena Group thought this to be a good idea, too. The Portfolio Manager expert system, which is targeted toward large institutional portfolios, makes recommendations on how to structure the optimal client portfolio.

Human portfolio managers base their recommendations on a combination of factors. They must be privy to how the market works, how the economy affects the marketplace, to quantitative methodologies for selecting portfolios, and a host of other interrelated variables. Not the least of which is the heuristics of an experienced veteran of the market.

Interfaces

The Portfolio Manager has a direct feed to databases that detail investment options. This information originates from places like the Dow Jones database or Value Line. On top of this, the Portfolio Manager permits the entry of personal variables such as the manager's threshold of risk, rate of return desired, total amount to be invested as well as other selection criteria.

This expert system exhibits a graphical interface permitting the manager the use of a mouse to override any of the input variables. This interface also provides a graphic display of its recommended portfolio relative to the capital market line. It also shows a second plot consisting of a lattice or decision tree showing exactly how the Portfolio Manager arrived at its conclusion. The lattice plot can be thought of as a justification. It shows all the combinations of different percentages of the various assets that the system reasons about and either selects or eliminates in order to create the optimal portfolio.

Viewpoints

To be able to handle the complexity of the portfolio management model, the designers used a concept known as "viewpoints" that is central to the ART expert system tool. ART (Automated Reasoning Tool), developed by Inference Corporation, uses viewpoints to permit the organization of facts that are closely aligned into one unit. For example, a viewpoint might consist of all facts related to the economy on the date of the October 1987 market break. This unique concept gives one the ability to hypothesize about the outcome of different scenarios. ART then picks the best of the litter, or the one that most closely aligns with the case being examined.

The Portfolio Manager uses a combination of viewpoints, rules, factual data, variable data, and economic models to analyze the holdings in the financial databases. The goal is to determine which one or combination of instruments would suit the purposes of the client. It also uses viewpoints and rules to reason about the regulations and restrictions of the particular institution, and generalized rules to reason about basic management of the portfolio.

Advisor/Assistant

The Portfolio Manager can be used in two different ways. As an assistant, it can work on its own to make a portfolio recommendation. As an advisor, the system can work in tandem with a human portfolio manager. Here the Portfolio Manager uses knowledge of the specific portfolio manager's selection criteria, such as risk. It then adds a modicum of its own knowledge and proceeds to a recommendation.

To arrive at a recommendation, the Portfolio Manager creates viewpoints for each of the possible combinations of different percentages of instruments that have passed muster as instruments that can be considered potential assets. Starting with one viewpoint that represents an empty portfolio of holdings, the system proceeds to show viewpoints that consist of one potential asset but each with a different percentage. If the viewpoint contains a percentage of less than 100 percent, then an arrow is drawn to another viewpoint, which has the effect of merging the two viewpoints to construct a new viewpoint. In this way, a portfolio actually consists of many viewpoints, some having one asset for a 100 percent allocation and some having a combination of assets together totaling up to 100 percent.

Obviously this procedure could generate a bit of the combinatorial explosion problem. However, Portfolio Manager is saved from this fate by use of rules that act as constraints to viewpoint proliferation. One rule might look like "IF it is true that the value of GOLD is declining steeply, THEN companies who have large holdings in GOLD should be eliminated from list."

It is possible that several different portfolios are created. In constructing a portfolio, remember, dozens of economic, technical, legal, and personal variables were factored into construction of holdings viewpoints. To accommodate this range of possible portfolios, the system can provide a ranking, which is called the "portfolio utility." This measure is based on quantitative and qualitative reasoning. If this is insufficient, the portfolio manager can always ask for a re-ranking of the portfolios by some criterion. This would serve to maximize or minimize some variable such as risk or tax considerations or any of a thousand other choices. At this juncture, the human manager would take over and make the final decision.

TAXCUT

The most important financial decision anyone has to make is in the area of filing an income tax form at the end of the year. For most of us this is a painful and confusing process.

It was in 1988 that I purchased my first automated tax-preparer program. With all the tax changes, doing it manually had gotten much too complicated for me. I was much too proud to go to a real accountant at first and then I was much too ashamed to show my botched-up attempts at tax preparation to any professional.

But even the automated programs I used left me high and dry. I had lots of questions. Did I qualify for this exemption? Did I have to pay the alternative minimum tax? It was all too confusing. Along with the software came a very thick tome containing the accountantese version of the tax code. I found myself reading and re-reading it trying to figure out just what they meant.

In desperation I called (in retrospect, an enormous mistake) the IRS to answer my questions. After waiting on indefinite hold, I was connected to someone who, I think, actually knew less than I did. So it was with a great relish that I opened the shrink-wrapped, Andrew Tobias TaxCut package (originally called ASK DAN).

At first, TaxCut looks like all of the other tax preparation software packages on the market. But first appearances are quite deceiving. This one is different. This one has an expert system.

The expert system portion of TaxCut was originally written by Daniel Caine, an attorney who founded Legal Knowledge Systems with his AI-maven wife, Claire. Claire was the technician on the original ASK DAN project. TaxCut uses a question-and-answer approach to smart tax preparation. The expert system is accessible through a pull-down menu or a hot key. And once you're into the expert system, you can get great tax advice just as if you're sitting face-to-face with your tax attorney. For example, on the 1040 (that scourge of forms), you might have questions about charitable contributions or miscellaneous deductions. Well, TaxCut is there for you on these items as well as for help in interest income, dividend income, and capital gains.

At times, TaxCut even chimes in with unsolicited suggestions on the ways and means of reducing your tax bill. And that's not all; it comes complete with hypertext explanation functions as well as an IRS checking facility that peruses your return looking for those very same things that would trigger an IRS audit.

The expert system works in the same way an accountant would were you in the office. For example, let's say that you recently sold your home. As would a good accountant, the system will ask you if you're over the age of 55 to see if you qualify for the once-in-a-lifetime exclusion of tax on gain. Since this exclusion has many options, TaxCut will keep probing until it finds one that works for you, or until all possibilities have been exhausted.

This series of questions and answers correlates to the rules in this rule-based system. Dan Caine chose expert system methodology over conventional methodology since the rule base or knowledge base is stored essentially as a separate entity. Since the tax code changes on a year-to-year basis this modularized knowledge base approach permits easy modification.

Perhaps the feature with the most pizzazz is the ability to play "What if" with up to 30 scenarios. For those of you who like to "manipulate" your tax responsibilities, this is truly a godsend. On the Big Picture pull-down menu, the option Scenarios need only be selected to get you into tax-payer bingo. "What if I deduct my new pool; after all, I bring clients around?" The TaxCut answer will surely be, "prepare for an IRS audit."

PLANMAN

Mel's son Junior was always asking for money. After paying all those back taxes because he didn't listen to TaxCut, Mel had none. Still, his son persisted. Ten dollars here, five dollars there. Mel's pockets were being emptied on a daily basis. Finally, he decided to teach Junior a thing or two about budgeting and planning.

These lessons went on for about two weeks. One day when Mel arrived home from work, his wife Peg met him at the door. Grabbing his briefcase and giving him a quick peck on the cheek she excitedly told him, "You'll never guess. You know those budget lessons you've been giving Junior. Well, they're finally beginning to pay off. He told me what he wants for his birthday—and it will only cost us one dollar!" "Hey, I guess I finally got through to him," the proud Dad boasted. "So what does he want?" "Something really small," Peg answered with a sly smile. "He wants his own set of keys to your Mercedes."

Budgeting. Financial planning. These are activities that are distasteful to the great majority of us. Even if we could figure out how to do it we still wouldn't. Oh, some of us diligently work out simple monthly budgets, balance our checkbooks, and even install software on our PCs to do all of the above. Unfortunately, our enthusiasm wanes with the waxing of interest for some new activity that we enjoy more. Like sitting glued in front of the television set during the baseball playoffs. Like our counterpart "couch potatoes," we "budget and planning potatoes" are saddled with enormous guilt. In this case the guilt concerns our future.

Into this void stepped an army of financial planners. Armed with calculators and more questionnaires than can possibly fill up an average sized briefcase, this legion of the financial plan spread out to spread the gospel.

In the middle 1980s a small financial planning company decided to join the fray. To set themselves apart they published a newsletter. One of the crew had the bright idea of including a questionnaire with the newsletter, promising a financial plan if one would only fill out the form. They expected half a dozen, a dozen, maybe two dozen responses at most. What they got was a deluge. Evidently they had found the sore spot with those "budget and planning potatoes."

Why Expert Systems?

What to do? It took at least forty hours of effort to complete one plan manually. They couldn't disappoint their subscribers; after all, they were a new start-up and they wanted to develop a reputation for excellence and for service. What to do?

So they did what many had done before, they went the route of automation. And thus the Sterling Wentworth Corporation was born.

Comfortably ensconced in his office near the great Salt Lake in (guess where) Salt Lake City, Utah, Chad Hortin tells the story of two

Brigham Young professors who had a vision. One was an expert in the area of financial planning and one a computer whiz; between the two they possessed the where-with-all to get their dream off the ground.

It made sense to go with expert systems. The two Ph.D.s wanted to build a series of systems filled to the brim with financial planning expertise and sell it to the financial advisor out in the trenches. They also knew there was nothing quite like this product out there, so they would surely be on the leading edge.

The selling points would be an increase in productivity, level of service, and professional image. And they wanted to reduce that 40 hours of labor to a more manageable quarter or half-hour, so the advisor could spend more time in front of the client instead of behind a calculator.

The Financial Planning Process

Their first product was called PLANMAN. With over seventy-five hundred rules, it's chock-full of knowledge. Most of it was gleaned from the expertise of Jim Jenkins, one of the two founders, who just happens to head a degree program in financial planning at Brigham Young. Sterling Wentworth didn't stop there. With their contacts in the academic world, PLANMAN had the benefit of a sterling education. Nor was the practical side forgotten. As Sterling Wentworth grew, they had the foresight to gather 'round them a board of advisors that was composed of experts among the Big Eight accounting firms, the insurance field and banking.

Hortin, who holds the title of Vice President of Operations, is noticeably proud of the intense effort put into the development of PLANMAN. Not only is the system heavy on the knowledge side, it's also a master explainer. No cryptic answers here, PLANMAN contains over ten thousand "source paragraphs," which are used in the formation of the tailored financial plan.

Three Points of View.   The plan is comprehensive. Producing somewhere around eighty pages of tables, conclusions, and explanations, the prepared plan makes observations, comments, and suggestions concerning the client's situation. Three points of view come into play here.

The client sits with the financial advisor in the comfort of the home. Working over a cup of coffee, the advisor whips out a thick pad of questions and proceeds to identify everything from financial particulars such as assets and liabilities to general estate planning. The client discusses preferences and other areas of concern.

The advisor, as does any financial planner, comes equipped with a personal philosophy and rules of thumb that come from years of experience. This inner set of rules is accommodated by planning parameters. Some five hundred "openings" into the system are provided, which are used to personalize the process.

The expert software is the grand integrator, permitting a tailoring of its knowledge base for the advisor's gut instincts as well as providing for the individuality of the client.

A Tailored Plan.   When the session is over, the advisor thanks the client and walks out the door. And heads straight for the office where PLANMAN sits waiting. Forms are entered quickly through the data entry facility, which provides a rough facsimile of the paper forms now crumpled from overuse.

This done, the advisor hits the run key and walks away for another cup of coffee. But PLANMAN stays behind chugging, chugging away. Twenty minutes later our financial advisor returns to find a personal financial plan printed prettily.

Back it is to the clients who, for purposes of this explanation, are two fictitious characters named Michael and Susan Oleson.

Michael and Susan have their financial history, present and future, right at their fingertips. The knowledge base covers such topics as income tax and cash flow planning, portfolio and debt management. There are also sections on management of wealth growth, estate planning, and planning for retirement. Or for those of us younger than that, planning for financial independence, which I think are heavenly words. The last stop on the financial planning train is personal risk management, which plans for such depressing, but necessary, events as income for survivors, income during disability, and other forms of insurance.

Mike and Sue entered the planning process with some concerns. They wanted to accumulate sufficient assets to provide a comfortable retirement income, provide educational funds for their children, and develop an appropriate investment strategy. They also wanted to provide an adequate standard of living for family members in the event of death. Finally, they wanted to minimize personal income taxes, which actually would be first in importance on my list. Yours, too?

Some of the recommendations that PLANMAN made concerning Mike and Sue's situation included recommending that they hire their children in a family business to take advantage of lower tax rates. It also suggested making some of their charitable gifts in kind. It advised them to use appreciated investment assets rather than cash. It tactfully suggested that they reduce their level of debt and recommended $30,000 of additional insurance on Sue's life.

Now, as someone who is as confused as anyone else on what to do with my money, I read the suggestions with increasing interest. They made really good sense considering the financial situation Mike and Sue had.

The plan is quite complex. A full eighty pages for Mike and Sue. The plan is filled, page after page, with charts and suggestions so Mike and Sue can forge ahead with their future with renewed vigor and confidence.

Rules numbering 7500 covering the spectrum of financial planning; 7500 rules plucked from the expertise of Sterling Wentworth itself as well as from members of their Board of Advisors who have tentacles into the real world and theoretical world of research. Written originally in Pascal but rewritten in C to run on IBM PCs, the system today is constantly being renewed.

"So, you want to show me that you can save money by only asking me for a paltry, dollar birthday gift," said Mel to his son Junior. "I'll do you one better. I'll be generous. I'm giving you your very own car."

"Gee, Dad. Thanks. Thanks a lot," said Junior happily. "It's out in the driveway. Here's the key. Go take a look." Mel smiled as he handed Junior a gold key.

Junior ran out to the driveway, heart pounding. "Wow, my very own car." But as he approached the driveway he stopped in his tracks. "Hey Dad," he yelled back at the house. "What's this?" Mel walked out the front door to the driveway and reached down and picked up the shiny, toy sports car. "Why son, it's your birthday gift. You see, I can save money, too."

SYNTELLIGENCE

It was a cold and bleak morning. The sky was white and low, like a freshly broken block of thick ice. A line of people, faces wrapped against the wind, huddled against the side of a small, one-story building. It was quiet except for the occasional whistle of a train in the distance. Eyes tired, they continually glanced at the big old clock across the street. Brought in from the East by stagecoach over one hundred years ago, the delicate scrollwork surrounding the clock's face was the only evidence that this town had seen better days. And still they waited. And hoped. Surely someone would come and give them their money. Bank closings. Sends shivers down your spine, doesn't it? But this isn't one for the history books. These are the 1990s and so far billions upon billions of dollars have been spent in bailing out the bankrupt thrifts.

Wait a second! How did this happen? Well, risky investments made by well-meaning and less than well-meaning bankers were a rather large nail in the coffin. Hey, you might say, extending credit is always a risky proposition. You win some and you lose some. C'est la vie! Besides, you say, unless you have an army of bankers joined at the hip working on every deal, there's just no way that every loan is going to be analyzed to the degree that it's risk-free. What's a small (or for that matter, a large) bank to do? Well you can be smart about it. Or to put it more precisely, you can be expert about it.

Syntel

In the middle of the 1980s a group of techno-gurus got together and made the momentous decision to apply AI technology to the financial services area. One of these techno-gurus just happened to be Peter Hart, who is the daddy of Prospector, one of the first expert systems. So if anyone had the technical know-how, it was these techno-gurus. The venture capitalists agreed and funded the four founders to the tune of a lot of dollars.

They decided early on to target both the insurance and the banking industries. Since they possessed no banking or insurance experience to speak of, they quickly hooked up to several big names and formed a sort of consortium. In the banking arena, Wells Fargo and Wachovia jumped in feet first while in the insurance arena the trio of Fireman's Fund, St. Paul and AIG scrambled to get on board. And they begat the name Syntelligence (which has a nice ring to it).

Four years and a bag of money later two products were christened. The Lending Advisor and the Underwriting Advisor were born of a dynamic new AI programming language, naturally called Syntel. It is unique among expert system tools.

Marketed as the first programming language specifically for financial risk assessment, it is priced way up there. The remarkable thing about Syntel is that the developers took the standard, ho-hum rule-based expert system and punted with it, adding probabilistic inference here, spreadsheet-like functionality there. And as an extra, added attraction, added relational database and application generator functionalities. Richard Watts, an assistant vice president at Wachovia, described his initial impression of the Lending Advisor as "a kind of electronic note pad for experienced loan officers and an on-line tutor for account officers with less lending experience."

Go into any bank, insurance office or securities firm. Go up the steps and into the back offices and watch the shirt-sleeve action. You'll see heavy Lotus 1-2-3 spreadsheet use as well as database access packages. In one way or another all this computer power is being used for one purpose and one purpose only: to calculate the risk factor of granting a loan, investing in a company, or underwriting insurance. What Syntelligence found was that even though the process of risk assessment might be performed differently in different business lines, there was much commonality in the methodology.

It was obvious, really. To anyone that really looked. And this is exactly what Syntelligence did. Then and there they decided to develop a language that would provide for a nice balance between qualitative and quantitative reasoning as well as provide for the "natural fit" of spreadsheet languages to the description of financial functional relationships. They saw to it that Syntel would be able to deal easily with incomplete, and worse, inaccurate information as well as heavily judgmental decisions. The team also was savvy enough to figure into the equation the need to access multiple internal and external reference databases. This permitted them to link to hazard ratings, financial reports for companies, and pricing data. Most importantly, they factored in the ability to perform multiattribute assessments. This was important since most problems of this nature are, by definition, complex and often involve interdependent considerations such as financial terms and management performance.

All of these ingredients were put into one big pot and stirred around. Added to the stew was a forms language that would enable the system developer to control the user interface. This nifty interface (Figure 10-4) is a natural for these forms-oriented users. Assessments are shown as gauges or meters providing a natural input for entering probability

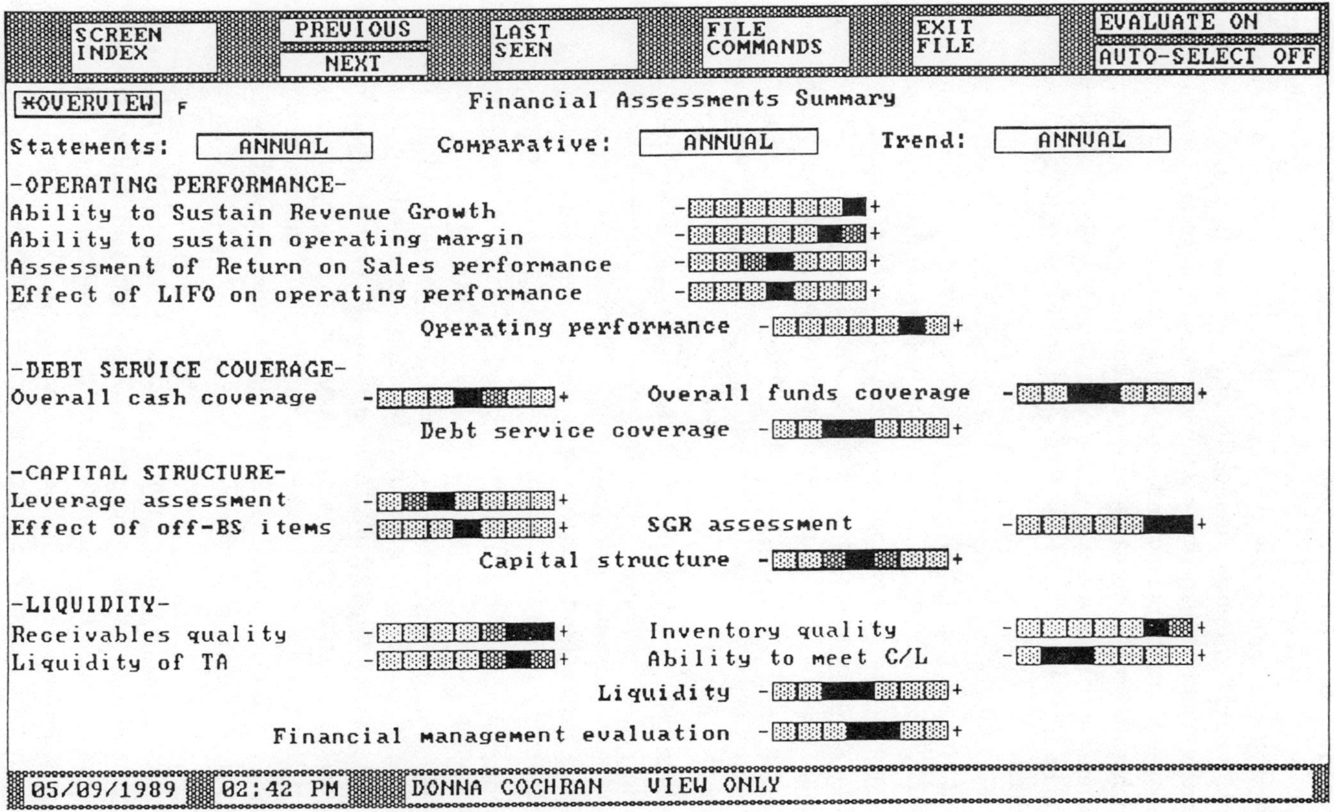

FIGURE 10-4. Syntelligence Lending Advisor.

SCREEN INDEX | PREVIOUS / NEXT | LAST SEEN | FILE COMMANDS | EXIT FILE | EVALUATE ON / AUTO-SELECT OFF

*OVERVIEW F

Financial Assessments Summary

Statements: ANNUAL   Comparative: ANNUAL   Trend: ANNUAL

-OPERATING PERFORMANCE-
Ability to Sustain Revenue Growth
Ability to sustain operating margin
Assessment of Return on Sales performance
Effect of LIFO on operating performance
Operating performance

-DEBT SERVICE COVERAGE-
Overall cash coverage
Overall funds coverage
Debt service coverage

-CAPITAL STRUCTURE-
Leverage assessment
Effect of off-BS items
Capital structure

-LIQUIDITY-
Receivables quality
Inventory quality
Ability to meet C/L
Liquidity of TA
Liquidity
Financial management evaluation

05/09/1989   02:42 PM   DONNA COCHRAN   VIEW ONLY

288

(i.e., judgment) about a particular variable. Everything else was as easy as answering yes or no by filling out an on-line questionnaire. This all-powerful Syntel language was embedded into the IBM mainframe operating environment and dubbed SynCore. Providing interfaces to standard insurance and banking systems gives the Syntelligence software a powerful punch that's hard to resist.

Syntelligence was smarter than just creating a souped-up, new expert system tool. Their real goal was to provide specific smart applications for the banking and insurance industries. Syntel was the bread. The butter would be the industry experience.

The Lending Advisor

Don Steele, CEO of Syntelligence, describes these products as "almost off the shelf." The Lending Advisor's innards contain the accumulated experience of the consortium members who helped bankroll Syntelligence's entry into the market. The techno-gurus went "to live" with the accountants for three whole years. They managed to drain the very essence of knowledge and expertise from their mentors. But there's always room for more. The product permits tailoring. So, for those banks that think that they have "that extra something" that makes them competitive—well, just add it to the system.

The Lending Advisor provides credit guidance by providing seasoned, multi-industry expert experience to the average commercial lender and credit reviewer. Not only does it go out and grab customer information and present it in one uniform display, it also permits industry comparisons using services such as Dun and Bradstreet or Standard and Poor.

Drawing on its large storehouse of experience, the system looks at such things as current financial condition. It compares this to historical performance as well as to the industry from a competitive analytical standpoint. It even looks at management competence, which is always a somewhat fuzzy issue. It also projects future performance. It doesn't just do a credit scoring. It does a thorough credit analysis, taking into account fuzzy or judgmental information. It does this by interfacing with the user in over twenty separate modules, each of which contains one or more screens.

As the loan officer walks through the screens with the system, the Lending Advisor is chugging away performing a comprehensive analysis that pretty much covers the spectrum.

The "big picture" is looked at first. What is the risk inherent in the industry? With this in mind the system begins to look at the specifics of the firm itself. These specifics are in the form of pro forma balance sheets, income statements, cash flows, and ratio analysis. All the things that make accountants mad with passion. Peer group and trend analysis is next on the agenda where industry norms are compared to. Getting down into the nitty gritty, we can cruise through a section on the firm's operating performance, historical capital structure, and historical debt service. If that isn't enough, we can hop over to liquidity and trading assets where such esoteric things as return policy and after-sales service can be addressed. The icing on the cake is the celebrated Management Competence module, which any employee worth their salt would willingly donate their free time to be a part of. Winding down now, we can get the system to produce a Financial Management Evaluation, which is one of the main determinants of the final and all-important borrower rating. A whole slew of other must-haves are spit out of the system from the Projections and Loan Structure worksheet to the Borrower Assessment Survey, to analysis of guarantor's financial strengths, to evaluation of multiple lines of business borrowers.

This process does not dispense with the loan officer. The loan officer controls the Lending Advisor every step of the way. This is done by using overrides and a special footnote feature where concerns, observations, and justification for overriding assessments can be easily and noticeably recorded.

Powerful. Complete. But still a hard sell. The banking industry is one of the most conservative groups in the financial services industry. Many look at this newfangled software and say, "why do I need it?" They look around and say, "wait a minute, my loan losses are better than the industry average. All my returns are better. We're not perfect, but we're okay. If I had $2 million to spend, hey, I'd spend it on a better loan accounting system."

The old town clock chimes five but the bank never did open. Light snowflakes begin to fall from the darkened sky. One by one they begin to drift away across silent, shadowy streets. Not so much as a word is exchanged. Maybe tomorrow. Maybe then.

Maybe smart systems could have prevented this very cold scene. If all credit lending had been uniform and expert judgment applied throughout, would the failed S&Ls have been in the predicament that they found themselves in? We'll never know but Syntelligence makes it a practice to ask a prospective customer to run its loans through the Lending Advisor. And guess what, the Lending Advisor's success rate has been 110 percent, with the 10 percent going to that unnamed bank where our smart system found a loan that had gone (shall we say) south. But *mum* was the word since the bank's president was as yet "in the dark" about this particular nasty mistake. Shades of savings and loans.

11

A Final Word

Stare at the black squares for a few seconds. Do you notice anything odd on the intersecting white lines? These blackish spots are after-images. This is known as an optical illusion.

LET'S SUM UP

The use of artificial intelligence in the financial services community is certainly no illusion, involves no sleight of hand and is no trick. From Wall Street's expert trading systems to Hartford's expert underwriting systems, everybody's dabbling. And for good reason.

There really is no other choice! The information explosion has financial services firms pinned under the weight of tons of claims forms, new applications, trade tickets, money transfer telexes. And the pile grows heavier every day. Of course newer and faster computers can easily digest this glut. It churns it around a bit and then spits out some shreds of illumination. But managements noted a remarkable anomaly. The pile of paper that came out was larger than the pile that went in. Something was missing!

That something was human judgment. The most that conventional computer systems can do is "input-calculate-output." Judgment is needed to make complex decisions about even more complex data. People, when faced with decisions concerning large amounts of information, employ subconscious filtering techniques to whittle down the task to a more manageable level. We do this every day. As an example, what do you do when you come home to find your mailbox crammed full of magazines, letters, junk mail, and the like? You employ your own inner rules of thumb and your best judgment to determine what to toss into the trash. Maybe your rules of thumb go something like this. Keep all magazines. Toss out all circulars. Toss out all requests for contributions. Keep all bills (unfortunately). If a letter does not fall into the categories above and you can't see through the envelope your rule of thumb might be, "if it has a stamp rather than a bulk mailing label keep it." Within a few seconds you have managed to make a whole host of decisions. How about a more difficult example. You're at work and you have to make a decision about whether or not a particular company is worth investing in. On top of your desk sits financial reports, 10Qs, 10Ks, press reports, press clippings, ad infinitum. An experienced person can sift through this mass of information fairly quickly and zoom in on just those items of significance. But most of the computer systems that we use today just can't cope with this level of judgmental complexity.

Enter AI. With its ability to reason, AI software certainly evokes computer magic. But it really isn't magic. AI software is just another tool in the software developer's toolbox. One that financial services firms must use in a large way if they hope to compete in a global environment characterized by increasing competition, some of it from the most unlikely places. Who would have thought, just a decade ago, that the banks would be trading securities? And who would have thought that the securities firms would be buying banks? With Europe 1992 looming just around the corner, these firms had better be prepared to become leaner and meaner financial machines.

FINANCIAL SERVICES' HIGH-TECH FUTURE

$\mathbf{W}$e've read about some remarkable uses of AI technology in financial services. But this is just the tip of the iceberg. More and more firms are beginning to understand that it is the "knowledge" workers who make up their most valuable resource. These are the people that create magic by working expertly with information. They are the largest and fastest growing segment of the industry. And just as these firms are beginning to understand the importance of these workers, they are also realizing the necessity of providing tools to magnify this expertise.

Wall Street

In the hallowed halls of the Chicago Board of Trade, AURORA will most certainly serve as a springboard to total off-floor trading. While the other exchanges have adopted a wait and see attitude, they will soon have no other choice but to follow AURORA's lead. Or they will be left out in the cold, sleeping while the rest of the world takes advantage of global 24-hour trading.

The securities firms themselves need to use smarter technology to retrench. The high volume of trading, the large number of instruments, the interplay of the various markets and increasing regulatory scrutiny will require these firms to trade smarter, better, and faster. Artificial intelligence is already being used in trading in various firms. This will be increased as the brokerages realize that no one person can process all of these variables quickly enough and carefully enough to make the most efficient trading decisions. And in a decade that will be noted for its conservativeness, in staffing levels as well as for decisions made, firms will need all the help they can get.

On the other side of the securities coin is the investing public. Off-floor trading, with its natural, built-in audit trail, might do wonders in luring this endangered species back. Add to this the emergence of expert trading software like AIQ's StockExpert and the small investors just might return in droves.

Since 1987 the securities firms have been in a slump. Fewer investors and a few bad investment decisions are but two of the factors causing this "securities winter." Perhaps technology that can even the odds a bit can do wonders to turn winter into summer.

The Banks

Banks, like Wall Street, lost a bit of luster in the 1980s. With the savings and loan scandal still fresh in everyone's mind, banks need to work hard to have some of this tarnish removed. Syntelligence and Peat Marwick among others have moved along the right road in developing software that the banks can use to assay the strength of their loan portfolios. The question now is, will the banks move in that direction as well?

In spite of a bit of tarnish, banks are moving forward with their strategy of joining technology to people. We saw it in Citibank's Pension Processor as well as their telex natural language processor. But they'll go even further.

American Express' Authorizer's Assistant will become the model for bank credit card processing. With the proliferation of credit cards and the growing tide of fraudulent use, no human reviewer can cope at a sustainedly high level.

Perhaps the most visible use of AI will be in the branch. For the first time, customers will be able to get the answers they need and fast. And the banks will be able to offer services that they couldn't offer before: financial planning, tax assistance, and even securities trading. And watch out for those smart ATMs.

Insurance

Medical insurers will follow Cigna's lead in providing clients with "smart" reports about their employees' medical claim patterns. In an era of sky-rocketing medical costs, this will serve as a much needed cost-containment device. Insurers might even go one step further, like Hartford Steam and Boiler Inspection and Insurance, and provide expert software for in-house client use so that these clients can do their own monitoring.

On the underwriting side, the use of AI will continue to infiltrate the life market. Expert underwriting systems will be rolled out into other forms of insurance as well. Automobile, home, and commercial will most likely be expert-systematized in that order.

AI can also be used as a marketing tool. I'm not talking about target marketing, which I mentioned in the chapter on insurance, I'm talking about bait. Luring a customer into an insurance office is often next to impossible. People willingly buy medical, automobile, and home insurance, but other forms of insurance are a harder sale. Outfitting a branch office with a terminal and access to a smart insurance advisor just might catch the fish. And providing smart assistance to an independent agent might just catch the big one.

The Off-the-Shelf Market

Much of the innovation will come from this sector. They have the money, the time, and the inclination. As I mentioned in Chapter 10, these innovators managed to corral the collective expertise of many specialists making off-the-shelf systems a hot commodity.

I would expect to find systems being developed for many of the different sectors of the financial services industry by these companies. But there will be a lot of competition in this market as the Big Eight and the AI tool marketers gain entry to this niche.

It's happening right now. Peat Marwick's Loan Probe, originally intended for internal use, is being marketed for external use. Several of the expert system tool manufacturers are adding domain knowledge bases to their systems for areas like manufacturing. It's just a matter of time before they realize what a large market financial services will be.

The Big Eight

Perhaps the biggest bang will come from the Big Eight. And the reason has little to do with AI expertise. The reason for this predominance will come from their expertise in the industry itself. Second after bankers in expertise in banking come the Big Eight. And securities and insurance, too. They know all of our secrets.

The industry will buy, not only the AI technical expertise but the industry experience as well. After all, that's what they're doing today. AI will just sweeten the pot.

Internally, you'll see AI tools spring up rather quickly in the Big Eight audit area. Audit planning will be first on the list, followed closely by in-field audit tools for sampling and interviewing.

The Big Eight will also delve into AI tools for management consulting, which is the flip side of their consultancies. This will take the form of planning tools, project management, as well as smart databases of domain knowledge. Consultancies "*are* what they know." Each Big Eight firm has pockets of industry knowledge that go unrecorded. AI technologies will be used to encode what was learned at a consulting assignment so that this knowledge can be reused elsewhere. This will not only benefit the Big Eight firm but it will benefit the customer as well.

A NATURAL EVOLUTION

The financial services industry has run out of paper to automate. Every conceivable form has been systematized and data entered into a computer until the computer is fairly bursting at the seams. For years we have concentrated on the numeric side of computing, which takes advantage of the quantitative power of the computer. But knowledge workers need more and computers can give it to them. Artificial intelligence systems exploit the qualitative side of computers, which is the next step in the natural evolution of computer systems. This coupled with the large repositories of information that we've amassed make for a dynamic duo.

Knowledge. That's the door we want to unlock and open wide. And artificial intelligence just might be the key.

APPENDIX A

Other Financial Expert Systems

Bank of Boston	Fed Funds Advisor. Designed to support the work of the Funds Trader in the Treasury Division. Reminds the trader of individual factors that must be taken into account in operating in the market. Also acts as a training aid to illustrate the effect of various technical factors on activity in the market.
Deutsche Bank	Increase Revenue. Used to perform 20 different analyses that assist in identifying areas where a company's revenue could be increased.
Arthur D. Little	Personal Lines Account Review (PLAR). Automates account review function that agents/brokers perform when recommending new products or adjusting coverages for their customers.
Arthur D. Little	Platform Manager's Assistant (PMA). Assists platform officers and customer account representatives in today's complex world of retail banking.

Arthur D. Little	Customer Account Review (CAR). Supports retail stockbrokers and their office managers. Reviews accounts that the broker is handling and makes recommendations regarding investments that are both promising and suitable for the customer. Works with customer profile developed from application data, margin data, holdings data and brokerage firm research.
AGS, Inc	Account Reconciliation Advisor. Assists bank personnel with corporate client bank statement reconciliation.
Applied Expert Systems with John Hancock Insurance	Client Profiling. Used for financial planning and support.
Applied Expert Systems	Plan Power. Financial planning tool aimed at banks, brokerages, and other financial institutionals that offer financial planning services.
Intelligent Technology Group	Intelligent Portfolio Manager. Advises on portfolio holding selections.
Cognitive Systems	Teller Trainer. Trains potential bank tellers in typical banking tasks.
Arthur D. Little	Trader's Assistant. Expert system with the goal to assist securities traders in determining the state of the market. Includes ability to evaluate rumors.
Palladian Software	Financial Advisor. Assists managers in the analysis of capital investment proposals.

Palladian Software	Management Advisor. Assists management staff in the creation of a business plan.
The Equitable	TIARA. Internal audit system.
Sanwa Bank	Best Mix. Portfolio Management System for conservative private accounts.
Nippon Life	Underwriter's Aid. Helps underwriter and physician determine whether to underwrite a policy for a difficult case and then determines how much to charge.
Bank of America (U.K.)	Letter of Credit Advisor. Detects discrepancies between the letter of credit and accompanying documents and recommends courses of action. In use in United Kingdom.
Bear, Stearns	Manager's Broker Monitoring System. Compliance system that monitors broker's discretionary accounts.

APPENDIX B

Software Vendors

This is a sampling of the products that are commercially available.

AICorp Inc.
100 Fifth Avenue
Waltham, MA 02254
(617) 890-8400

KBMS
First Class
expert system shell:
IBM PC/Mainframe/VAX

AION Corp.
101 University Avenue
Palo Alto, CA 94301
(415) 328-9595

Aion Development System
expert system shell:
IBM PC/Mainframe/DEC

Artificial Intelligence
Technologies
40 Saw Mill River Road
Hawthorne, NY 10532
(914) 347-3182

Mercury
expert system shell:
DEC/Unix Workstations

Arity Corp.
30 Domino Drive
Concord, MA 01742
(508) 371-1243

Arity/Expert
expert system shell:
IBM PC

California Intelligence
912 Powell Street #8
San Francisco, CA 94108
(415) 391-4846

XYSYS
expert system shell:
IBM PC/VAX/HP/SUN

Carnegie Group
650 Commerce Court
Station Square
Pittsburgh, PA 15219
(412) 642-6900

Knowledge Craft
expert system shell:
Workstation

CIM Solutions
P.O. Box 7041
Provo, Utah 84604
(801) 374-5626

Socrates
expert system shell:
IBM PC/DEC

Expert Systems International
1700 Walnut Street
Philadelphia, PA 19103
(215) 735-8510

ESP-Advisor
expert system shell:
IBM PC/VAX

ExperTelligence Inc.
559 San Ysidro Rd.
Santa Barbara, CA 93108
(805) 969-7871

ExperLISP
ExperOPS5
ExperProlog
AI development languages

EXSYS Inc.
P.O. Box 11247
Albuquerque, NM 87192
(505) 256-8356

EXSYS
expert system shell:
IBM PC/VAX

Gold Hill Computers
26 Landsdowne Street
Cambridge, MA 02139
(800) 242-5477

GoldWorks
expert system shell:
IBM PC
also sells Golden Common LISP

Hecht Nielson Corp.(HNC)
5501 Oberlin Dr.
San Diego, CA 92121
(619) 546-8877

Anza board
KnowledgeNet
neural net products:
IBM PC

IBM
P.O. Box 10
Princeton, NJ
(201) 329-7000

ESE
Knowledgetool
TIRS
expert system shell:
IBM Mainframe/PC

Inference Corp.
5300 W. Century Blvd.
Los Angeles, CA 90045
(213) 417-7997

ART
expert system shell:
IBM PC/Mainframe/
Workstation/VAX

Information Builders Inc.
1250 Broadway
New York, NY 10001
(212) 736-4433

Level 5
expert system shell:
VAX/Workstation/
IBM PC/Mainframe/Macintosh

IntelliCorp
1975 El Camino Real W.
Mountain View, CA 94040
(415) 965-5500

KEE
expert system shell:
IBM PC/Mainframe/
Workstations/Macintosh

IntelligenceWare Inc.
9800 S. Sepulveda Blvd.
Suite 730
Los Angeles, CA 90045
(213) 417-8896

Auto-Intelligence
IXL: Machine Learning
Intelligence/Compiler
expert system shells:
IBM PC

Jeffrey Perrone and Associates
3685 17th Street
San Francisco, CA 94114
(415) 431-9562

Expert-Ease
Expert-Edge
expert system shell:
IBM PC

Knowledge Garden Inc.
473A Malden Bridge Road
Nassau, NY 12123
(518) 766-3000

KnowledgePro
KnowledgeMaker
expert system shell:
IBM PC

Logicware International
2065 Dundas St. E
Suite 204
Mississauga, Ontario
Canada L4V 1T1
(416) 672-0300

MProlog
programming language:
IBM PC/Mainframe/
Workstation/VAX/HP

mdbs Inc.
P.O. Box 248
2 Executuve Drive
Lafayette, IN 47902
(317) 463-4561

Guru
expert system shell:
IBM PC/Workstations/DEC

NeuralWare Inc.
103 Buckskin Court
Sewickley, PA 15143
(412) 741-5959

NeuralWare Professional II
expert system shell:
IBM PC/NEC/Workstation

Nestor Inc.
1 Richmond Square
Providence, RI 02906
(401) 331-9640

Nestor Development System
neural network

Neuron Data
444 High Street
Palo Alto, CA 94301
(415) 321-4488

Nexpert Object
expert system shell:
IBM PC/Mainframe/VAX/
Workstations/Macintosh

Paperback Software International
2830 Ninth St.
Berkeley, CA 94710
(415) 644-2116

VP-Expert
expert system shell:
IBM PC

Softsync Inc.
162 Madison Ave
New York, NY 10016
(212) 695-2080

SuperExpert
Expert Ease
expert system shell:
IBM PC/Macintosh

Software Architecture and
Engineering
1600 Wilson Blvd.
Suite 500
Arlington, VA 22209
(703) 276-7910

KES
expert system shell:
IBM PC/Mainframe/
Workstations/VAX

Teknowledge, Inc.
1850 Embarcadero Rd.
P.O. Box 10119
Palo Alto, CA 94303
(414) 424-0500

M.1
S.1
expert system shell:
IBM PC/Mainframes/HP/VAX

Texas Instruments
P.O. Box 809063
Dallas, TX 75380
(800) 527-3500

Personal Consultant Series
Procedure Consultant
expert system shell:
IBM PC

APPENDIX C

Financial Services' AI Products

Applied Artificial Intelligence 1620 Gregg Ave. #14 Florence, SC 29501 (803) 667-1986	Expert Trading System
Applied Expert Systems, Inc. Five Cambridge Center Cambridge, MA 02142 (617) 492-7322	APEX Client Profiling
Brattle Research 55 Wheeler St. Cambridge, MA 02138 (617) 492-1982	Who-What-Ware text retrieval
Cognitive Systems Inc. 234 Church Street New Haven, CT 06510 (203) 773-0726	ATRANS deciphers funds transfer telex

EBG & Associates Inc.
70 E. Lake St.
#1400
Chicago, IL 60601
(312) 580-2260
	Coach, A Guide to Permitted
	   Disparity
	pension plan integration
	   with social security

General Intelligence
3008 Hillegass
Berkeley, CA 94705
(415) 548-8873

XYZ
peer group financial
  analysis

Integrated Analytics Corp.
13315 Washington Blvd.
Los Angeles, CA 90066
(213) 578-5052

MarketMind
alert system for traders

JS&A Products
1 JS&A Plaza, Dept. CR
Northbrook, IL 60062
(312) 564-7000

Halographix
analyzed fluctuations in
  stock prices

Mortimer & Associates
7900-27 Baymeadows Circle E.
Jacksonville, FL 32216
(904) 739-2424

Software Development Joint
  Ventures specialized software
  for traders

National Computer Systems
400 Northridge Road
Atlanta, GA 30350
(404) 641-4141

ULTRUST
integrated asset
  management system

The Partners Group
3108 Oxford Road
Madison, WI 53705
(608) 238-2301

The Bodway Model
econometric model

Providence Research Group
999C Edgewater Blvd. Suite 212
Foster City, CA 94404
(415) 593-0257

Intelligent Trading System

Raden Research Group
P.O. Box 1809
Madison Square Garden Station
New York, NY 10159
(212) 696-4476

PRISM
financial market prediction system

TRT Telecommunications Corp.   Intelligent Banking System
1331 Pennsylvania Ave. N.W.   process unformatted telex
Washington, D.C. 20004
(202) 879-2373

Glossary

Algorithm. A procedure that is systematized which results in a correct outcome. In developing a conventional program the programmer must specify the algorithms that the program will follow.

Artificial intelligence. A subfield of computer science aimed at pursuing the possibility that a computer can be made to behave in ways that humans recognize as "intelligent" human behavior.

Attribute. A property of an object. For instance, cold is an attribute of ice cream.

Automatic programming. The field of AI dealing with creation of programs that in turn write other programs.

Back-End. Usually refers to that portion of the system run after-hours (i.e. batch reports).

Backward chaining. A control strategy that regulates order in which inferences are drawn. In backward chaining the system attempts to determine if the goal rule is correct. It backs up to the *Ifs* and tries to determine whether or not they are correct.

Breadth-first search. In a rule hierarchy, this strategy refers to having all of the rules on the same level being examined prior to any rules on the next lower level.

CAI. Computer-Aided (or Assisted) Instruction. Another subfield of AI where the computer is used to present instruction.

Certainty factor. A numerical weight given to a fact or relationship to indicate confidence in that fact or relationship.

Class. A set of information similar to a file.

Class member. The elements of information within a class, similar to a record within a file.

Common LISP. The standardized version of the most prevalent AI language.

Conflict resolution. The process by which a rule is chosen to fire.

Conflict set. Eligible rules to fire. In other words, rules whose LHS (Left-Hand Side) were satisfied.

Consultation paradigm. These paradigms describe generic types of problem-solving situations.

Control. Within the context of a knowledge-based system, *control* refers to the regulation of the ordering in which reasoning occurs. Examples are backward or forward chaining.

Demon. A procedure that is automatically triggered when a value is changed within an object.

Depth-first search. In a hierarchically controlled system, a depth-first search refers to a strategy where one branch of the hierarchy is thoroughly searched. This is the opposite of breadth-first search.

Domain. An area of knowledge.

Download. To move data from one computer system to another. Usually refers to moving data from a mainframe to a PC.

Embedded expert system. An expert system run under the control of a conventional data processing system.

Encapsulation. Refers to the fact that an object can be considered a miniprogram. It is independent from other objects, with its own attributes, values, and procedures.

End user. Ultimate user of expert system.

Expert system. A computer system that can perform at or near the level of an expert.

Forward chaining. One of several control strategies that regulate the order in which inferences are drawn. It begins by asserting all of the rules whose *if* clauses are true. It continues this process, checking on what additional rules are true until the program reaches a goal or runs out of possibilities.

Frame. A knowledge representation scheme that associates an object with a collection of facts about that object.

Front-End. Usually refers to the on-line processing portion of a computer system.

Fuzzy logic. Knowledge representation techniques that deal with uncertainty.

Garbage collection. How a programming language manages the storage of unused variables.

Hardwire. In the 1990s this refers to the programming practice of coding all details within a program. The flipside is to use variables that can be entered at run time.

Heuristic. A rule of thumb.

Heuristic rules. Rules written to capture the "rules of thumb" of an expert. Usage of these rules does not always lead to correct solutions.

High-level Languages. FORTRAN, COBOL, C, and others written for more conventional data processing.

Induction. Some expert system shells have the capability of using examples to gather the knowledge that goes into the knowledge base. This eliminates the need to go through the formal knowledge acquisition process.

IF...THEN Rule. A statement of relationship in the form of IF A THEN B.

Inference. The process by which new facts are derived from known facts.

Inference Engine. The working program of the knowledge system that contains inference and control strategies. The term has also become linked with the attributes of user interface, external file interface, explanation features as well as other attributes.

Inheritance. Attributes of the parent object can be inherited by the child. For example, in the object CAR, a parent attribute is that it has four wheels. The child object, MERCEDES, inherits this attribute from its parent CAR.

Instantiations. The rule and the list of class members that satisfy the left-hand side of the rule.

Interface. The linkage between the computer program and the outside world.

Knowledge acquisition. The laborious process of collecting, documenting, verifying, and refining knowledge.

Knowledge base. That portion of an expert system that consists of the facts and heuristics about an area (called a domain). Can be composed of rules, objects, and other methodologies for storing knowledge.

Knowledge engineer. That individual whose role is to assess problems, acquire knowledge, build expert systems.

Knowledge representation. Methods used to encode and store facts and relationships. Examples are rules, frames, objects-values-attributes.

LHS. Left-hand side of rule. Often thought of as the condition that must be met. For example: IF salary > 25000 THEN . . . with the IF clause being the LHS.

LISP. A programming language, favored by American AI researchers.

Meta-rule. A rule about a rule rather than about the knowledge application. This type of rule is used to control how the system operates.

Mid-run Explanation. An expert system has the ability to stop during a consultation run and explain what it is doing.

MYCIN. One of the first backward-chaining expert systems. Developed at Stanford in the middle 1970s, it was developed as a research tool in the domain of diagnosis and treatment of meningitis and bacteremia infectious diseases. When researchers emptied all of the medical information out of MYCIN, the first *shell* was born. This was called EMYCIN.

MIPS. Acronym for Millions of Instructions Per Second. This is a measurement of computer speed.

NLP. Natural Language Processing. Using English to converse with the computer.

Neural net. Another branch of AI, where software tries to mimic the interconnected neurons of the human brain. Here the net is trained by use of examples.

Object. Building block of the newer AI-based systems. Similar to frame in concept.

Object-attribute-value. A method of knowledge representation. An example would be object is sweater, attribute is color, value is blue—thus, the blue sweater.

OPS5. One of the original AI languages. Used to build DEC's XCON. Most terminology used within Knowledgetool is derived from OPS5.

PROLOG. A symbolic programming language based on predicate calculus. Most popular AI language outside of the United States.

Prototype. Initial version of expert system.

Pseudocode. Writing rules in English language.

Recognize-act. A looping or iterative process whereby the inference engine determines the conflict set, picks a rule to fire, and performs the actions of that rule found on the RHS (Right-Hand Side). This methodology was first used in OPS5. Knowledgetool is based on this methodology.

RETE. Algorithm that optimizes the searching process of rule-based systems. Systems that have this feature are much more efficient than systems that don't.

RHS. Right-Hand Side of rule. The executable actions performed as a result of the LHS being true. For example: IF salary > 25000 THEN salary = salary * .10 with the THEN clause being the RHS.

Robotics. Branch of AI dealing with robots. Robots can sense and manipulate their environment.

Rule. A conditional statement of two parts.
IF... is the condition
THEN... is the premise

Rule-based system. A program that represents knowledge by means of rules.

Shell. A prewritten expert system tool. Includes interfaces and inference engine.

Speech recognition. Ability of computer to understand human speech.

Symbolic language. A computer language designed for expressing manipulation of complex concepts.

Uncertainty. Conventional systems cannot deal with uncertainty. Expert systems, on the other hand, can deal with the vagueness and fuzziness that comes with the processing of human judgment.

Bibliography

MAGAZINES

AI MAGAZINE. Official journal of AAAI.
AAAI
445 Burgess Drive
Menlo Park, CA 94025

EXPERT SYSTEMS. Auerbach publication.
Auerbach Publications
Division of Warren, Gorham & Lamont
210 South Street
Boston, MA 02111

IEEE EXPERT. Publication of IEEE.
IEEE Computer Society
10662 Los Vaqueros Circle
Los Alamitos, CA 90720

AI EXPERT. Commerical publication, available at newstands.
Miller Freeman Publications
500 Howard Street
San Francisco, CA 94105

PC AI. Commercial AI magazine.
PC AI
3310 West Bell Rd.
Suite 119
Phoenix, AZ 85023

NEWSLETTERS

"Applied Artificial Intellignece Reporter"
ICS Research Institute
P.O. Box 12308-EP
Fort Lee, NJ 07024

"EXPERT SYSTEM STRATEGIES"
Cutter Information Inc.
1100 Mass Avenue
Arlington, MA 02174

"AI WEEK"
AIWEEK INC.
P.O. Box 2513
Birmingham, AL 35201

"Artificial Intelligence Report"
Booz-Allen Hamilton
4330 East-West Highway
Bethesda, MD 20814

"Spang-Robinson Report"
3600 West Bayshore Rd.
Palo Alto, CA
94303

"TECHINSIDER"
2170 Broadway
Suite 2290
New York, NY 10024

BOOKS AND ARTICLES

Arend, Mark. 1988. "Expert System Is AE's Latest Commodity." *Wall Street Computer Review,* (June): 24.

Aronson, David R. 1988. "What Neurocomputers Can Do for Wall Street." *Financial Technology Forum,* (December): 22–23.

Ashmore, G. Michael. 1988. "Containing the Information Explosion." *The Journal of Business Strategy,* (January-February): 52–54.

Barr, Avron; Edward A. Feigenbaum and Paul Cohen. 1981. The Handbook of Artificial Intelligence, Vols. I, II and III. Los Altos, CA: William Kaufmann.

Barth, James R. and Michael G. Bradley. 1989. "The Ailing S & Ls: Causes and Cures." *Challenge,* (March-April): 30–43.

Buchanan, Bruce G. and Edward H. Shortliffe. 1984. *Rule-Based Expert Systems.* Reading, MA: Addison-Wesley.

Chithelen, Ignatius. 1987. "Teaching Computers to Emulate Great Thinkers." *Wall Street Computer Review,* (June): 33–56.

Connell, N. A. D. 1987. "Expert Systems in Accountancy: A Review of Some Recent Application." *Accounting and Business Research* 17, no. 67 (Summer): 221–233.

Ely, Bert. 1988. "Technology, Regulation and the Financial Services Industry in the Year 2000." *Issues in Bank Regulation* (Fall): 13–19.

Ernst, Christian J. 1988. *Management Expert Systems.* Wokingham, England: Addison-Wesley.

Feigenbaum, Edward A. and Pamela McCorduck. 1984. *The Fifth Generation.* New York: Signet.

Francis, Ted. 1989. "Expert System Tools Are Wall Street's Newest Creation." *Wall Street Computer Review,* (June): 27–40.

Frenzel, Louis E. 1987. *Understanding Expert Systems.* Indianapolis, IN: Howard W. Sams.

Hansell, Saul. 1989. "The Wild, Wired World of Electronic Exchanges." *Institutional Investor,* (September): 171–195.

Harmon, Paul, Rex Maus, and William Morrissey. 1988. *Expert Systems. Tools and Applications.* NY: Wiley.

Harmon, Paul and David King. 1984. *Expert Systems.* NY: Wiley.

Hayes-Roth, Frederick, Donald A. Waterman and Douglas B. Lenat. 1983. *Building Expert Systems.* Reading, MA: Addison-Wesley.

Howman, Paul M. 1988. "Freeing Underwriters for the Tough Jobs." *Best's Review,* (November): 54–56.

Kick, Russell C. 1989. "Auditing an Expert System." *Expert Systems,* 1, no. 2, (Summer): 33–38.

Kwong, K. Kern and Donald Cheng. 1988. "A Prototype Microcomputer Forecasting Expert System." *The Journal of Business Forecasting,* (Spring): 21–25.

Laurance, Robert. 1988. "Bold New Theory Could Make Investors' Day." *Wall Street Computer Review,* (June): 8–12.

Martin, Thomas J. 1988. "Investment Advice from the Experts." *Best's Review,* (November) : 48–52.

McConnell, Nancy Belliveau. 1989. "Can Phony Performance Numbers Be Policed?" *Institutional Investor,* (June): 91–104.

Mishkoff, Henry C. 1985. *Understanding Artificial Intelligence.* Dallas, TX: Texas Instruments.

Mui, Chunka and William E. McCarthy. 1987. "FSA: Applying AI Techniques to the Familiarization Phase of Financial Decision Making." *IEEE Expert,* (Fall): 33–41.

Nagy, Tom, Dick Gault, and Monica Nagy. 1983. *Building Your First Expert System.* NY: Halstead Press.

Peat, F. David. 1988. *Artificial Intelligence: How Machines Think.* NY: Bean Publishing.

Popolizio, John J. and William S. Cappelli. 1989. "New Shells for Old Iron." *Datamation,* (April): 41–48.

Prietula, Michael J. and Herbert A. Simon. 1989. "The Experts in Your Midst." *Harvard Business Review,* (January-February): 120–124.

Ribar, G. "Loan Probe: The Development of an Audit Expert System." Unpublished paper, KPMG Peat Marwick.

Rich, Elaine. 1983. *Artificial Intelligence.* NY: McGraw-Hill.

Schoen, Sy and Wendell Sykes. 1987. *Putting Artificial Intelligence To Work.* NY: Wiley.

Smith, Murray. 1988. "Neural Networks: Do They Compute?" *Best's Review,* (November): 70–74.

Shwartz, Steven C. 1987. *Applied Natural Language.* NY: Petrocelli Books.

Silber, Ken. 1989. "Distinct Business Requirements Spur AI Evolution." *Bank Systems & Equipment,* (May): 40–42.

Socha, Wayne J. 1988. "Problems in Auditing Expert System Development." edpacs XV, no. 9 (March): 1–6.

Stock, Michael. 1988. *AI Theory and Applications in the Vax Environment.* NY: Multiscience Press.

Tam, Kar Yan. 1989. "Information Systems for Security Trading." *Information and Management* 16, no. 2 (February): 105–114.

Tanimoto, Steven L. 1987. The Elements of Artificial Intelligence. Rockville, Maryland: Computer Science Press.

Tello, Ernest R. 1988. *Mastering AI Tools and Techniques.* Indianapolis, IN: Howard W. Sams & Company.

Waterman, Donald A. 1985. *A Guide to Expert Systems.* Reading, MA: Addison-Wesley.

Wolff, Mark R. 1989. "A Look at the National Council's 1988 Operations Survey." *Bottomline* (March): 19–24.

Index